BEING THERE

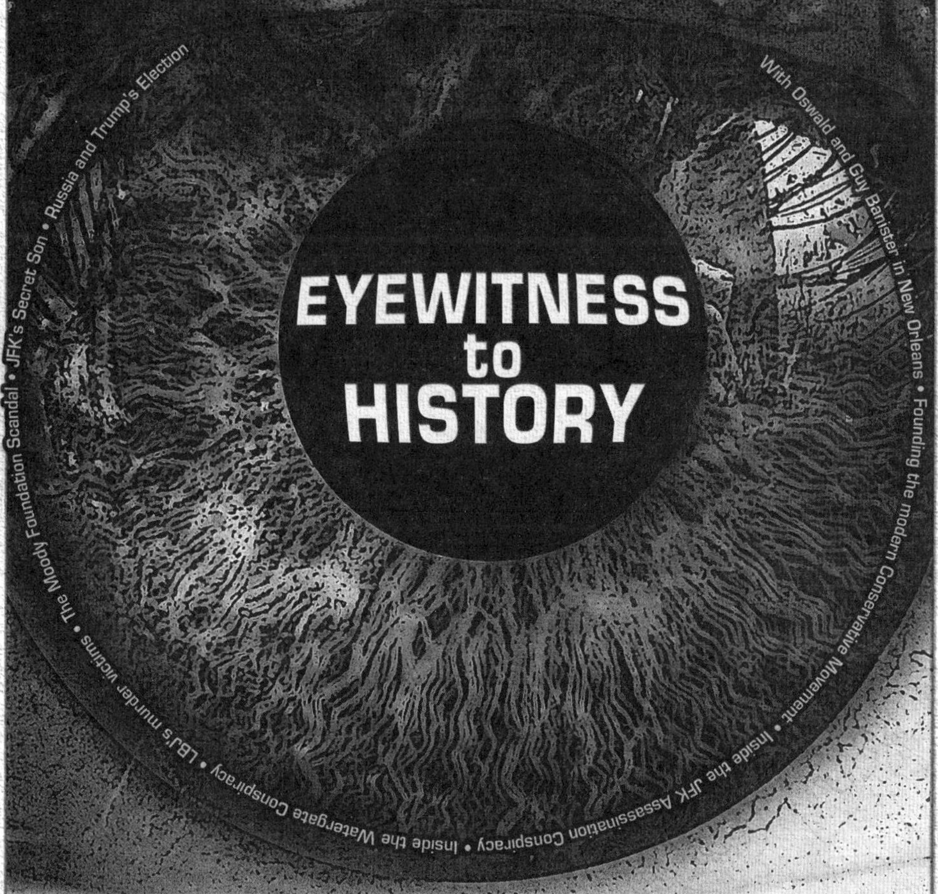

DOUGLAS CADDY

ATTORNEY

Published by:
Trine Day LLC
PO Box 577
Walterville, OR 97489
1-800-556-2012
www.TrineDay.com
TrineDay@icloud.com

Library of Congress Control Number: 2018932323

Caddy, Douglas.
–1st ed.
p. cm.

Epub (ISBN-13) 978-1-63424-115-1
Mobi (ISBN-13) 978-1-63424-116-8
Print (ISBN-13) 978-1-63424-114-4
1. Caddy, Douglas -- 1938- . 2. Watergate Affair, 1972-1974 -- Personal narratives. 3. Merrit, Robert. 4. United States -- Politics and government -- 1969-1974. 5. Conservatism -- United States -- History. 6. Kennedy, John F. -- (John Fitzgerald), -- 1917-1963 -- Assassination. 7. Estes, Billie Sol. 1925-2013. 8. Park, Tongsun. 9. Trump, Donald, -- 1946- . I. Caddy, Douglas. II. Title

First Edition
10 9 8 7 6 5 4 3 2 1

Printed in the USA
Distribution to the Trade by:
Independent Publishers Group (IPG)
814 North Franklin Street
Chicago, Illinois 60610
312.337.0747
www.ipgbook.com

Publisher's Foreword

At any given moment, public opinion is a chaos of superstition, misinformation and prejudice.

– Gore Vidal

Douglas Caddy has lived an eventful life that has touched publicly upon many episodes of America's "secret" past. You will be amazed at where he shows up, what he has done and "heard." Myself, I am intrigued by his story, but have problems with the veracity and motives of confidential informant Robert Merritt. TrineDay released *Watergate Exposed* by Merritt "as told to Douglas Caddy" in April 2011. As soon as it was published, Merritt was on the radio decrying the book and expanding his tale of covert action to include incredible scenarios and revelations about his alleged involvement in the deepest enigmas of America's "hidden history."

Caddy, himself, was accused of having confidential connections by Mae Brussell in a 1971 article entitled "Why Was Martha Mitchell Kidnapped?" in *The Realist* published by satirist and comedian Paul Krassner in August of 1972:

> Money to manage an election campaign is difficult to separate when you mix CIA funds with Republican party dollars. Robert Mullen, chairman of Mullen & Company, shared his office space at various times with Howard Hunt, Robert Bennett and Douglas Caddy, all possibly CIA agents.

Not being shy, I have asked Doug directly about this and he has told me that he is not CIA, and during his time in the public eye, there was official speculation and denial. From a 1978 Senate Select Committee on Intelligence report dealing with 1976 "Koreagate" scandal:

> [Tongsun] Park's activities in the United States first came to the attention of the intelligence community in 1962 when one of the domestic components reported that Park and his Georgetown roommate, Douglas Caddy, were forming "a new and hopefully potent international anti-communist youth organization," called the International

> Federation of Free Youth. The intelligence officer who reported this information noted that his source, a close associate of Park, had not asked for support or guidance, but had passed the information along because U.S. intelligence "should be informed of this type of activity from the beginning." Although the intelligence officer told his superiors he would "appreciate an expression of interest in pursuing the development," there is no indication in intelligence files that any further action was taken. Although U.S. intelligence funded various student organizations during the 1960s, there is no indication that this particular organization was ever utilized in any fashion by U.S. intelligence. Moreover, relevant intelligence components have informed the Committee that *they have never had any relationship with Mr. Caddy*. [Emphasis added]

Our American Constitution's First Amendment gives us the right to a free press, but it doesn't guarantee truth. As a publisher I can do my best, but I can not guarantee truth. In this era of "Fake News," truth appears elusive at best, and I am reminded of what my repentant OSS/CIA father told me: "Read it all." He explained to me that you can learn interesting things from dubiously-sourced information. Do not be afraid to read something, but be careful of what you believe. Caveat Lector!

Our intelligence community has many components, civilian, military and a combination of both. It has successes and mistakes, but the secrecy, compartmentalization and subterfuge (for my thinking) allow it sometimes to be used and abused for purposes beyond its lawful duty.

TrineDay is proud to bring you Douglas Caddy's amazing life-story: a very real eyewitness to history, and I thank Doug for shining a light in dark places, but I must admit: I wonder about how and why he was there, and what he and Merritt are telling me now.

Onward to the Utmost of Futures!

Peace,
Kris Millegan
Publisher
4/14/18

I dedicate this book to my parents,
Tabitha Miles Caddy, (1905-1994)
Frank Edward Caddy (1908-2002)

Acknowledgements

I wish to express my appreciation to Kris Millegan, Trine Day publisher, and to Philip S. Dyer, and Andy Thibault for their assistance in the preparation of this book

Table Of Contents

PREFACE

The world's population is 7.6 billion people, each of whom has a unique life story to tell. This book is my unique story, which I relate at age 80 years.

We live in an age of information overload. For that reason I have written my autobiography to reflect this. I attempt only to provide new information on historical events not found elsewhere and to do so in a limited manner so as not overburden the reader. However, I do list additional research sources should the reader desire to pursue a subject further.

An example is my chapter on Watergate.

Watergate, like the Kennedy Assassination, still has unsolved questions. Many of the most tantalizing ones with possible answers can be found in *Watergate Exposed: How the President of the United States and the Watergate Burglars Were Set-Up* (Trine Day, 2010) by Robert Merritt, confidential informant, as told to me as the original attorney for the Watergate Seven.

A second source is Len Colodny's book, *Silent Coup* (Trine Day, 2016), and his website, watergate.com. Colodny has donated his voluminous materials on the scandal compiled over decades to Texas A&M University where they are being put in digital form under the able supervision of Professor Luke Nichter and will soon be available for public viewing. Colodny's files are a treasure trove that at some future time will be examined by historians and undoubtedly be used in writing revisionist histories of that seminal event.

Another landmark source that on the whole has withstood the test of time for information and credibility is *Secret Agenda: Watergate, Deep Throat and the CIA* by Jim Hougan (Random House, 1984).

Finally, I recommend *Haig's Coup* by Ray Locker, the Washington enterprise editor of *USA Today,* which is scheduled to be released in 2018. I have been advised that it will contain startling new information about General Alexander Haig's role in Watergate and will be the perfect supplement to Locker's prior book, *Nixon's Gamble: How a President's Own Secret Government Destroyed His Administration* (Lyons Press, 2016).

These books together with Robert Merritt's new disclosures of 2018 that are found in Part Three of Chapter Three on Watergate in this book present the strong case that Congress should establish a Select Committee to Reinvestigate Watergate. There is precedent for this. In 1976 Congress, dissatisfied with the Warren Commission Report of 1964, created the House Select Committee on Assassinations to investigate the murders of President John F. Kennedy and of Martin Luther King, Jr.

One of the great mysteries of Watergate is the role played in it by the controversial Huston Plan. Robert Merritt was the sole employee of the secret Huston Plan. White House Counsel John Dean took over administration of the Huston Plan after Tom Huston was eased out. Merritt recently recounted to me a key aspect of the plan that has never before been revealed. This was the existence of a secret court that convened in a secret location in Washington before which Merritt appeared on at least twelve occasions in 1971 and 1972. Each time he submitted to a three judge panel there an affidavit sworn to by him but which was actually written by the FBI that was shown to him only fifteen minutes before the court convened. Invariably the court would issue a warrant for wiretapping or search or surveillance or a combination of these aimed at a specific target. In at least three cases the target was a law firm. The only law firm Merritt remembers today was Arnold & Porter for which a wiretap warrant was issued. Another target was the Institute for Policy Studies. The secret court always convened a 1 A.M. and was located beneath an apartment building on P Street, NW, three blocks west of Rock Creek Park in Washington, D.C. Entrance was gained through the garage beneath the apartment building. Inconspicuously located there was a small elevator that held only three persons that descended two stories further down beneath the apartment building. The elevator opened onto a small corridor that led to a door that had three separate locks on it, each of which required a separate key. Once that door was opened there were two other unlocked doors that ultimately led to a small courtroom. On each side of where the three judges sat were American flags. The judges wore black suits, not judicial gowns. "In God We Trust" appeared on the wall behind the judges. Merritt, following the orders of the FBI agents, recited to the judges the basic contents of the affidavit prepared by the FBI of which he had no personal knowledge. He then submitted the affidavit to the judges who read it and then handed it back to Merritt to sign. Lawyers from the U.S. Department of Justice were always present. The proceeding usually lasted 45 minutes after which Merritt was escorted out by the FBI agents and subsequently driven back to his residence.

When President Richard Nixon fired John Dean as White House Counsel in April 1973, Dean took the only copy of the 31-page Huston Plan with him and submitted it to Chief Judge John Sirica. To this day this copy has remained among the federal court's sealed records beyond the reach of a subpoena. Its contents are unknown to the public.

Merritt's work under the Huston Plan was exemplary in the words of President Nixon, which is why Nixon was to entrust him to carry out a clandestine mission dealing with one of the nation's most vital secrets as herein described in Chapter Three.

Chapter One

The Early Years

My most important life changing event took place three months before I was born.

There is an historical record of it published in the Eureka, California, *Humboldt Times,* "Thrills of 'Wash-Out' Adventure During Flood Written by Scout Chief" of December 13, 1937. Raymond O. Hanson, its author, was a regional Scout executive en route from San Francisco to Eureka on the Northwestern Pacific Railroad to give the principal address at the annual Boy Scout meeting of the Redwood Area Council. The train on which he was a passenger got trapped by a rock slide near Bell Springs, south of Eureka.

My mother was on the same train with my brother age four and sister age two. She was traveling to visit a relative in Eureka and was six months pregnant with me.

Hanson wrote in part:

> Trapped for three anxious days and four long December nights, in a canyon of the Big Bend, with the turbulent Eel River rising sixty-four feet toward the tracks, which held the Northwestern Pacific overnight train to Eureka, was a novel if not harrowing experience of twenty-five passengers who emerged today into the open country and the prospects of home-coming reunions.
>
> Caught in the early hours of Friday morning between two great slides, with road beds washed out by torrential rains, and tons of rock, gravel and dirt covering the rails, the train, thanks to the efficiency of the railroad service, escaped precipitation into the rushing and roaring river below.
>
> Two mothers with children claimed major attention for naturally the little ones find it difficult to adjust to unusual situations.
>
> Little did the party realize the extent of the danger which had threatened them earlier until this morning as railroad officials began transporting passengers toward Willits in motor speeders. About nine miles south there suddenly loomed a scene that struck terror in the hearts of all for three hundred feet of track hung suspended in mid air above the river. A few hours after the train had passed Thursday night, the slide had begun to take formation.
>
> Gradually the small cars made the forty-eight mile trip, stopping here and there at one washout after another, while men, women and children walked around the depressions and train men carried the equipment to other track extensions.

> It was a cheerful and grateful group which finally arrived in Willits, realizing from radio and newspaper reports that others in flooded areas throughout the state had fared far worse.

When my mother, decades ago, gave me a copy of Hanson's article she talked about the stress that she had endured during the traumatic event, foremost of course worrying about the imminent danger in which the passengers and train crew found themselves, and also about her two small children being hungry due to the small amount of food that was available for the three days.

The event was traumatic for me also, being in my mother's womb for six months and born three months later on March 23, 1938 in Long Beach, California.

The personal significance of this intense experience for me was brought home in a recent article by Hemley Gonzalez, "Science has a New Explanation for Homosexuality," published on May 7, 2017, at unitedhumanists.com. The article was based on a TED talk given by medical doctor James O'Keefe. O'Keefe had an 18-year old son who had come out publicly as gay. As his father, O'Keefe "wondered about the genetic and evolutionary factors that made his son gay."

Gonzalez wrote that "epigenetics basically states that similar genes express themselves in different ways based on external circumstances." O'Keefe declared in his TED talk found at https://youtu.be/4Khn_z9FPmU that: "If the family is flush with plenty of kids and/or it's a stressful place in time, nature occasionally flips these epigenetic switches to turn on the gay genes. This alters brain development that changes sexual orientation."

> "You probably have gay genes in your DNA," O'Keefe told his audience, "but unless they were activated in your mother's womb, they remained coiled up and silent."

I was born gay, my sexual orientation having been determined three months previously by the stress endured by my mother in a harrowing experience that lasted three days, one that she remembered her entire life. In the back of my mind I have a feeling that she gave me the Hanson article because she and my father had come to realize that I was gay through no choice of my own. While they were alive we never discussed the subject of my sexual orientation, and I never publicly acknowledged that I was gay until after their deaths, not wanting to embarrass them in any way. None of my brothers and sisters are gay, nor are any of their children.

So this is my story of being an eyewitness to history, born gay, and as a result, having to overcome the immense difficulties encountered in being dealt such a hand in life. Among these was my being targeted for murder because of my sexual orientation by military intelligence Agent Carl Shoffler under the Huston Plan in the early days of the Watergate scandal, who also feared that I knew too much, not only about Watergate, but also the assassination of President John F. Kennedy. This was because of what my close friend, Howard Hunt, a key figure in both historical scandals, might have told me about the role of military intelligence and the CIA in both events. But I am getting ahead of my story.

Both my mother and father were born in the early 1900s. My mother was raised on rural land that is now the Nashville, Tennessee airport, and my father grew up in sparsely populated Wyoming, attending a one room school with 25 students, half of whom were Indians. He rode to school on horseback. He later attended Stanford University from which he graduated with a degree in chemistry in the early years of the Great Depression and soon got a job with Shell Chemical Company. During World War II the government exempted him from military service because he was a key chemist at the Torrance, California plant of Shell Chemical that manufactured synthetic tires for our armed forces. My two brothers and two sisters and I at the time attended public schools in the Long Beach area.

I had an Aunt Nina who lived in Hollywood, just off Hollywood Boulevard and four blocks from Hollywood and Vine. I stayed with her and my uncle frequently during the war years and we would occasionally go to the movies at the neighborhood theaters: Graumann's Chinese, The Egyptian and the Pantages. My aunt was a member of the Hollywood Beverly Christian Church that was directly across the street from where she lived on Gramercy Place. Ronald Reagan attended services at the church. In 1946 when I was eight years old my aunt decided to take me to the Spiritualist Church in Hollywood. At one point in the service she had me stand on a chair and asked the spiritualist to predict my future. I can still see the scene in my mind's eye these many years later. The spiritualist looked at me for a full minute and then pronounced that I would never reach society's first level to become a national leader, but would reach the level directly underneath where I would know and work with many who did and witness how the world works.

The summers of my formative youth were spent in Mill Creek Canyon, part of the San Bernardino National Forest, above Redlands where our family had a mountain cabin not far from Lake Arrowhead. These were my happiest early years.

Shell Chemical in 1954 transferred my father to Louisiana, where he had the responsibility of building a new chemical plant at Norco. Our family took up residence nearby in New Orleans.

I attended Alcee Fortier High School in New Orleans from September 1954 until June 1956, when I graduated. The school provided its students with a superior education and nourished us on school days with the same lunch of red beans and rice.

In late 1954 two local activists, Kent and Phoebe Courtney, announced that they were holding a public meeting in a pavilion in Audubon Park to enlist citizens who opposed the censure of Senator Joseph McCarthy pending before the U.S. Senate. Our residence was only a few blocks from Audubon Park, so I decided to attend as my parents admired McCarthy's spirited fighting against communism.

An enthusiastic crowd of about 40 persons attended the Courtneys' meeting and assignments were handed out. My assignment was to set up a card table in the plaza in front of St. Louis Cathedral in the French Quarter to collect signatures on a petition that opposed the censure of McCarthy as part of a national petition drive headed by General Bonner Fellers. I had little difficulty in collecting signatures as the Catholics who attended services at the Cathedral were sympathetic towards McCarthy who was a fellow Catholic.

A few months later Kent and Phoebe announced they were starting a monthly conservative publication, *Free Men Speak*, which subsequently became *The Independent American*. I volunteered to work on the publication after high school. As a result Kent started taking me to meetings such as Toastmasters International and to a radio station where he had a weekly radio show. Several times during the period of 1955-1956, while still in a high school student, I would accompany Kent to meetings with Guy Banister, a former FBI agent, then Assistant Supervisor of the New Orleans Police Department. The topic at these meetings was the extent of organized crime in the city and more particularly the efforts of the Metropolitan Crime Commission of New Orleans headed by Aaron Kohn to combat it.

So how did Lee Harvey Oswald manage to enter into the picture during this period? Well, he was living with his mother in the Vieux Carre section of the French Quarter, less than a five minute walk from Banister's office. Oswald was then about 16 years old and enrolled in a different high school than the one I attended.

> During his early childhood and adolescence in New Orleans, Lee Oswald lived with his divorced mother at a number of different locations, usually in small rented houses or apartments in a moderate-to-lower-income section of the city. While the record of residences is not complete, one address was 126 Exchange Alley. During her testimony before the Warren Commission, Mrs. Marguerite Oswald indicated that she and her son lived there when Oswald was about to 16-years old, roughly the years 1955-56. They were "living at 126 Exchange Place, which is the Vieux Carre section of the French Quarter of New Orleans." During her testimony, Mrs. Oswald noted that "the papers said we lived over a saloon at that particular address ... that is just the French part of town. It looks like the devil. Of course I didn't have a fabulous apartment. But very wealthy people and very fine citizens live in that part of town." ... While Mrs. Oswald correctly

> noted that "wealthy" citizens resided in some sections of the French Quarter, Exchange Alley was well known as the location of other elements; it was an area notorious for illicit activities. As the managing director of the Metropolitan Crime Commission of New Orleans, Aaron Kohn recalled, "Exchange Alley, specifically that little block that Oswald lived on, was literally the hub of some of the most notorious underworld joints in the city." He noted further that Exchange Alley was the location of various gambling operations affiliated with the Marcello organization. Noting the openness with which such activities were conducted there, Kohn said, "You couldn't walk down the block without literally being exposed to two or three separate forms of illicit activities and underworld operations."[1]

Guy Banister and I continued to be involved in joint activities even after I enrolled at Georgetown University after graduating from high school in 1956:

> In1959, a New Orleans man, Richard C. Bell, in conjunction with a Chicago group, organized a group of students to attend the 1959 World Youth Conference in Vienna. His plans attracted opposition from the local American Legion, especially Kent Courtney, Festus Brown and James Pfister. The Legion organized a Free Enterprise Seminar "to alert local college students to the dangers involved in attending the communist-sponsored World Youth Festival in Vienna." Speakers at the seminar include Guy Banister, Medford Evans and Douglas Caddy. Bell and his group did make it to Vienna.[2]

In 1963 President John Kennedy was assassinated in Dallas. Oswald was branded the alleged assassin. Banister gained instant fame as someone who had interacted in a mysterious way with Oswald in New Orleans in the months before the assassination – allegedly being his handler (they shared the same business address). Years later I ended up representing Howard Hunt, an alleged key figure in the assassination, who claimed that Lyndon Baines Johnson was at the top of the conspiracy. Later, I also was destined to represent Billie Sol Estes, LBJ's bagman and silent business partner, who maintained to his death that LBJ killed JFK.

But in 1955 Oswald, Banister and I were within walking distance of each other but, of course, none of us had any inkling of what the future held.

Endnotes

1. http://jfkassassination.net/russ/jfkinfo/jfk9/hscv9b.htm#res
2. https://groups.google.com/forum/#!topic/alt.assassination.jfk/7fKgzfeYtpI

The NEW GUARD

THE MAGAZINE OF YOUNG AMERICANS FOR FREEDOM

OCTOBER 1961 • 25 CENTS

When Freedom is Threatened by William F. Buckley, Jr.

Fall Book Issue

four pages of reviews

- ★ The Foxglove Saga
  by Auberon Waugh
- ★ Citizen Hearst
  by W. A. Swanberg
- ★ House Without a Roof
  by Maurice Hindus
- ★ The Quest for Being
  by Sidney Hook

Where the Iron Curtain Begins by Lee Edwards

Chapter Two

Birth Of The Modern Conservative Movement

In 1956, after graduating from high school, I enrolled at the School of Foreign Service at Georgetown University in Washington, D.C., the oldest Catholic and Jesuit university in the country. My ultimate goal was to join the country's diplomatic corps. I was a Protestant and so was the first student that I met, Tongsun Park, who was from a wealthy Korean family. He had an engaging personality and our talk soon turned to campus politics. With two other newly enrolled students we formed "The Four Freshmen" and in a class election Tongsun was elected president of the freshman class and I was elected class treasurer. Tongsun years later was the major figure in the Koreagate scandal that followed on the heels of Watergate in which a number of members of Congress were implicated and resigned – one went to prison. Still later Tongsun got caught up in a scandal involving the buying and selling of oil from Saddam's Iraq and was sent to prison.

In my sophomore year I became class president and editor of the *Foreign Service Courier,* the school's student publication. I never met John F. Kennedy, but he did enter my life for a brief moment in a most unusual way. Three of the girls on the *Courier's* staff had baked a birthday cake and planned to surprise me with it at a staff meeting. Senator Kennedy and Jackie lived on N St., N.W., just a few blocks from the university's campus. By chance Senator Kennedy came out of his Georgetown townhouse just as the girls walked by and seeing them carrying the cake inquired what the occasion was. Once that was explained to him to the shock and delight of the girls he took a finger and pushed it part way into the cake, tasted it and pronounced the cake "delicious." Then with a smile and a wave of his hand JFK entered his vehicle and was driven away. The girls were beside themselves with excitement when they arrived shortly thereafter at the *Courier's* office, and we sat around for awhile trying to figure how the cake could be preserved for posterity. In the end the cake was eaten and since it was my birthday I got the piece that bore the hole where JFK's finger entered. Today I wonder if I got some of JFK's DNA in me when I ate that piece, since beyond the grave he has continued to play a role in my life.

Jackie Kennedy attended night classes at Georgetown and took a course in government under Professor Jules Davids, who wrote a first draft of several chapters of what later became JFK's Pulitzer Prize winning book,

Profiles in Courage. Years later Professor Davids' son, Paul, a prominent Hollywood producer, and I engaged in correspondence about his father's role in launching JFK's famous book that propelled him towards the presidency.

In my second year at Georgetown I was offered a part-time working scholarship at *Human Events,* the conservative publication. The conservative movement at that time was non-existent. David Franke, my roommate who was also a scholarship holder at *Human Events,* and I believed that a national conservative movement could be organized and to achieve this we decided to form the National Student Committee for the Loyalty Oath to keep the oath in the National Defense Education Act. Senator John Kennedy was sponsor of legislation to remove it. The *New York Times* published a letter-to-editor on February 5, 1960, that I wrote about our group's effort that brought us some publicity, some favorable and some not. Gerald Johnson wrote a scathing article in *The New Republic* titled, "A Plea for Servility." William Shannon, columnist for the *New York Post,* interviewed Franke and me and by his reaction we could tell that he was surprised at how dedicated we were to our mission.

I received letters from around the country addressed to me c/o Georgetown University that prompted the Jesuit Vice President of the university to open my mail without permission and to initial it after doing so before I got it. He did this until a large envelop arrived in the mail bearing a letter from Republican Senator Styles Bridges of New Hampshire, who enclosed a copy of the *Congressional Record* that contained a speech that he had made on the floor of the Senate endorsing our Committee. Thereafter he ceased opening mail addressed to me. It was one thing to run roughshod over a mere student, and yet another to be caught illegally opening personal mail sent to him by a powerful U.S. Senator.

Professor Carroll Quigley, who later wrote the famous book *Tragedy and Hope* taught a course titled "Civilization," and I was fortunate to study under him. He was charismatic and a favorite of all the students. William Clinton years later took Quigley's course while a student at the Foreign Service School, and as president returned for years to the university to give a lecture in honor of the professor.

The formation of our committee in 1958 put Franke and me in contact with several dozen other students and young people around the country who considered themselves conservative. In 1959, when it was widely acknowledged that Richard Nixon would be the GOP Presidential candidate the next year, Franke and I formed Youth for Goldwater for Vice President as our next step towards creating a national conservative movement. After I made a speech publicizing our group the *Washington Star* carried an article titled, "A Solid Goldwater Caddy."

In 1959 while I was a junior at Georgetown William Buckley's magazine, *National Review,* published an article by me, "What's At Stake In Louisiana," about the gubernatorial race there. As a result I got to know Buckley and we became great friends.

In my senior year at Georgetown I worked with Forrest Davis on a book opposing the admission of Communist China into the United Nations. Davis was a prominent author and longtime writer for *The Saturday Evening Post.* The Texas oil magnate H.L. Hunt at one time visited Davis and Davis asked if I wanted to be interviewed by Hunt for a position in his Facts Forum organization. However, in doing so Davis described H. L. Hunt to me as "having the mind of a brute," and a result I turned down Hunt's offer of employment after we had the interview. In retrospect I am glad I did so – for many reasons.

Upon graduating from Georgetown in 1960, I went to work for Marvin Liebman Associates in New York City in charge of the McGraw-Edison Company account. Marvin had arranged funding for the book on which Forrest Davis and I worked. One of Marvin's key clients was former New Jersey Democratic Governor Charles Edison, the chairman of McGraw-Edison Company, who lived in the Towers of the Waldorf Astoria. His neighbors in the Towers were Herbert Hoover and General Douglas MacArthur with whom he occasionally played bridge. Governor Edison, who had served in the Roosevelt Administration as Secretary of the Navy, was the son of Thomas Edison and looked exactly like his father. His political philosophy was that the American eagle should have two strong wings, a right wing and a left wing, if it is to fly and soar. He believed the country's right wing at the time was too weak and needed strengthening.

One memorable experience in 1961 was being invited by Governor Edison to join him and William Buckley to tour Thomas Edison's famous laboratories in West Orange, New Jersey. As our limousine was driven through Manhattan en route to New Jersey we passed a townhouse that caused Buckley to shiver visibly. Both Governor Edison and I were surprised and asked what had caused this and he responded: "There is where Ayn Rand lives." Buckley was one of Rand's most vehement critics not only for her extreme view of cutthroat free enterprise but for her outspoken atheism. Buckley was an avowed practicing Catholic.

With a donation of four hundred dollars from Governor Edison, our Youth for Goldwater for Vice President Organization opened headquarters in the Pick Congress Hotel during the July 1960 Republican National Convention in Chicago at which Nixon was nominated for president. The *New York Times* carried an article about our effort there in which I was characterized as a "young fogey" The mass media did not foresee that a groundswell for conservatism was in the making. Senator Goldwater came to our committee's headquarters during the convention and urged us not to let the organization die but to form a permanent conservative youth group. Buckley was present and offered his family estate, Great Elm, in Sharon, Connecticut, to be the site for the founding of the new organization.

I sent out a letter [copy in Appendix] to our small list of known young conservatives. Its letterhead was "Interim Committee For A National Conservative Youth Organization." In September 1960, about 60 young conservatives from around the country gathered to found Young Americans for Freedom (YAF). I was elected as its National Director. Robert Schuchman, a brilliant student at Yale Law School, was elected chairman and Howard Phillips, president of the Harvard Student Council, was elected to the board of directors.

Claire Vaile's essay about this period that provides a general overall view:

> While at the [1960 Republican National Convention] Buckley and Liebman met with Douglas Caddy and David Franke, both of whom attended as representatives of Youth for Goldwater for Vice President. Together, these four men would turn their disappointment in Goldwater's loss [in not being nominated as Vice President] into a national conservative youth movement. Impressed by the passion of Caddy and Franke and their attempts to organize conservative youth in the past, including the creation of the Student Committee for the Loyalty Oath in 1958, Buckley and Liebman decided to mentor them. The loss of Goldwater for the Vice Presidential nomination convinced Buckley that young conservatives in the GOP needed to be fostered from the top down. He believed that young conservatives, with his guidance, could change the American political discourse. Consequently, Buckley hired Franke to intern at the *National Review* and Caddy worked for Liebman in public relations. Their first major task was to organize a national youth group for conservatives funded by Buckley. In September of 1960, on the Buckley family estate in Sharon, Connecticut, over 100 students from 44 different colleges and universities across the country assembled to devise a plan to capitalize on the growing conservatism of American youth and turn it into an organized political movement. The result created the Young Americans for Freedom, officially chartered on September 11, 1960, and the adoption of the Sharon Statement at the conference…
>
> Buckley announced the birth of the Young Americans for Freedom to his readership in the *National Review* and reaffirmed the dual goal of YAF as not only to establish chapters on college campuses across the nation but to also promote the truths manifested in the Sharon Statement. "Every chapter of YAF," he wrote, "in every college will shape a program rooted in the principal concerns of its own campus; except that no one will be accepted as a member who does not endorse the Sharon Statement." The Sharon Statement, like the New Left's Port Huron Statement, announced YAF's ultimate vision for the county. It contained the broad principles all young conservatives, Libertarians and Traditionalists, wanted to incorporate into a national political debate. More than anything, the Sharon Statement expressed a pronounced fear about the fate of the United States. It felt personal to young conservatives because they saw their futures

> hanging in the balance, as the US federal government continued to grow and Communism continued to spread across the world. Contrary to popular belief about the 1960's and the New Right, the appeal of the Young Americans for Freedom was not simply a young conservative's reply to the widely publicized Radical Left but an attempt to build a movement for young people, based on the ideals of the Sharon Statement.[1]

On March 3, 1961 YAF sponsored a Conservatives Rally at Manhattan Center on 34th Street in Manhattan that had three thousand six hundred persons crammed inside the Center, which was its capacity, and another three thousand on the outside. Prominent conservative leaders addressed the rally, including Senator Goldwater. The *New York Times* the next day carried a front page article about the event with its unexpected turnout. The rally marked the birth of the modern Conservative Movement.

The rally led to more publicity about the burgeoning conservative movement and that same year *The New Leader* magazine carried an article about YAF with a picture of me on its cover. *Life* magazine in its June 9, 1961 issue published an article "A Liberal Meets Goldwater" in which Goldwater singled me out for special attention to interviewer Gore Vidal. This was heady stuff for someone who had only graduated from college the year before.

Two books about this period are: John A. Andrew III, *The Other Side of the Sixties: Young Americans for Freedom and the Rise of Conservative Politics,* (New Brunswick: Rutgers University Press, 1997; and M. Stanton Evans, *Revolt On The Campus,* (Regnery, 1961).

From Prof. Andrew's book:

> Born March 23, 1938 in Long Beach, California, [Douglas] Caddy attended high school first in Houston, Texas and then in New Orleans, where he graduated in 1956. Caddy had admired Senator Joseph McCarthy, circulated petitions supporting McCarthy's efforts in New Orleans while a sophomore in high school, and was an inveterate writer of letters to the editor in support of such conservative causes as the Bricker Amendment. He later became a volunteer worker for Phoebe and Kent Courtney's early publication, *Free Men Speak,* which grew out of that petition drive.

While YAF was quickly taking off as a powerful voice for conservatism, I faced a personal dilemma. The U.S. was not engaged in a war but nevertheless young men of my age were still being drafted. I had registered for the draft, but chose in June 1961 to join voluntarily the National Guard and saw active duty for six months at Fort Jackson, South Carolina, and served in the U.S. Army Reserves for another seven and a half years until I received an Honorable Discharge at the end of my tour of duty. When I left for basic training Buckley sent me a long handwritten letter counseling me as to what

I should expect based on his own tour of duty in the Army. He wrote of the pleasure of having a clean pair of socks to put on after being on a forced march through treacherous terrain. Actually I found South Carolina to be a beautiful state and enjoyed my six months there.

After I was released from active duty in the Army in December 1961, I discovered the board of directors of YAF to be engaged in a bitter internal dispute. The issue was how close YAF's relationship should be to the Young Republican National Federation. Those who favored a close relationship prevailed. This was dispiriting to me because I had always believed YAF's purpose was to promote conservatism independently and not become an appendage of the Federation. So I ceased active participation in YAF, and in 1962 I enrolled in night school at New York University Law School. During the day I worked in Governor Nelson Rockefeller's private Manhattan office at 22 West 55th Street, where I served on the staff of Lieutenant-Governor Malcolm Wilson, who was as conservative as Rockefeller was liberal.

A memorable event occurred while I was working there. On November 22, 1963, I received a phone call from John Holmes, a close friend who was also an evening law school student at NYU. He worked in the daytime for a Wall Street financial firm. In an excited voice he told me in our brief 15 second phone conversation that he had just received news that President Kennedy had been shot in Dallas and then hung up. I walked thirty feet to the office of Lt.-Gov. Wilson and told him of Holmes' call. He said, "Go downstairs to the press office and check on this." So I rode on the elevator from the fifth floor to the ground floor where Governor Rockefeller had his press office. I entered and found only a receptionist on duty as Carl Spad, the press secretary, was out of the building at lunch. I blurted out: "President Kennedy has just been assassinated." The receptionist gave me a look like I was out of my mind but did point to a closet. I went over to it, opened the door and found a Telex machine whose bells were ringing endlessly as it typed out the news of the assassination in Dallas. At this point the receptionist made a call to summon Spad back to the office. Rockefeller's personal townhouse office on 55th Street had only thirty employees. I walked through each floor alerting everyone of what had occurred. This is how the Rockefeller inner sanctum first heard the news of the Kennedy assassination, not from the famous Rockefeller intelligence organization but from a law school student who worked on the fifth floor for the Lieutenant Governor.

While going to night law school and working during the day, I lived in a spectacular coop on East 72nd Street owned by journalist Alice Widener that had sweeping views of Manhattan and the East River. I had written an article for Alice's newsletter, *USA*, while still at Georgetown. *Barron's Financial Weekly* often published articles by Alice and she had Robert Bleiberg, its editor, and James Dines of *The Dines Letter* as a frequent dinner guests. I learned a lot about the world listening to the discussions over dinner of these wise persons.

Alice also was in direct contact with FBI Director J. Edgar Hoover because posing as Alice Berezowsky, widow the famed Russian orchestra conductor Nicholas Berezowsky, who was her first husband, she attended inner sanctum meetings of the Communist Party unbeknown to those in attendance that she was a clandestine FBI informant. Alice was a true unsung patriot.

Upon graduating from law school I went to work for General Foods Corporation at its corporate headquarters in White Plains, New York. The company in 1969 sent me to Washington to be its Washington representative. For the first year I was to work out of the Robert Mullen Company, which General Foods had retained for years as its public relations firm. In 1970 Howard Hunt joined the Mullen Company staff, having been placed there by Richard Helms, the CIA director, upon Hunt's alleged retirement from that agency. Hunt and I soon found we had Buckley as a friend in common: he was godfather to Hunt's four children and had worked under Hunt as an agent for the CIA in Mexico City years earlier. Buckley had left Mexico City and returned to the U.S. to write *God and Man at Yale*, which became a famous book.

It wasn't until 1974 that I learned definitively from a Senate Watergate Committee supplementary report issued by Senator Howard Baker that the Mullen Company was a CIA front and had been incorporated by the CIA in 1959. My employer, General Foods Corporation, knew this, but kept the information from me on a need to know basis when I was transferred from its headquarters to Washington, D.C. to work out of the Mullen Company. I was outraged that the corporation had deliberately placed me as an innocent employee in a CIA front.

In 1971 I left General Foods and became an attorney employed by the Washington law firm of Gall, Lane, Powell & Kilcullen. Hunt became an early client and Robert M. Scott, a partner of the law firm, and I represented him for more than a year on sundry personal legal matters. It was during this period that Hunt joined the White House staff upon the recommendation of Charles "Chuck" Colson, one of Nixon's key advisers. Hunt and Colson both claimed Brown University as their alma mater and had bonded as members of the university's alumni association. Hunt asked me to write a letter of reference to the White House to supplement Colson's recommendation. I was pleased to be asked and promptly did so.

Then the Watergate case broke on June 17, 1972. One casualty of the Watergate case would be that the Conservative Movement that I had been instrumental in founding evolved over the succeeding years into something far different from what its founders had envisioned. It got hijacked by hypocrites and opportunists, so that today I no longer consider myself a conservative.

Endnotes

1. https://www.slideshare.net/ClaireViall/rebels-with-a-causethe-growth-and-appeal-of-the-young-americans-for-freedom-in-the-1960s

Chapter Three

Watergate

Part 1

From there I drove to the White House Annex – the Old Executive Office Building, in bygone years the War Department and later the Department of State.

Carrying three heavy attaché cases, I entered the Pennsylvania Avenue door, showed my blue-and-white White House pass to the uniformed guards, and took the elevator to the third floor. I unlocked the door of 338 and went in. I opened my two-drawer safe, took out my operational handbook, found a telephone number and dialed it.

The time was 2:13 in the morning of June 17, 1972, and five of my companions had been arrested and taken to the maximum-security block of the District of Columbia jail. I had recruited four of them and it was my responsibility to get them out. That was the sole focus of my thoughts as I began talking on the telephone.

But with those five arrests the Watergate affair had begun…

After several rings the call was answered and I heard the sleepy voice of Douglas Caddy. "Yes?"

"Doug? This is Howard and I hate to wake you up, but I've got a tough situation and I need to talk to you. Can I come over?"

"Sure. I'll tell the desk clerk you're expected."

"I'll be there in about 20 minutes," I told him, and hung up.

From the safe I took a small money box and removed the $10,000 Liddy had given me for emergency use. I put $1,500 in my wallet and the remaining $8,500 in my coat pocket. The black attaché case containing McCord's electronic equipment I placed in a safe drawer that held my operational notebook. Then I closed and locked the safe, turning the dial several times. The other two cases I left beside the safe, turned out the light and left my office, locking the door.

– E. Howard Hunt,
Undercover: Memoirs of an American Secret Agent (Berkley, 1974)

Howard Hunt accurately describes how I got involved as his attorney in Watergate within hours after the burglars were arrested. Yet to my mind my entry in the case began indirectly two months earlier, in April 1972, when I was called into the office of John Kilcullen, a partner in the Washington law firm of Gall, Lane, Powell and Kilcullen where I worked. Kilcullen, a loyal Republican as was I, declared, "Doug, our firm has been asked to volunteer an attorney to work for the Lawyers Committee for the Re-Election of the President and you are being volunteered. Call George Webster, the Committee's chairman, and get your assignment." So I called Webster, who told me to report to John Dean, Counsel to the President.

During my first meeting with John Dean in his White House office, shown on his appointment calendar as April 25, he gave me my first assignment. This was to research contributions to candidates for the Democratic presidential nomination, one of whom was certain to oppose Richard Nixon in the November election. Over the next two months Dean gave me additional run-of-the-mill legal assignments. The last one that his office gave me took me to syndicated columnist Jack Anderson to get any background information that Anderson might have not used in a recent newspaper column he wrote about Democratic Senator Edmund Muskie, one of the presidential contenders. This was on the day before the arrests of the burglars at Watergate.

The significance of my doing volunteer work, under the direction of John Dean, beginning in April 1972 will become apparent as I relate here how Watergate evolved in the first weeks of the case, and how the ultimate outcome of the case could and should have been vastly different but for Dean. This will include Dean selecting me to be the first person approached to pass "hush money" to the five arrested burglars and to Hunt and Gordon Liddy, and my refusal to do so; Dean withholding vital information from President Nixon, as shown by the Oval Office tapes of July19 and 20, 1972, about my volunteer campaign work under Dean's direction and his attempt to get me to distribute the hush money. This untold story of Watergate is vital history, because the entire case could have been resolved in the first month or so, had it not been for Dean devising a secret agenda for his own purpose to protect himself from the legal consequences of certain of his activities prior to Watergate, even if ultimately it meant the betrayal of President Nixon and of the nation.

Dean tells his latest version of Watergate in his most recent book, *The Nixon Defense: What He Knew and When He Knew It* (Viking, 2014). The book's publication was timed with the 40th anniversary of President Nixon's resignation. Critics of the book attacked it for being misleading and deficient in its history of the scandal. We shall have to wait and see if, somewhere down the road, Dean repudiates what he has written as he did with his first book, *Blind Ambition.*

The *Washington Times* of February 12, 1996, in an article headlined "Dean Disavows much of 'Blind Ambition,'" reported that Dean:

> [W]ho brought down President Nixon in the Watergate scandal, has disavowed his best-selling book on the cover-up.
>
> The book, "Blind Ambition," portrayed Mr. Dean as a hero of conscience who eliminated "a cancer on the presidency." In its for-

> ward, Mr. Dean vouches for the book's accuracy, offering to take a lie-detector test.
>
> Now Mr. Dean says he didn't write key portions. Nor did he even read the entire book. "I have never gone through the book cover to cover," he said.
>
> In sworn depositions that have been obtained by *The Washington Times,* Mr. Dean said that key elements of the book were actually pure "speculation," "reasonable conjecture" and "distortion."

Another significant event for me also happened in April 1972 besides that involving Dean. Hunt asked me to join him and Lawrence Houston, General Counsel to the CIA, at a restaurant on the Maryland side of the Potomac River. Houston asked if I was interested in going to work for the CIA and said that if I did, my assignment would be to construct a luxurious hotel on the seashore in Nicaragua into which the Communist Sandinista leaders would be lured and compromised. I told Houston and Hunt that I would have to think about their proposal, but in my mind I already knew it was something I could not pursue for personal reasons.

The Burglars' Arrests at Watergate

The arrests of the burglars at Watergate took place sometime directly after midnight. As recounted by Hunt in his autobiography, he called me from his White House office after he and Gordon Liddy had fled their room in the Watergate Hotel, upon being alerted that the police had caught the five burglars. Shortly after calling me, he arrived at my apartment located less than a mile from both the White House and Watergate.

Hunt explained to me what had occurred inside the Democratic National Committee headquarters at Watergate culminating in the arrests of James McCord and the four Cuban-Americans. I was appalled at what I heard and immediately realized the dire threat it posed as a criminal case to the survival of the Nixon Administration.

From my apartment Hunt telephoned Gordon Liddy, whom I had come to know because George Webster at one point had assigned me to do election law research for Liddy in the latter's capacity as Legal Counsel to the Finance Committee for the Re-Election of the President. Shortly before 5 A.M. both Hunt, in my apartment, and Liddy, on the telephone with me, retained my services as their attorney to represent them and the five arrested burglars in the case. I telephoned Robert M. Scott, the partner of the law firm who in the past had worked with me on Hunt's personal legal affairs, briefed him on what had transpired, and told him I needed to obtain an attorney skilled in criminal law to assist me in the case.

Scott's spontaneous reaction was "they must have been set up." He said that he would immediately call his nephew. He soon called back and said that he did talk to his nephew and also had arranged for a criminal law attorney, Joseph Rafferty, to assist me.

Hunt departed my apartment, some four hours after the burglars' arrests, and proceeded to his home, Witches Island, in Potomac, Maryland. His son, Saint John Hunt, has recounted what happened upon his dad's arrival home and in the days immediately thereafter in his illuminating book, *Bond of Secrecy: My Life with CIA Spy and Watergate Conspirator E. Howard Hunt* (Trine Day, 2012).

My intent and Joseph Rafferty's was to get the five arrested burglars out on bail as soon as possible without attracting undue publicity. That proved impossible because, as I learned later, Carl Shoffler, the police officer who arrested them, had telephoned the *Washington Post* within a few hours of the arrests and alerted the paper to the significance of the event at the Watergate. Shoffler, who was a 27-year-old military intelligence officer assigned to the Washington police, had, as his goal bringing down President Nixon. Those wishing additional information about a nefarious and clandestine military intelligence apparatus operating inside the Nixon White House without the President's knowledge should consult *Silent Coup* by Len Colodny (Trine Day, 2016).

As the five were being arraigned in court late that Saturday, a *Post* reporter named Bob Woodward, himself a former military intelligence agent assigned to the Nixon White House, sought me out. I found myself in the awkward position of providing evasive answers, because at that point few persons knew of the involvement of Hunt and Liddy, and anything I might say could place them in legal jeopardy. The *Post* the next day carried an article that Woodward helped write, "5 held in Plot to Bug Democrats." The article described me as "one of the attorneys for the five men" and noted that "Caddy, who says he is a corporate lawyer, attempted to stay in the background at yesterday's 4 p.m. court hearing. He ... brought another attorney ... who has experience in criminal law, to do the arguing."

While I was in the federal courthouse working on the case on June 28, Assistant U.S. Attorney Donald Campbell approached me and handed me a subpoena to appear "forthwith" before the federal grand jury that had been convened to investigate the case. Campbell then grabbed me by the arm and physically pulled me into the grand jury room. Principal Assistant U.S. Attorney Earl Silbert immediately began asking me questions and demanding answers as the grand jurors looked on. The *Post* on July 2 carried another article, "Jury Probes Lawyer in 'Bug' Case," that reported,

> During an extraordinary court proceeding yesterday, it was revealed that the attorney, Douglas Caddy, has been questioned at least twice about the possible involvement of the Central Intelligence Agency in the case. And Caddy was ordered to testify before a federal grand jury about his relationship with Howard Hunt, the one-time White House consultant.

> When asked about Hunt, Caddy invoked the attorney-client privilege, refused to testify, and then asked to leave the grand jury room to consult with his own attorney, Silbert said.
>
> He [Silbert] told Judge Sirica that Caddy's conduct was "specious, dilatory and ... an obstruction of justice."

I answered hundreds of questions, and even had my bank account subpoenaed by the prosecutors, but I refused to answer 38 key questions that had been publicized by the prosecution and which attempted, through my lips as their defense attorney, to implicate and incriminate Hunt and Liddy. My refusals to answer were based on the advice of five senior attorneys that included three former Assistant U.S. Attorneys, all of whom strongly believed that my answering the 38 questions would violate the attorney-client privilege. For example, two questions asked were: "At what time did you receive a telephone call in the early morning hours of Saturday, June 17, 1972?" and "From whom did you receive a telephone call in the early morning hours of June 17, 1972?" Obviously if I answered these and the remaining 36 questions Hunt and Liddy would inevitably have been implicated in the break-in, although they had not been arrested.

Judge Sirica Holds Me in Contempt of Court

On July 12, less than a month after the arrests of the five burglars, Chief Judge John Sirica, in a courtroom packed with the press, viciously attacked me and impugned my professional integrity. The Judge declared:

> You see, to put the matter perfectly bluntly, if the government is trying to get enough evidence to indict Mr. Caddy as one of the principals in this case even though he might not have been present at the time of the alleged entry in this place, I don't know what the evidence is except what has been disclosed here, if the government is trying to get an indictment against Mr. Caddy and he feels that way and you feel it and the rest of your attorneys feel it, all he has to say is I refuse to answer on the grounds what I would say would tend to incriminate me. That ends it. I can't compel him to say he knows Mr. Hunt under the circumstances. He doesn't do that, understand? He takes the other road. He says there is a confidential communication. Who is he to be the sole judge whether or not it is confidential or not? That is what I am here for.

Sirica then declared that unless I answered the 38 questions the next day before the grand jury he would hold me in contempt of court and jail me. Woodward in an article in the *Post* the next day, "'Bug' Case Attorney to Testify,' wrote:

> After Sirica announced that Caddy must answer or go to jail, Robert M. Scott, one of Mr. Caddy's attorneys, said, "This is very harsh treatment."

> Caddy's attorney did disclose to the court that Caddy has been before the grand jury three times for a total of about 14 hours and answered all but roughly 10 percent of about 14 hours of the 300 to 400 questions asked him.

The next day, July 13, I again went before the grand jury and refused to answer the 38 questions on the grounds that to do so would violate the attorney-client privilege. A short time later I was back before Judge Sirica.

John Powell, whose reputation as a leader of the Bar had been praised by Sirica during the hearing the day before, spoke on my behalf:

> Your Honor, the professional burden I carry at the moment weighs very heavy on me and I shall be extremely glad when these issues are resolved. Mr. Caddy has been asked questions pertaining to his relations with a number of people, all of whom have been his clients, some of whom are his friends. It is therefore apparent that the answers he gives may have long-lasting and profound effect on both his professional and his private life. After much soul-searching and prolong conferences last night after we left this courthouse, with some six or eight attorneys present, Mr. Caddy was advised that in light of these foregoing factors and the seriousness of the legal questions involved he should not answer until the United States Court of Appeals for this circuit has ruled on the matter. He is prepared once the Court of Appeals has ruled to follow that ruling and to appear immediately before the grand jury and answer the questions according to the Court of Appeals' ruling. We on our part are prepared to file an appeal upstairs with the Clerk of the United States Court of Appeals and have papers present here in the courtroom. The only request I have, Your Honor, is in view of these circumstances Your Honor would commit Mr. Caddy to my custody pending the ruling of the Court of Appeals. Needless to say, I warrant that he will be here when the Court wants him.

Judge Sirica, before holding me in contempt of court, then asked me if I had anything to say. I responded tersely, "I would just indicate that I did invoke the lawyer-client privilege to these questions, and I did so upon the instructions of my clients who asked me not to waive the privilege." After reading his order holding me in contempt, Sirica told me to step back and placed me in the custody of the U.S. Marshal. I was immediately led from the courtroom. After spending a short time in the cell block directly behind Sirica's courtroom, I was taken down the elevator to the basement and placed behind bars in the central cell block imprisoning people awaiting their various trials upstairs.

The *New York Times* article of July 14, "Lawyer Held in Contempt in Democratic Raid Inquiry," written of course the day before, said in part:

> A 34-year-old lawyer was found in contempt of court in refusing to answer a series of grand jury questions about the June 17 raid on the offices of the Democratic National Committee...
>
> Late this afternoon, the United States Court of Appeals for the District of Columbia Circuit stayed the penalty pending a hearing ... Mr. Caddy was then released without bond.

On July 18, the U.S. Court of Appeals affirmed Judge Sirica's order holding me in contempt. Its order was gratuitously insulting regarding my attorney-client privilege relationship with Howard Hunt. The court declared: "Even if a relationship does exist, certain communications, such as a consultation in furtherance of a crime, are not within the privilege."

The Oval Office Tapes

My going back before the grand jury was the subject of a discussion between President Nixon and John Ehrlichman on July 19, 1972, as disclosed in the Oval Office tapes:

> **Ehrlichman**: That fellow [Douglas] Caddy, the lawyer who wouldn't answer questions because it was privileged communications, refused to answer, the Judge cited him for contempt. He appealed it to the local Court of Appeals. They affirmed the trial judge and he's now down there answering questions, as far as I know.
>
> **President Nixon**: That's probably what's breaking it up.
>
> **Ehrlichman**: It could well be.
>
> **President Nixon**: Who is Caddy the lawyer for?
>
> **Ehrlichman**: Caddy is a 37-year-old lawyer who was very active in the YAFs, the very conservative Young Americans [for Freedom].
>
> **President Nixon**: Who does he represent?
>
> **Ehrlichman**: He represented the five guys who got caught the night they were caught, and he was at the police station within minutes after the police brought the prisoners there. He'd obviously been called by someone from the outside. Well, I think what had happened is that Hunt was in the neighborhood, and when he saw those guys get caught or heard it over the bug, he called Caddy and Caddy went down and tried to arrange bail and advised them not to talk and so forth. So he's been asked by the grand jury, who called you? And he's refused to answer.
>
> **President Nixon**: That would bring Hunt into it...
>
> **Ehrlichman**: It would bring Hunt in, it would bring Liddy in. And this guy [Caddy] has an indirect connection with [Charles "Chuck"]

Colson because he is the attorney for Colson's secretary, who is in the process of getting a divorce. But that's as close as it comes to the White House.

President Nixon: Well, I don't think that a problem.

Ehrlichman: No, that's not a problem. That's sort of a tangential thing. But he will not, Caddy will not disclose much beyond what was already going to be disclosed. So it isn't going to add too much to the trouble...

President Nixon: Do you mean that the Circuit Court ordered an attorney to testify?

Ehrlichman: It [unintelligible] me, except that this damn Circuit that we've got here, with [Judge David] Bazelon and so on, it surprises me every time they do something.

President Nixon: Why didn't he appeal to the Supreme Court?

Ehrlichman: Well, he could, I suppose. They don't have to grant *certiorari*. I don't know. I don't know the answer to that.

President Nixon: But he's now testifying?

Ehrlichman: My understanding is that he was going to go in this morning. Now, he may go down there and refuse and take it to the Supreme Court. I don't know. I just don't have those facts.

How Dean Misled Nixon

As disclosed in the tapes, President Nixon did not think there was a "problem" for the White House in my testifying because my being the attorney for Colson's secretary in her divorce action was as "close as it comes to the White House." Actually there were two very big problems for the White House.

First, Dean had withheld from Nixon the information that I had been working as a volunteer lawyer under Dean's direction from April 25, when George Webster and I met with him in his White House office, until the Watergate case broke on June 17. It doesn't get much closer to the White House than that.

Second, beginning about two weeks after the case broke, I started to receive mysterious phone calls from someone I never met who called himself "Mr. Rivers." The purpose of the calls, if I was to believe the caller, was to arrange for me to pass "hush" money to the five arrested burglars and Hunt and Liddy. When I comprehended what Mr. Rivers was apparently talking about, I consulted with Jerome Powell, the managing partner of the law firm where I worked and a former Assistant U.S. Attorney. Powell said that while the precise intentions of Mr. Rivers remained unclear, as well as, who he was and whom he actually represented, and that if I accepted any money for any purpose from him, subsequently I could be blackmailed to do anything Mr. Rivers and those associated with him wanted done – I would no longer be a free man. When Mr. Rivers called back on July 6, a partner of the law firm was in my office. I told Mr. Rivers I wasn't at all certain what his intentions were and what he wanted me to do, but I wanted no further contact with him. As I hung up I heard Mr. Rivers give a big exasperated "aaugh."

Later, I learned that Mr. Rivers was actually Anthony Ulasewicz, a former New York City detective, who before Watergate had carried out numerous assignments for the White House primarily but not exclusively from Dean. Ulasewicz disclosed that one assignment in April 1972, two months before the June 17 break-in, was to visit and case the layout of the Democratic National Committee headquarters using the guise of a casual visitor.

Here is the testimony of Herbert Kalmbach, President Nixon's personal attorney, before the Senate Watergate Committee as he was being questioned by Samuel Dash, the Committee's Chief Counsel on July 16, 1973:

> **Mr. Dash**: Now, what was the first instruction you received to give the money?
>
> **Mr. Kalmbach**: Again, as I have tried to reconstruct this, Mr. Dash, the first instruction that I received, which I passed to Mr. Ulasewicz, was to have Mr. Ulasewicz give $25,000 to Mr. Caddy. I don't know much of Mr. Caddy. I understand he is an attorney here in Washington. And as I recall it, this was probably from approximately July 1 through July 6 or 7. There were a number of calls. I would either talk to Mr. Dean or Mr. [Fred] LaRue [a presidential aide.] I would then call Mr. Ulasewicz who, in turn, would call Mr. Caddy. He would have some response from Mr. Caddy, and I would call back up to Mr. Dean or Mr. LaRue.
>
> **Mr. Dash**: What was the response from Mr. Caddy?
>
> **Mr. Kalmbach**: Well, the sum and gist of it was that Mr. Caddy refused to accept the funds.
>
> **Mr. Dash**: In that manner?
>
> **Mr. Kalmbach**: That is correct. That was the end-all. There were several telephone calls, but the final wrap-up on it was that he refused to receive the funds.

Back Before the Grand Jury

On July 19, the day after the U.S. Court of Appeals had affirmed Sirica's contempt citation, I met with the prosecutors before going in front of the grand jury. Our meeting had barely got underway when the office door burst open and William Bittman, Hunt's new attorney who had succeeded me, strode in and thrust a one-page letter from Hunt into my hand. The letter read:

> July 19, 1972
>
> Dear Doug:
> I have just had an opportunity to review the Court of Appeals' opinion, in docket 72-1658, which affirms the District Court's Order directing you to testify. It appears the Court of Appeals' opinion is predicated on the assumption that the existence of a bona fide attorney-client relationship between you and myself has not been established before the grand jury.
>
> As you know, you have represented me in various matters over a considerable period of time. In addition, during the months of June and July, 1972, I consulted you, in your capacity as an attorney, seeking legal advice concerning matters which are now apparently under investigation by the Federal Grand Jury sitting in the District of Columbia. At no time during the confidential discussions that we had were we involved in any way in matters that could possibly be construed as on-going criminal activity. As I am sure you are aware, I sought your advice only in your capacity as an attorney, and we therefore discussed many things that were confidential and which I would not have discussed with you but for the attorney-client privilege.
>
> This letter is to advise you of my understanding of the relationship which we had, of my understanding that the discussions which you had with me during June and early July 1972 were in your capacity as my attorney, and in connection with matters which are apparently now under investigation by the Federal Grand Jury, and my desire and instruction that you not, in any way, waive the attorney-client privilege.
>
> Very truly yours,
> /s/ Howard
> E. Howard Hunt, Jr.

I granted permission to the prosecutors to make a copy of Hunt's letter.

Before going into the grand jury room, I had decided to disclose my volunteer work for John Dean, which, for a reason that one could only surmise, was not among the 38 questions publicly listed by the prosecutors and had never come up in my prior appearances. Neither had the "mysterious" phone calls I had received from Mr. Rivers. I answered all the questions posed to me by the prosecutors from their list of 38 queries. The opportunity then arose in my testimony to begin telling about the "mysterious" phone calls. I was beginning to describe the calls about the "hush" money, when one of the three prosecutors, Seymour Glanzer, peremptorily cut me off and switched to another line of questioning.

I was stunned. Here I had been falsely accused by the prosecutors of engaging in conduct that was "specious, dilatory and ... an obstruction of justice," falsely accused by Sirica of being "one of the principals in this case even though he might not have been present at the time of the alleged entry in this place," and my professional reputation gratuitously insulted by the U.S. Court of Appeals declaring: "Even if a relationship does exist, certain communications, such as a consultation in furtherance of a crime, are not within the [attorney-client] privilege." Now when I attempted to testify about being approached with the "hush" money, my grand jury testimony was cut off by the prosecution. The question arises: who was behind this scheme to prevent me from so testifying?

An answer is found in the Oval Office tapes. On July 19, 1972, there was this exchange regarding Henry Petersen, the Assistant Attorney General for the Criminal Division of the Justice Department, and Richard Kleindienst, the U.S. Attorney General:

> **President Nixon**: What is the situation, what is the situation on Petersen, Kleindienst and the rest?
>
> **Ehrlichman**: Petersen, pretty good. Kleindienst is one step removed from it. Petersen's always been very good with Dean in trying to help to evaluate the thing as it goes along and in keeping Dean informed of the direction that things are going.
>
> **President Nixon**: What the U.S. Attorney is up to, and so forth?
>
> **Ehrlichman**: Yes. And he's managed to keep a hold of the U.S. Attorney better. It is a better situation than it was.

Then there is the Oval Office tape of the next day, July 20, 1972, of a discussion between President Nixon and H.R. Haldeman:

> **Haldeman**: Another thing I didn't know that [John] Mitchell told me is that John Dean ... went into [Henry] Petersen and laid out the whole scenario to him of what actually happened, who was involved and where it all fit. Now, on the basis of that, Petersen is working with that knowledge, directing the investigation along the channels that will not produce the kind of *answers we don't want produced*. Petersen also feels that the fact that there were some lines in this case that ran to the White House is very beneficial because it has slowed them down in pursuing things, because all of them are of the view that they don't want to indict the White House, they only want to indict the – they want to tighten up that case on the criminal act and limit it to that to the degree that they can ... [Italics added].

There can be no doubt that the "we" here is John Dean, who had his own personal agenda that conflicted with serving President Nixon. Dean, having kept vital information from President Nixon, was behind the scenes orchestrating the investigation through Petersen, including circumventing my attempt to tell the grand jury about Dean's involvement with me, so as to assure that my testimony on July 19 "would not produce the kind of answers we don't want produced."

After I refused to accept the "hush" money on July 6, the prosecutors increased their abusive handling of me. In retrospect I believe that Dean, who was micro-managing the cover-up, ordered through Henry Petersen that this be done without the latter knowing why, and that Petersen obligingly passed the word to the prosecutors who were also ignorant of the reason behind it. I was to be punished because I had refused to participate in Dean's "hush" money criminality.

FBI Internal Report on Watergate

Evidence to support this is found in an FBI memorandum of July 5, 1974, from O.T. Jacobson to the FBI Director, the subject was "Watergate Investigation – OPE Analysis," OPE being Office of Planning and Evaluation. The following is from the memorandum:

> Pursuant to the Director's instructions of 5/14/74 for the Office of Planning and Evaluation (OPE) to conduct a complete analysis of the FBI's conduct of the Watergate and related investigations the enclosed study has been prepared. The General Investigative Division participated in major portions of the study...
>
> IV. Areas of criticism and comments
>
> 1. Allowing John Dean to sit in on interviews of White House personnel; submitting copies and/or reports of the FBI investigative results to Dean, and clearing proposed investigative activity through Dean.
>
> Comments: On June 19, 1972, WFO [Washington Field Office] by teletype requested authority to interview Charles W. Colson since information had been developed that Hunt had worked for Colson in the White House. On June 22, 1972, Mr. Gray [Acting FBI Director L. Patrick Gray] telephonically authorized then Assistant Director Bates to have WFO contact John Dean to set up an interview with Colson. Dean subsequently indicated that he would sit in on interviews of White House personnel and all requests for investigation at the White House had to be cleared through him.
>
> Criticism of FBI interviews in the presence of Dean and clearing proposed investigative activities through him is justified. However, there appeared to be no alternative to WFO and to the Accounting and Fraud Section to following this procedure since the decision

concerning this had been made between Mr. Gray and Dean, and neither Bureau supervisors nor field agents were in a position to overrule decisions of the Acting Director.

With respect to the submitting of copies of FBI reports to Dean, this is probably the most serious blunder from an investigative standpoint made by Mr. Gray. The facts concerning this development became known outside Mr. Gray's staff for the first time on February 5, 1973. This is long after the substantive investigation into the Democratic National Committee Headquarters (DNCH) break-in was completed and, in fact, was after the trial of those originally implicated was completed. While Dean's role as the master manipulator of the cover up was unknown, and, in fact, the cover up itself was unknown during the investigation, obviously the furnishing to Dean by Mr. Gray of our reports allowed Dean the total opportunity to plan a course of action to thwart the FBI's investigation and grand jury inquiry. There was no way that FBI personnel could have avoided this situation since it was unknown that Mr. Gray was furnishing the reports to Dean.

The principal lesson to be learned from this is that rarely should we conduct interviews in the presence of an attorney and never should we allow the same attorney to sit in on all interviews relative to a certain situation. Further, FBI reports should be disseminated only to the prosecutor and certainly never to the White House.[1]

Dean's New Book

How does Dean handle my role in the Watergate case as it relates to him in his new book, *The Nixon Defense: What He Knew and When He Knew It?* The book is misleadingly subtitled because Dean himself kept Nixon from knowing, among other key information, about the two big "problems" that I presented to the White House. A more appropriate title for his book would be, *The Nixon Defense: What He Did Not Know And Why He Did Not Know It.*

Dean in this book writes on page 106, first quoting Nixon:

> "...I hate to see it, but let me say, we'll take care of [Jeb] Magruder [Deputy Director of Nixon's reelection committee who had prior knowledge of the break-in plan] immediately afterwards." The president reassured Ehrlichman that '[i]n his case it would be easy as pie, it'd be a case of [unclear], you could treat him like those Vietnam Veterans Against the War, and I mean, you could just give amnesty to all of 'em."
>
> "That'd do it. We'll have to lay that foundation, but as I say, I think Bob [Haldeman, Nixon's Chief of Staff] and Dean will have a better feel for this a little later, after they talk to [John] Mitchell, see where we are," Ehrlichman said, and changed the subject to a morn-

> ing lead story in the *Washington Post* about the lawyer who showed up to bail out the Watergate burglars without being called, Douglas Caddy. Caddy had refused to answer questions, because he claimed the information was privileged communications, but Judge Sirica cited him for contempt; Caddy's appeal had been denied by the local court of appeals. Ehrlichman explained how this could draw in not only Hunt and Liddy, but Colson as well, because Caddy was handling the divorce of Colson's secretary. Both concluded that that was too remote to be a problem and returned to the Magruder situation.

That's Dean's version in its entirety. Nowhere in his new book does Dean acknowledge our meeting in his White House office on April 25, 1972, where as a volunteer lawyer I received my first campaign research assignment. Nor does he mention his effort to get me to distribute "hush" money to the defendants starting less than two weeks after Watergate broke.

More important, Dean does not acknowledge in his new book that he withheld this vital information from President Nixon.

What if Nixon had been informed of the two "problems"?

It is a fair question to ask. What if Nixon had known of the two big "problems" that led right to the White House, before I testified in front of the grand jury on July 19, problems kept from him by Dean? Nixon, being a shrewd lawyer and shrewd politician, might have analyzed the situation as follows:

> Caddy will disclose to the grand jury that for two months before Watergate broke he was working as a volunteer lawyer doing ordinary campaign legal work under the direction of Dean. This leads directly to the White House, but does not present an insurmountable problem. Caddy will also disclose that he was approached to pass "hush" money to the burglars and Hunt and Liddy, but from whom he does not actually know. So that remains murky. The blunt truth of the matter is that the five burglars were caught red handed. There is no possibility that they will be found innocent at trial. Ditto for Hunt and Liddy because Caddy's testimony coerced by Sirica and the U.S. Court of Appeals will clearly implicate them in the crime.
>
> So let Caddy, who is Hunt's attorney and friend, disclose to the grand jury the failed attempt to pass "hush" money to him as the burglars' lawyer. This gets Hunt off our back if he presses for future cash payments or tries to blackmail us. He can only blame his own attorney for the disclosure. The cover-up, even if there is one, is in its incipient stages. Let's end whatever it is right now, and just characterize those involved in the break-in as a bunch of reckless campaign rogues who engaged in a third-rate burglary.
>
> Let Caddy testify to the grand jury as to what he knows, and let the burglars and Hunt and Liddy stand trial and be convicted. Then what? The question arises, why didn't Caddy appeal Sirica's con-

> tempt order and that of the Appeals Court to the Supreme Court? I think the answer Caddy would give is that he and his attorneys built a strong enough court record that if Hunt, Liddy and the five arrested individuals were found guilty, their convictions could be overturned on appeal because of Sirica's and the Appeals Court's abuse of him as their attorney.
>
> Clearly the record shows he was mistreated and as a result the defendants will not receive a fair trial. Of course, if the convictions are not overturned on appeal, I can always pardon or grant clemency to the seven after the trial, which will take place when the November election is behind us, although I can only do so in a manner that does not constitute obstruction of justice. The Democrats will make a big deal of all of this, but we control the Justice Department and its investigation. They will be relegated to filing a civil lawsuit that will take years to litigate and to holding committee hearings in the Senate and House. We'll take some heavy blows but we shall survive.

If Nixon had taken this approach the Watergate case may likely have been essentially wrapped up within the first two months. There would have been no lengthy cover-up. Hunt would have been precluded from making any further demands for hush money. Hunt's wife might not have died in a mysterious plane crash. James McCord would not have written his explosive letter to Sirica exposing the cover-up. There would have been no Senate Watergate hearings. The Oval Office tapes would never have been made public. Nixon could have served out his second term, somewhat bruised, but still wielding power.

But Nixon never had the opportunity to explore this legal avenue early in the case. Why? Because John Dean was micro-managing the criminal investigation through Henry Petersen at the Justice Department and L. Patrick Gray at the FBI, and while doing so keeping vital information from the President.

Why was Dean doing this? For two principal reasons: (1) Dean had comprehensive prior knowledge of the Nixon White House plans to target and subvert the Democrats in the 1972 presidential campaign, of which the Watergate break-in was an outgrowth, and (2) Dean's girlfriend, Maureen Biner, had a unique roommate relationship with Erika L."Heidi" Rikan, the madam who ran prostitution ring allegedly operating out of the Democratic National Committee headquarters, a ring that was managed behind the scenes by Rikan's boy friend, Joseph Nesline, a Mafia figure. Dean married Maureen in October 1972, four months after Watergate broke, and it has been widely alleged that this was done so that neither could be forced to testify against the other under the marital privilege. Heidi Rikan was bride's maid at their wedding.

Those who want additional information about this crucially important aspect bearing on the cover-up, which was never investigated because of Dean's masterful manipulation of the scandal, should consult three books that discuss it in detail: *Silent Coup* by Len Colodny, *Nixon's Secrets* by Roger Stone (Skyhorse, 2014) and *White House Call Girl: The Real Watergate Story* by Phil Stanford (Feral House/Process Media, 2013). The last contains the list from "Heidi" Rikan's little black book of the clients of her prostitution ring which included well known persons from the Nixon White House and the Committee for the Re-Election of the President in addition to prominent Democrats. (Trine Day released another book, *Confessions of a D.C. Madam: The Politics of Sex, Lies and Blackmail,* by Henry W. Vinson, that deals with the female and male prostitution rings operating in Washington.)

Len Colodny has donated his treasure trove of voluminous Watergate files and depositions to Texas A&M University where they are available to the public. Anyone wishing to examine these should contact Professor Luke Nichter at the university. A list of the files and depositions can be found here: http://watergate.brightpixelstudio.com/Content/Colodny%20Collection%20tape%20Interview%20list.pdf

The First Watergate Trial

In early December 1972 at William Bittman's request, one of my attorneys and I met with him. Bittman was the lawyer who succeeded me in representing Hunt. The meeting was to discuss the pending trial of Hunt, Liddy and the five burglars scheduled for January. Bittman had previously been a high level Justice Department lawyer; among cases he had prosecuted was that of Jimmy Hoffa.

After we were seated, Bittman said, "Your testimony is going to be crucial at the trial. It will be gone over with a fine tooth comb. The government is worried now that it may have fatally tainted its case against the defendants by calling you before the grand jury." He continued that shortly before the trial to refresh my recollection, the prosecutors would call me to their office to have me read my five grand jury transcripts.

"Doug," Bittman then said, "when you read your grand jury transcripts, check carefully to see if anything has been altered."

My attorney and I stared at him in amazement, both of us speechless.

"Yes," Bittman added, " check your transcripts to see if the questions and answers have been tampered with."

In a low voice I managed to ask, "And if they have been?"

"Then," Bittman replied, "I plan to call Silbert to the witness stand to question him about them. Hunt deserves a fair trial, and I am going to see that he gets one." Bittman was worried that the transcripts had been altered to weaken the attorney-client privilege so as to benefit the government's case.

Indeed, a few weeks later Silbert asked me to come to the U.S. Attorney's office to read the transcripts of my five appearances before the grand jury. In reading the final one I found to my astonishment that at least one key question and answer had been altered and did not reflect what I has testified. It boggled my mind that after all Sirica and the Court of Appeals had done to me, forcing me to testify under threat of contempt of court, that my final grand jury transcript had been altered. Soon thereafter my attorney and I again met with Bittman and informed him. A court transcript of an interview of Alfred Baldwin, a key Watergate witness, was also changed. There may have been other witnesses whose testimony was altered by the original prosecutors, but who never knew it.

Later in December 1972, Howard Hunt's wife, Dorothy, was killed in a mysterious plane crash in Chicago. This left Hunt psychologically almost a basket case. His attorney, William Bittman, pressured him to plead guilty at the start of the trial the next month, which he did, and the four Cuban-American defendants followed his lead and did so also. Hunt later came to believe that he had been pressured wrongfully to plead guilty by Bittman because the latter was worried that at trial it might be disclosed that he accepted the initial $25,000 "hush" money from Ulasewicz after I had turned it down. Bittman had a major conflict of interest: was he representing Hunt or protecting himself from prosecution?

This left James McCord and Gordon Liddy as the defendants who stood trial. I was called as a witness by both the prosecution and the defense. I was an involuntary witness for the prosecution as Silbert reminded Sirica of my prior assertion of the attorney-client privilege for which he had held me in contempt.

At the beginning of the trial I had a conversation with prosecutor Silbert in which I told him that I expected to be asked about the work as a volunteer lawyer that I had done for John Dean and for his assistant, David Wilson, in the two months before Watergate. Silbert's short response was that he had never heard of David Wilson. When I testified, Silbert failed to ask me about Dean or Wilson. I wondered why.

At the trial Liddy's attorney adamantly contended that Liddy's Sixth Amendment constitutional right to effective assistance of counsel was being violated by my being forced to testify.[2] He argued:

> ... If Mr. Liddy or any citizen of the United States or any person under the jurisdiction of the United States has a Sixth Amendment right to the effective assistance of counsel ... it ought not to matter one whit whether he exercises that right at three in the morning or three in the afternoon and what Mr. Silbert is suggesting is that there should be some limitation as to the hours when one can consult with an attorney and have no adverse inference drawn there from. I submit that it would have a chilling effect on the right to effectiveness of counsel.

Sirica openly sneered at this argument, declaring:

> How do I know Mr. Caddy in the context of the facts of this case is truly Mr. Liddy's attorney? The simple fact that he says he is my

> attorney does not make him his attorney, does it? Then, if he wants to take the stand and go into detail when he consulted him and how Mr. Caddy became his lawyer, what fee he paid him, and anything like that, I will listen to him, and then make a ruling. He hasn't made any showing. Does your client want to take the stand? He will be cross-examined as to the relationship between Mr. Liddy and Mr. Caddy.

Liddy's attorney responded,

> Is your honor requiring that the only method in which I can establish the attorney-client relationship is to put my client on the stand?

Judge Sirica retorted,

> I am not saying anything but you have offered no evidence and your argument is not evidence to me. It is simply a statement by you.

At this point the prosecution began to worry that Liddy's attorney was building a good case for appeal. So Silbert called upon his second in command, Seymour Glanzer, to pollute the record with a tantalizing smear. Glanzer told the judge:

> There are many cases even though there is a relationship of attorney-client, the court can lift the confidentiality where it is in furtherance of a criminal venture although we are not saying it here. I am just citing an example where lawyers are called to testify or testimony is admitted with respect to lawyers of defendants at trial. There are no Sixth Amendment claims raised in those cases. It is preposterous.

Sirica, his innate viciousness barely concealed, jumped at Glanzer's smear:

> I think you are right.

The jury took little time in finding McCord and Liddy guilty.

Robert Jackson in the *Los Angeles Times* of January 29, 1973, caught the flavor of the trial:

> A clubby atmosphere has prevailed in federal court during the three weeks it has taken the government to present their case in the Watergate bugging trial.
>
> The questioning of Republican officials and others has been more polite than penetrating. Entire areas have been left unprobed.
>
> In the corridor discussions, prosecutor Earl Silbert has been asked repeatedly by newsmen why he has not posed additional questions to the witnesses or called higher Republican officials to the stand.

> Silbert's contention is that the government is submitting only evidence that is necessary to prove charges in its indictment of the original seven defendants last September.
>
> There is no evidence of a wider conspiracy, he has told reporters. Additional testimony could be immaterial and irrelevant, he has said.
>
> Not only have the prosecution's questions been limited but the defense attorneys at times have waived their opportunity to cross-examine.

In March 1973 McCord, fearing Sirica would impose a long sentence on him, wrote his famous letter to Sirica alleging that there had been a cover-up and hush money paid. Soon thereafter I was called by the prosecutors to appear again before the grand jury. This was my sixth and final appearance before the grand jury. Before going into the grand jury room, I reminded the prosecutors how my attempt to tell the grand jury on July 19, 1972, in the early weeks of the case about the "mysterious" phone calls I had received from Mr. Rivers had abruptly ended when Glanzer had cut my testimony off.

Months later, after the Special Prosecutor had been appointed to investigate the case, I requested an appointment to inform that office of the details of my July 19, 1972, grand jury transcript being altered. I started the meeting by remarking about how it was obvious that Silbert, Campbell and Glanzer had purposely limited the case to the original defendants so as to make certain it would not reach the higher-ups. The Special Prosecutor's representative smiled broadly at this and nodded his head vigorously in agreement. However, as I got deeper into the details of my grand jury transcript, his face took on a serious and then alarmed look. When I finished he looked somewhat shocked and said that he would relate what I had said immediately to the Special Prosecutor himself. However, I was *never* contacted afterward by the Special Prosecutor.

Watergate defendant James McCord later testified before the Senate Judiciary Committee in its 1975 hearing on confirmation of Silbert to be U.S. Attorney for the District of Columbia that he had been told there was a complete circuit of grand jury minutes from the grand jury to Silbert to an attorney for the Committee for the Re-election of the President and to the White House.

Senator John V. Tunney in the same confirmation hearing made public a White House tape conversation of April 26, 1973, that contained the following exchange:

> **Nixon**: I considered the special prosecutor. I considered the Presidential Commission. I considered, you know, three judges et cetera and so on. And, uh, I decided that I was satisfied myself so in and in so doing the job, and uh, of course on the uh.

Haldeman: That's it – you prob – well you see, they're going to undermine that through saying Silbert was covering up earlier, earlier.

Nixon: (unintelligible) He may have been.

Haldeman: He was limiting the investigation.

How Everything Turned Out For Me

After all was said and done with the Watergate case, notwithstanding the vicious attacks and false accusations against me by the prosecutors and Judge Sirica, I was never indicted, named an unindicted co-conspirator, disciplined by the District of Columbia Bar, named as a defendant by the Democrats in their civil lawsuit after Edward Bennett Williams had taken my deposition, or even contacted or called as a witness by the Senate Watergate Committee.

Sirica wrote a book *To Set the Record Straight* (Norton, 1979) for which he was paid $1 million (about $4 million in today's dollars), which he pocketed instead of donating it to charity. Professor Stanley Kutler of the University of Wisconsin has acknowledged that he had been approached to ghost-write the book. Nowhere in his book did Sirica discuss what he had done to me, or how he shaped the trial to achieve the outcome wanted, while being paid with taxpayer dollars so that he could profit from it.

Neither Sirica nor the U.S. Court of Appeals ever acknowledged their injustice meted out to me and, through me, to the seven defendants that caused Hunt to realize early on he would never receive a fair trial, and led him instead to choose the cover-up route.

Hunt later wrote in *Undercover: Memoirs of an American Secret Agent*:

> On the 19th of June, 1972, Gordon Liddy told me that his superiors – the White House – had decided I should leave the country and join my vacationing wife and children in Europe until things settled down.
>
> I was reluctant to follow such unexpected instructions, feeling I might be regarded as a fugitive even though no warrant had been issued for me (nor ever was). However I went home and began to pack, and soon afterward Liddy phoned me to rescind his previous orders. But shaken by the appearance of confusion and indecision among our sponsors, harassed by the press and lacking even basic legal guidance, I decided to fly to California and quietly await developments.
>
> From there I placed frequent calls to Washington in order to obtain legal counsel. Douglas Caddy, my first – until then only – lawyer, was reluctant to speak with me, as was my employer, Robert Bennett. Through press accounts I learned that Caddy had been summoned before a grand jury and then hauled off before Judge John J. Sirica who ruled no attorney-client privilege existed between Caddy and myself. He ordered Caddy to answer the grand jury questions and subsequently thrust my attorney in jail.

> Sirica's savage handling of Caddy made me realize how desperately I needed expert criminal counsel. Moreover, the cognomen "Maximum John" had begun appearing in the press, and the combined implications were clear: if Sirica was treating Caddy – an Officer of the Court – so summarily, and Caddy was completely uninvolved in Watergate, then those of us who were involved could expert neither fairness nor understanding from him. As events unfolded, this conclusion became tragically accurate.
>
> Among the many legal scholars who were later to criticize Judge Sirca's conduct of the Watergate proceedings, Dean John Roche of the Fletcher School of Law and Diplomacy has this to say: "...there is one sinister relic of that era: Watergate 'justice.' One appalling aspect of Watergate was the extent to which liberals and civil libertarians deserted traditional principles of due process. The slogan was: 'No due process for the bad guys: get the bastards.' What Sirica did was clearly cruel and unusual punishment forbidden by the Bill of Rights. He used the sentencing process as a medieval rack."
>
> And Douglas Caddy was his first victim.

On September 25, 2014, Bob Woodward and Carl Bernstein spoke at the Brilliant Lecture Series in Houston. At a reception before the event, I renewed my acquaintance with the two famed reporters whom I not seen in the four decades since Watergate. We reminisced about the early days of the scandal, and Bernstein disclosed that Judge Sirica had personally encouraged them to pursue the case. This was typical of Sirica's abuse of the judicial process so as to deny the seven defendants a fair trial. One wonders what other persons he interacted with in the case in violation of judicial ethics in his maniacal and insatiable quest for fame and money.

One landmark book that focuses on this is, *The Real Watergate Scandal: Collusion, Conspiracy, and the Plot that Brought Nixon Down,* by attorney Geoff Shepard (Regnery, 2015). A description of its contents is as follows:

> Geoff Shepard's patient and persistent research has uncovered shocking violations of ethical and legal standards by the "good guys" – including Judge John Sirica, Archibald Cox and Leon Jaworski. "
>
> The Watergate [Special] prosecutors' own files reveal their collusion with the federal judges who tried their cases and their appeals – professional misconduct so extensive that the pretense of a fail trial is now impossible to maintain.[3]

When I read Shepard's book I was disappointed that he did not include among the egregious examples of how the Watergate case was rigged what happened to me. My disappointment was short lived, however, because none of the countless books on Watergate with the exception of *Watergate*

Exposed have described what happened to me as the original attorney for the Watergate seven. In fact none of these authors, before writing their books, ever interviewed myself or Robert Merritt about what we knew.

In November 1974, while the second Watergate trial was underway that dealt with the cover up, the U.S. Court of Appeals issued its decision on Liddy's appeal of his conviction. Liddy had listed as one of his five grounds for reversal that Sirica's "instructions improperly allowed the jury to consider the time and circumstances under which the appellant retained an attorney as bearing on his state of mind." In its decision, the Appeals Court declared:

> We agree with the Third Circuit's analysis that admission of a request for counsel raises Sixth Amendment problems.... In the present case, even it is assumed that there was error in the admission of evidence, the prosecutor's summation, or the instruction, or all of these, the error would be harmless beyond a reasonable doubt. The evidence against appellant ... was so overwhelming that even if there were constitutional error in the comment of the prosecutor and the instruction of the trial judge there is no reasonable possibility it contributed to the conviction.

The Court of Appeals in its Liddy decision made no reference to its upholding Judge Sirica's contempt citation against me two years earlier, after he had falsely accused me of being a "principal" in the crime. Both Judge Sirica and the Court of Appeals were complicit along with Silbert in denying Hunt, Liddy, McCord and the four Cuban-Americans a fair trial and in effect causing the cover-up in so doing.

Ironically, among the most telling criticism was that from Bob Woodward, who in a post-Watergate speech to the Young Lawyers Section of the District of Columbia Bar declared that a "Sirica Myth" had developed around the whole Watergate matter despite the fact that "the job of a trial judge is not to conduct a grand jury session and to some extent he did." Woodward left the impression that he believed *Time* magazine misspoke when it named Judge Sirica "Man of the Year," and that "revisionist historians will re-evaluate and downplay Sirica's role."

These comments by Woodward are welcomed. That said, this is how *Newsweek* reviewed the acclaimed film *All The President's Men*, in which Bob Woodward was played by Robert Redford and Carl Bernstein by Dustin Hoffman:

> That tenacity takes on a new rhythm in the performances of Redford and Hoffman, a rhythm that doesn't romanticize the reality but choreographs it into a compelling dramatic shape. This happened immediately as Redford is assigned to the routine story of the break-in at the Democratic National headquarters. Sitting behind a mysterious defense lawyer at the arraignment, Redford strains forward, trying to see right through the guy's shoulder blades. His alert body, his glancing eyes, his tense, open mouth, ex-

> press inquisitiveness so acute that the audience laughs in delighted complicity. This is more than a hungry young reporter smelling a story – it's a Good guy spotting a *Bad Guy*. [Italics added].

I am especially proud of the backhanded accolade accorded me by the *Washington Post* in its August 4, 1972, editorial: "The lawyer for the five suspects fought fiercely to avoid being questioned by the grand jury." This memoir explains why this "Bad Guy" fought so hard in behalf of his clients.

Woodward was not alone in voicing criticism of Judge Sirica. Conservative columnist James J. Kirkpatrick wrote:

> It would be pleasant if someone really would set the record straight about this tin pot tyrant. Sirica is a vainglorious pooh bah, as ill-tempered and autocratic as any judge since Samuel Chase of Maryland 180 years ago. When the Watergate criminal trials were assigned to him in the fall of 1972, he set out to enjoin the whole countryside with an encompassing gag order that perfectly reflected his lust for power. The order was patently absurd – it embraced even "potential witnesses" and "alleged victim" – and had to be watered down.
>
> During the trial the following January, Sirica was seldom content to let the prosecutor Earl J. Silbert do his job. He repeatedly took over the questioning, hectored witnesses, postured to the press. Sirica's grandstand performance provoked attorney Gerald Alch to the kind of biting criticism seldom heard from a practicing lawyer about a sitting judge; he charged that Sirica "permeated the whole courtroom with prejudice."

Joseph H. Rauh, Jr., a Washington attorney and former national chairman of the liberal Americans for Democratic Action, concurred:

> It seems ironic that those most opposed to Mr. Nixon's lifetime espousal of ends justifying the means should now make a hero of a judge who practiced this formula to the detriment of a fair trial for the Watergate Seven. Indeed, Sirica was quite frank about all of this with statements during the trial such as "I could care less about what happens to this case on appeal" and "I could care less what the Court of Appeals does, if this case ever gets up there."

In response to a letter that I had written the FBI, I received a reply from that agency dated April 18, 1978, that stated, "A thorough search of our central indices revealed that you never have been the subject of an investigation by this Bureau." I wonder how the venomous and venal Judge Sirica would have reacted upon learning this.

The issue of my being gay

A spectre behind the facade of the prosecutors and the judiciary in Watergate concerning me was: "Let's teach this faggot a lesson he will not soon forget." America was still a deeply homophobic nation.

The point man in orchestrating this was Washington, D.C. police detective Carl Shoffler. Shoffler was the officer who arrested the burglars. He had asked to work overtime instead of going off duty to attend a family birthday party and was very conveniently parked in a police vehicle one block from Watergate when the call came into the police headquarters about a possible burglary in progress. In the book, *Secret Agenda* (Random House, 1984), Jim Hougan wrote:

> Adding to the suspicions surrounding Shoffler is the fact that he is no ordinary cop. Prior to joining the police department in Washington, he had served for years at the Vint Hill Farm Station in Virginia. This is one of NSA's most important domestic "listening posts." Staffed by personnel assigned to the Army Security Agency (ASA), Vint Hill Farm is thought to be responsible for intercepting communications traffic emanating from Washington's Embassy Row. By itself, this proves nothing, but it is ironic that the police officer responsible for making the most important IOC (Interception of Communications) bust in American history should himself have worked in the same area only a few years before.
>
> Shoffler's work at Vint Hill was mentioned in passing in the staff interviews for the Ervin committee. This occurred as the result of an allegation against Shoffler by his former commanding officer at Vint Hill, Captain Edmund Chung. According to Captain Chung, he had occasion to dine with Shoffler in the aftermath of the Watergate arrests. Chung claimed that Shoffler told him the arrests were a tip-off, that [Alfred] Baldwin and Shoffler had been in contact with each other prior to the last break-in, and that if Shoffler ever made the whole story public, "his life wouldn't be worth a nickel."

Shoffler, who was a military intelligence agent assigned to the Washington police, in 1969 recruited an informant, Robert Merritt. Merritt's assignment was to infiltrate the "Left" and sabotage its activities using illegal and unscrupulous schemes devised by the FBI, military intelligence and the Washington police. In *Watergate Exposed,* Merritt provides a lengthy and detailed account of what he did as informant for the government, which was Cointelpro on steroids.

Merritt claims he and Shoffler, who was married and had children, had a gay sexual relationship for two years that lasted until the Watergate scandal broke. He also maintains that through a gay friend, "Rita" Reed, who worked as a telephone operator at the Columbia Plaza Apartments where "Heidi" Rikan's prostitution ring was located near the Watergate, he learned of the plan for the June 17 break-in at Watergate two weeks before it happened. His gay friend had overheard it being discussed while surreptitiously listening in on a telephone conversation from an outside caller, who asked to be connected to a supposedly non-working number on the switchboard. Merritt claims that he immediately told Shoffler about the planned break-in, which is why Shoffler was purposely parked a block away from Watergate when the burglary telephone call to police headquarters was made by, Frank Wills, a guard there.

Shoffler, whom I came to believe was a classic self-hating homosexual and blackmailer, expressed his outrage at the original attorney for the Watergate Seven turning up as a closeted gay. He determined different ways to destroy my reputation and career, and even allegedly planned to have me killed in the first few weeks of the case using a poison suppository in a staged sexual encounter, according to a sworn affidavit signed by Merritt. Merritt has stated that Shoffler dropped his plan after the prosecutors subpoenaed me on June 28, 1972, to appear before the grand jury because, as he told Merritt, my murder was no longer needed since the prosecutors would effectively destroy me through the grand jury process.

Some of Shoffler's other measures included arranging for Merritt to telephone key Senators on Capitol Hill to spread the word that I was gay, and also to expose my sexual orientation to the media. A popular alternative newspaper in Washington, *The Daily Rag,* in its October 5-12, 1973, issue carried the headline "FBI Informer Confesses" in which Merritt recounted sundry and many illegal activities that he carried out under the direction of the FBI, military intelligence and the Washington Police. In the publication Merritt was asked, "What was your contact with the Watergate affair?" He responded:

> In June 1972, a few days after the Watergate break-in and arrests, MPDC [Metropolitan Police] Intelligence [officers] Shoffler and Leaper approached me and tried to get me to do one last job. They said that it was the most important thing I had ever done, that it was for my country...
>
> They wanted me to get close to Douglas Caddy, who was alleged to be gay. They wanted me to get to know him socially, sexually, and any other way. They said he had been born in Cuba, that he liked Cubans and was associated with communist causes.

The Advocate, a national gay publication, carried a two-part lengthy interview, "Revelations of a Gay Informant," with Merritt in its February and March 1977 issues in which he reiterated and elaborated upon what had told the Washington alternative newspaper five years earlier.

U.S. National Archives documents

When Merritt asked me in 2008 to work with him on a book that became *Watergate Exposed,* I suggested that he contact the U.S. National Archives for any material it might have on him.

One of the documents released by the Archives was from a box labeled, "Senate Select Committee on Presidential Campaign Activities, Staff Files, James C. Moore, Box B186, Bob Merritt." It was a memorandum to assistant chief counsel of the Watergate committee, Terry Lenzner, from Watergate investigator Jim Moore with its subject being "Interview with Earl Robert Merritt, Jr." dated July 24, 1973. The document states in part:

> On July 13, 1972, Merritt's one association with the Watergate affair began. Detective Schaffler [sic] and Sergeant Leper [sic] of the DC police visited Merritt and asked him to find out all he could about Douglas Caddy, who was representing some of the Watergate defendants. Caddy lived at 2121 P Street, N.W., across the street from Merritt's residence at the time. Merritt did not know Caddy. Schaffler and Leper told Merritt that Caddy was homosexual and pro-Cuban. In response to Merritt's questions, Schaffler and Leper said that this assignment did not come from the police intelligence unit or the FBI or Alcohol, Tobacco and Firearms Division or the CIA. They further denied that the assignment was involved with the Justice Department in any way. They would not tell Merritt who authorized their request, but Schaffler laughingly said it could possibly come from sources higher than the Justice Department. They told Merritt that it would be his biggest job and that it was one of the best things he could do for his country. Merritt refused to carry out the assignment. He said he was periodically asked during 1972 to find out about Caddy, these requests coming from Schaffler or Leper. As recently as February 22 or 23, 1973, Schaffler asked him if he knew anything about Caddy or could find out anything about him. According to Merritt ... on May 16 or 17, 1973, Leper testified before the Senate Watergate Committee that there was no police involvement in Watergate in any way after the apprehension of the burglars on the night of the break-in. Merritt says that Leper was personally involved in the effort to enlist him, Merritt, in the investigation of Caddy. Consequently, Leper committed perjury before the committee. Isbell [David Isbell, Merritt's attorney] and Merritt are interested in pursuing possible perjury committed by Leper and in pursuing the more general question of possible DC police involvement in post-break-in investigations and activities.

Frank Martin of the Watergate Special Prosecution Force interviewed Carl Shoffler and afterward wrote a memorandum dated December 20, 1973, which contained the following:

> Schoffler [sic] was questioned about the incident involving [redacted]. Schoffler stated that at some time after the Watergate arrests, Schoffler and Leper [sic] were in their car and met Merritt near his residence at 2121 P Street. Schoffler stated that he had first seen [redacted] the day after the arrests when [redacted] came to represent the Cubans. When Schoffler and Leper met Merritt, Merritt stated that he might know [redacted] and Merritt had an article from the newspaper with a picture of [redacted] on it. Schoffler told Merritt to let him know if Merritt found out who [redacted] was and if he was "funny", i.e., homosexual. Schoffler stated that this was an off-hand comment and he never expected Merritt to do anything, and Merritt never told Schoffler anything about Caddy.
>
> Schoffler stated that in the summer of 1973, after he had testified in the Watergate hearings, Schoffler met Merritt. Merritt stated that he had made all sort of calls to Senators concerning Watergate and the Caddy incident with Schoffler. Schoffler stated that he told Merritt that if he, Merritt, reported a crime that was one thing, but if he reported something that was only in his head it was going to come back on him. Schoffler said that he did not in any way threaten Merritt.

The *New York Times* of July 2, 2014, carried an article by reporter Michael Powell about Merritt, "Takeover of Kenmore Hotel: Informer Recalls His Complicity." The article quotes a former New York police officer who knew Merritt as saying,

> ... Mr. Merritt loved to tell tall tales of his supposed connections to intelligence agencies and Watergate.
>
> But as it happened, those tales were true.
>
> Federal records confirm that Mr. Merritt worked with the Washington police and the F.B.I. to infiltrate left-wing groups in Washington in the early 1970s; that his police handler apprehended the Watergate burglars; and that he was interviewed by investigators for the Watergate Special Prosecutor, Archibald Cox.

I guess that it is a singular distinction that my sexual orientation as a closeted gay man became an issue in Watergate and that evidence of this can be found in the U.S. National Archives. After all, Watergate occurred only three years after the Stonewall riots and the gay revolution was still not thought of as being a realistic possibility. What effect the knowledge that I was gay had in the vicious actions of the politically corrupt original prosecutors, the venal Judge Sirica and the biased Court of Appeals in their attempt to set me up will never be known, though their abusive actions speak for themselves.

President Nixon's cosmic downfall because of Watergate was, in my opinion, blowback or what goes around, comes around, or perhaps a morphed form of Karma. This was because the alleged principal purposes of the burglars going into the Democratic headquarters, in addition to getting lists of the clients of both the female and male prostitution rings thought to be there and to plant a new wiretap bug, was also to copy secret Cuban government intelligence reports suspected to be there. The documents, through a chain of events decision by Vice President Nixon in 1960, linked him to the assassination of President John F. Kennedy three years later. It was about that "Bay of Pigs" thing. Possible possession of these reports by the Democrats, which included additional intelligence as to persons involved in JFK's assassination, if released publicly during the 1972 presidential campaign, posed a serious threat to Nixon's reelection, but an even far more serious one to the CIA.

But that story will be told in next chapter on the assassination of President Kennedy.

Part 2

Robert Merritt and Carl Shoffler

Understanding what happened in Watergate is impossible without considering the roles of two persons whose significance in the case has never been appreciated. These are Washington, D.C. Metropolitan Police Department (MPD) Detective Carl Shoffler and Robert Merritt. When Watergate broke in 1972, Shoffler was 27 years old and Merritt was 26. This is how Shoffler described his life in a deposition in 1995 in the case of *Maureen K Dean and John Dean, Plaintiffs vs. St. Martin's Press, Inc. et al., Defendants:*

> After high school, shortly after high school, I joined the military. I spent four years in the military. I became a member of the Metropolitan Police Department in '69. I retired from the Metropolitan Police Department in 1989 and was immediately employed in Prince George's County.

Here is how Merritt described his early life in *Watergate Exposed*:

> I became fed up with my mother's alcoholism, my two bigoted uncles, my lying and conniving Aunt Tiny and, most of all, being sexually abused by Catholic priests, So I dropped out of high school just two months short of being graduated in 1962. Hurt, humiliated and ashamed, I ran away from West Virginia to begin a new and hopefully more peaceful life with a new identity in the nation's capital, Washington, D.C.

Both Shoffler and Merritt lacked any formal education other than high school. The fate of the nation in Watergate was to rest in the hands of these two uneducated but bright young men.

In 1969 Shoffler recruited Merritt as a "Confidential Informant." He told Merritt at the time that military intelligence had been profiling Merritt for months and had concluded that Merritt was a flawed individual because of the abuse he had suffered back in West Virginia, especially the sexual abuse by the two Catholic priests. Military intelligence viewed Merritt as a pliable sociopath through no fault of his own, and because he was the flawed product of this abuse, he was someone who could be used and manipulated. However, Merritt turned out to be street-wise to the ninth degree and talented and inventive in his own right.

Shoffler also was a flawed individual. He was a sociopath, even borderline psychopath, and given to acts of extreme cruelty against innocent strangers as Merritt recounts in *Watergate Exposed*. Even though Shoffler was married and had two children, he initiated an intense gay sexual relationship with Merritt that lasted for two years until Watergate broke, when he realized that it was too dangerous to continue.

Merritt described his work as a Confidential Informant for the Washington police and FBI in *Watergate Exposed*:

> From the spring of 1970 until October 1971 I worked both for Carl [Shoffler] and for the MPD Intelligence Division. While in the employ of the latter I received many orders from Sgt. Scrapper and Sgt. Robinson, although most were from Sgt. Scrapper, who sometimes issued them through Connie Fredericks. These instructions included engaging in multiple criminal acts, such as planting drugs (they gave me about 500 "dime" bags of pot valued at $10 each and 5 or more ounces of cocaine) to clandestinely place upon unsuspecting protesters against the Viet Nam War or radical political foes of the Nixon White House, bugging, instigating violence at demonstrations by throwing the first rocks at the police, cutting wires to sound equipment at left-wing public events and protests, giving misinformation to protesters, spreading lies and rumors, creating racial friction, causing thousands of protesters to be arrested, engaging in theft, burglary, mail fraud, filing false police reports against individuals, and many other crimes against citizens who were merely exercising their First Amendment rights.
>
> Sgt. Scrapper specifically ordered me to break into the Community Book Store, the Third Day Book Store and various offices at 1029 Vermont Avenue, N.W. in order to remove anti-Viet Nam war petitions, plant drugs, steal files, photograph documents and destroy office equipment. He also instructed me to steal thousands of names, addresses and phone numbers of directories of citizens who were supporting and financing these left-wing organizations.

On one occasion Sgt. Scrapper ordered me to break into the Red House Book Store. This was actually to test my prowess in carrying out an intelligence operation because the radical book store was in reality a police front operation. The test was whether I could break in and steal records under the very eyes of the police. I passed it with flying colors.

Because I was gay I was ordered to seduce and engage in sexual acts, including sodomy, with over 70 targeted individuals. The MPD Intelligence Division was especially interested in my being able to establish sexual contact with Senator William Proxmire, a Democrat from Wisconsin, whom they said was bisexual. While I was able to worm my way into jogging with the Senator on one morning, nothing more came of this.

The MPD Intelligence Division also ordered me to break into the embassies of two foreign countries, which I successfully did. My attempt at one embassy, which was timed to occur during its Christmas party, was made easier when I was invited inside by the daughter of the ambassador who asked me to smoke pot with her in the library.

In October 1971, after working with the MPD Intelligence Division for about a year, Carl arranged for me to be transferred to the Washington, D.C. field office of the Federal Bureau of Investigation. I was delegated to work with Special Agents Terry O'Connor and Bill Tucker. The FBI assignment primarily dealt with targeting the Institute for Policy Studies and the Weatherman Underground, two organizations deemed radical and dangerous under the government's COINTELPRO program, although no organization in the country was immune from investigation. COINTELPRO stood for co=counter, intel=intelligence and pro=program. The FBI assigned me the code names of the Reverend, then Eric and eventually Top Cat.

Under the FBI's expert training I became an even more proficient CI. I was trained to be a spy, eaves-dropper, saboteur, infiltrator, provocateur, instigator, male prostitute, thief and burglar. Activities that normally would be considered to be illegal became routine, any means to an end. I could become your confidante and cut your throat at the same time. My task was to demoralize, dehumanize and deprive my targets and ordinary American citizens of their lives, freedom and liberty. I had no gun or badge, but I literally had the power to destroy anyone whom I targeted or got in my way. I was your best friend or your worst enemy.

All this time Carl was interacting with any number of federal law enforcement and intelligence agencies, such as the FBI, Department of Justice, Central Intelligence Agency, National Security Agency and military intelligence. One time I chose to resurrect the forbidden topic between us, joking with Carl about his being a federal agent himself, and not merely a lowly police detective, to which he replied, "How do you know that I am not?" My suspicion that this might be so was heightened by Carl always having large wads of cash, and I mean really large wads, on his person for use in his intelligence gathering activities.

As recounted earlier and related in *Watergate Exposed,* CI Merritt had his own informants, one of whom tipped him off on June 1, 1972, of the burglars' plan to break into the Democratic National Committee two weeks later. He passed the information along to Shoffler who set up an entrapment scheme that caused the burglars to change their break-in date from June 16 to June 17 because the latter date was his birthday. His plan was to become the most famous detective in the world on his birthday. He then arrested the burglars inside the DNC at Watergate on Saturday, June 17, 1972, shortly after midnight.

I became an obsession and target of the closeted-gay Shoffler even though I never met him. Here is Merritt's affidavit of June 29, 2009, as to Shoffler's deadly actions towards me:

AFFIDAVIT

1972 CONSPIRACY TO ASSASSINATE DOUGLAS CADDY, Original Attorney for the Watergate Seven

I, Robert Merritt, attest to the following facts regarding my involvement with the Watergate attorney Douglas Caddy, who represented the burglars known as the Watergate Seven. On Saturday, June 17, 1972, five burglars broke into the Democratic National Committee offices in Watergate and were arrested at 2:30 a.m. by Washington, D.C. Police Officer Carl Shoffler. At the time the Washington, D.C. Metropolitan Police Department employed me as a Confidential Informant and assigned me to work directly with Officer Shoffler. Two weeks before the arrests at Watergate I provided information to Shoffler about the planned break-in of the DNC that I had obtained as a Confidential Informant from a highly unusual source. By using this advance information, Shoffler developed a successful triangulation strategy that in effect set the burglars up in a form of entrapment. The Watergate scandal thus began and ultimately forced the resignation of President Nixon.

Shoffler came to my apartment in Washington, D.C. late in the morning of the day of the events at Watergate and exulted in having made the arrests. He told me that he had secretly telephoned the *Washington Post* soon after the arrests to tip the newspaper off to what had occurred. He then demanded his special birthday present from me, which I was only too happy to perform.

(*First meeting*) Three days later, on June 20, 1972, Shoffler showed up at my apartment with his supervisor, Police Sgt. Paul Leeper. They asked me if I knew someone by the name of Douglas Caddy, who lived at the Georgetown House, a high-rise apartment, at 2121 P St., N. W., which was directly across the street from my apartment. They told me Douglas Caddy was an attorney who was representing the Watergate burglars and that Douglas Caddy was a communist and pro-Cuban and was a leader of the Young Americans for Freedom.

They wanted me to establish a sexual relationship with Douglas Caddy to find out how Douglas Caddy knew to show up for the arraignment of the burglars after their arrest. They asserted that Douglas Caddy had to be in on the conspiracy with the burglars and that in the past he had been shadowed when he frequented a leather-Levi gay bar in Greenwich Village in Manhattan.

Shoffler and Leeper related that Douglas Caddy had been working as a White House attorney in a sensitive position. They claimed that I was butch enough to entice Douglas Caddy, a masculine gay guy, into a sexual affair to obtain the information they wanted. They told me that this was the most important thing that I could do for my country and that I would be well-paid if I undertook the assignment. Their initial offer was $10,000.

I asked Shoffler about who it was that so desperately wanted this information from Douglas Caddy and he said that it was from very high up sources in the Department of Justice and the U. S. Attorney's office.

I did not commit to doing the assignment.

Two days later, on June 22, 1972, which was my birthday, Shoffler came to my apartment to give me my birthday present. He spent the entire day with me. Afterwards, when we were relaxing in bed, he gently tried to persuade me to cooperate with him and Leeper regarding the Douglas Caddy assignment. I emphatically told him *"No."* I didn't know Douglas Caddy and I didn't know how to get to know him and I was bothered that undertaking the assignment could lead to the destruction of another gay person who apparently was still in the closet and merely attempting to represent his clients.

We talked about the break-in and Shoffler told me straight out that the burglars were hired indirectly by one of the 100 families of America, which Shoffler named as the Kennedy Family.

Shoffler said, "The intention of the Watergate break-in was to destroy the Nixon presidency. President Nixon was guilty of nothing in its planning."

Shoffler said that there were hidden motivations involved, such as the fear of law enforcement agencies that their turf would be reduced by President Nixon through a scheme known as the Huston Plan, the CIA's concern that President Nixon planned to reorganize the intelligence agencies and their operations, and the Defense Department's opposition to President Nixon's new China policy.

I asked Shoffler if he was angry at me for refusing to take the Caddy assignment and he smiled at me and said he was glad that I didn't.

(*Third meeting*) In the March 1973, nine months after the initial overture and a month after the first Watergate trial ended, I met with Shoffler and Leeper, FBI agents Terry O'Connor and Bill Tucker and their FBI Agent-In-Charge, whose name escapes me. Leeper did most of the talking. He again tried to persuade me to take on the Douglas

Caddy assignment, making an initial offer of $25,000. I refused outright. The group then said that I could be paid as much as $100,000 if I took the assignment but I still refused without providing any explanation. Once it was understood that I would not accept the offer, Leeper declared that the least I could do was to spread the rumor around Washington, D. C. that Douglas Caddy was gay in an effort to force him to come out of the closet. Their intention was to defame Douglas Caddy. This was the last attempt to persuade me to take the Douglas Caddy assignment. The group departed angrily, with the exception Shoffler, who secretly winked at me as he went out the door.

DISCLOSURE OF SECOND MEETING

On June 17, 2009, 37 years after Watergate, I notified Douglas Caddy, now an attorney in Houston, Texas, of a well kept secret and informed him of a new Watergate revelation. (Previously I had disclosed to Douglas Caddy that there had been two meetings regarding the Caddy assignment as discussed above.)

I then informed Douglas Caddy that there had been a *second meeting* about the Caddy assignment. It took place on June 28, 1972, with Shoffler and four others agents who were never introduced to me. I am quite certain that these agents were from either military intelligence or the CIA. I know that they were not FBI agents from their manner and the special type of assignment they asked me to do regarding Douglas Caddy.

Shoffler and these agents met with me in my apartment at 2122 P Street, N.W. Douglas Caddy did in fact live across the street from me in the Georgetown House at 2121 P St., N.W.

One of the agents, whom I will never forget, had two plastic bags, one containing two small blue pills and another that had a laboratory test tube with a small gelatin substance that was approximately ¼ inch in diameter. He referred to it as a suppository.

The assignment was to become intimately acquainted with Douglas Caddy as quickly as possible.

The exact description of the assignment was to engage in oral sex with Douglas Caddy and in doing so I was suppose to fondle his balls and ass, and at the same time insert the small gelatin like suppository into his rectum, which would have caused death within minutes.

If there were any delay in the lethal process that would prevent me from leaving fast from his presence, then I was to take the small blue pills, which would have caused me nausea, providing me with an excuse to leave for home immediately.

The agents told me that Douglas Caddy had to be eliminated without fail.

My first reaction was that they were "nuts." But then Shoffler pulled me aside and whispered that this was a very real and serious situation and the decision was entirely up to me.

The agents were planning a pre-arrange way for me to meet Douglas Caddy, which they did not disclose at the time.

I asked the agents what the reason was that they wanted for me to go to this length and why they and the government were taking such a risk. I was told that this matter involved a high national security situation that they were not at liberty to disclose. The agents stated that their orders did not allow them to know the answers and that they were only following orders from their superiors who sometimes did not know the answers either and merely implemented instructions from those above. However, from the agents' comments I inferred that because Douglas Caddy was gay, that was reason enough.

The agents informed me that I would be well taken care of for this assignment. They also said that I would never have to worry about anything for the rest of my life.

I was totally repulsed by the entire assignment and proposition. After I emphatically refused, the agents swore me to secrecy and left.

Only in July of 1986 when I was subpoenaed by Shoffler to testify before the grand jury in the Lenny Bias case in Upper Marlboro, Maryland did he ever discuss this subject again. At that time he said, "Butch, I am glad that you did not go through with that Douglas Caddy assignment because I found out that those two little blue pills would have caused your instant death."

I regret that I never disclosed these facts until now. I suppressed this information out of fear for my life.

Some of the background information in this affidavit about my relationship with Shoffler as a Confidential Informant was disclosed by Jim Hougan in his 1984 best-selling book, *Secret Agenda: Watergate, Deep Throat and the CIA* (see pages 320-323). Some was also disclosed in the Watergate Special Prosecution Force Memorandums of its two interviews of me and one of Officer Carl Shoffler in 1973.

This sworn statement is the truth, the whole truth and nothing but the truth, so help me God.

I, Robert Merritt, swear in this affidavit that the facts are true to the best of my knowledge under the penalty of perjury.

Robert Merritt

Subscribed and sworn to before me on the 28th of July, 2009,
to certify which witness my hand and seal of office.
Notary Public in and for the State of New York
Ricardo S. Castro
Notary Public, State of New York
No. 01CA5041272
Qualified in Bronx County
Comm. Exp. 08/29/09
7/29/09

Part 3

Robert Merritt's Secret Files Disclosed in 2018

While I was writing this book Merritt contacted me and asked that certain new alleged information, known to him alone, be included in the book. Here is what he told me:

> (1) Martin Luther King was on the train in 1962 that took Merritt from West Virginia to Washington, D.C. after he had dropped out of high school two months short of being graduated and became a runaway. Merritt's mother was white and his father was black. His father was a solder in the Korean War and was killed. This background allowed him to make the longtime acquaintance of several key members of King's entourage on the train.
>
> (2) A few years after Merritt arrived in Washington he got a job as a soda jerk in a drug store that was just around the corner from the Chancery of the Soviet Union. An attaché at the chancery named Boris became a regular customer at the fountain each day and he and Merritt became friends. This evolved into them having breakfast together at the drug store each morning. Merritt found Boris to be a kind man who had tears in his eyes after Merritt recounted the sexual abuse by the two priests and familial abuse he had suffered that caused him to flee West Virginia.
>
> One afternoon Merritt was sitting not far from the drug store in Dupont Circle that was known as a gathering place for anti-war activists and radicals of all stripes. Two men approached him and quietly flashed the CIA credentials. They showed him a dozen photographs that had been taken of him and Boris having breakfast at the drug store on various occasions. Then the two men made veiled threats against him that slowly evolved into strongly advising him that it was in his best interest to become an undercover agent for the CIA. They assured him that he would be well paid if he agreed.
>
> Merritt so agreed and signed on as an undercover agent for the CIA and worked for the organization for over a year. He was given two assignments during that period: (a) monitor and report on anything of substance that Boris might tell him, and (b) monitor and report on the activities of L. Ron Hubbard who regularly hung out at Dupont Circle. Hubbard lived nearby in a townhouse and also had a building in the neighborhood where a dozen followers were engaged in the planning stages of Hubbard's Scientology. The CIA was intensely interested in Hubbard's Scientology. Merritt knew a beautiful girl from Georgia who regularly hung out at Dupont Circle and introduced her to Hubbard who promptly invited the girl to his townhouse. She accepted the invitation on the condition that Mer-

ritt accompany her. Hubbard and the girl on various occasions had sex upstairs in the townhouse while Merritt waited downstairs. The girl later disclosed to Merritt that she had been authorized to tell him that she also was working undercover for the CIA.

(3) Shoffler raped a 13-year old girl whose mother was a drug dealer who lived on the edge of the Georgetown section of Washington. When Shoffler returned to the undercover police vehicle after the rape Merritt expressed his shock. Shoffler replied, "If they are old enough to bleed, they are old enough to be butchered." This was classic Shoffler behavior.

(4) Shoffler ordered Merritt to murder an attorney and provided him with the means to do so under a Huston Plan operation. The innocent victim was killed in Alexandria, Virginia, across the Potomac River from Washington. Shoffler pointed out the target to Merritt as the target walked down the street and the killing was carried out using a poison dart in a closed umbrella that caused the victim to have a fatal heart attack that left no evidence of it being a homicide. Merritt was never given the victim's name.

(5) The Federal Government refuses to release its full file on Shoffler, who is now deceased. Merritt says that the file would reveal that Shoffler engaged in activities that would shock the general public to its core.

(6) Merritt was the sole employee of the Huston Plan that Nixon set up as a clandestine auxiliary and competing organization to the FBI, CIA, NSA and Military Intelligence. Merritt was paid in cash that came from the White House and was doled out to him by Sergeant Dixie Gildon, an officer in the Intelligence Division of the Washington Metropolitan Police Department.

(7) On one occasion Merritt was with Shoffler in front of the Ol' Stein Restaurant on Connecticut Avenue in Washington while Shoffler waited for the arrival of General Alexander Haig and John Dean from the White House. When Dean stepped out of his vehicle, Shoffler introduced him to Merritt, saying, "Butch, this is J.D., your boss." Dean looked startled and disturbed that his cover had been blown by Shoffler. Just then General Haig arrived, and Haig, Dean and Shoffler watched a large anti-war gathering at nearby Dupont Circle before the three entered the restaurant.

(8) Both Bob Woodward and Shoffler received training in military intelligence at the same time at the Vint Hill Station in Virginia operated by the NSA. Each was enrolled under an alias. As a result they knew each other before Watergate broke. Vint Hill Station was one of the NSA's most important listening posts, regularly monitoring Embassy Row. Part of the military intelligence training there was becoming skilled in wire-tapping and electronic eavesdropping.

(9) Woodward served in military intelligence before he went to work at the *Washington Post*. He was a Yale educated officer [also a member of the Yale secret society "Book & Snake"] with a top security clearance. The Chairman of the Joint Chiefs of Staff assigned Woodward to brief members of the President's National Security Council staff and in particular General Haig in the White House on military intelligence matters. It is interesting to note in passing that after both Woodward and Shoffler left military intelligence around the same time. Woodward ended up working for the *Post* and Shoffler ended up working for the Washington Metropolitan Police Department, two key positions in the campaign that destroyed Nixon. Were they "sleeper agents" of Military Intelligence who were placed in these positions?

(10) The Joint Chiefs of Staff and military intelligence began monitoring Nixon when he became the Republican nominee for president in 1968. A scandal broke out in 1971 when Nixon's Plumbers Unit discovered that Navy Yeoman Charles Radford in his capacity as the Pentagon's liaison to the White House had secretly copied thousands of national security documents, many of them from Henry Kissinger's briefcase. Radford's assigned task was to funnel these so that they went up the chain of command to Admiral Thomas Moorer, Chairman of the Joint Chiefs of Staff. This Pentagon secret endeavor was part of a plan to bring Nixon down that ultimately succeeded through Watergate in which (former) military intelligence Agents Woodward and Shoffler played key roles. The Pentagon was vehemently opposed to Nixon's opening to China and his attempt to engage in nuclear disarmament talks with the Soviet Union.

(11) Woodward and Haig worked together in orchestrating Nixon's downfall. Haig gave the order to John Dean who in turn gave the order to Gordon Liddy to burglarize the Democratic National Committee in June 1972.

(12) The CIA had its own operation inside the White House to monitor both the activities of Nixon and Kissinger and also the Pentagon's secret intelligence operation inside the White House. The CIA's plan was allegedly known as Crimson Rose. Merritt says he was involved in an operation of military intelligence headed by Shoffler that stole the Crimson Rose file from within the CIA by blackmailing the CIA's General Counsel. Military intelligence wanted possession of the file for fear that the Senate's Church Committee investigating the CIA would get hold of it and expose its spy operation inside the White House.

(13) Dean and Jeb Magruder, who was a top official in the Committee to Re-elect the President, directed Gordon Liddy to have the burglars break into the Democratic National Committee on June 17, 1972 pursuant to an order from Haig. One goal of the burglars was

to get the list of clients of the prostitution ring operating out of the DNC for use in the campaign to re-elect the president.

(14) Dean had a personal interest in the break-in. His name allegedly appeared in the clients list of a prostitution ring on Capitol Hill that was exposed early in June 1972. Four months after Watergate broke he married Maureen Biner, who was the roommate of Heidi Rikan, the madam in charge of the prostitution ring. Joseph Nesline, a Mafia Capo, ran the ring. Dean might have been compromised.

(15) Merritt allegedly met with President Nixon on three occasions. The first occurred in a few days before J. Edgar Hoover died on May 2, 1972. Merritt was awakened from a sound sleep around 2 A.M. in the morning in his apartment about a mile from the White House by a Secret Service Agent knocking on his front door. The agent told him the President wanted to see him immediately. Merritt hurriedly dressed and was driven by the agent to the White House. Once there he was led through a secret entrance and then into an elevator. The elevator appeared to go down, then sideways, then up, and then down and eventually opened onto a long corridor deep beneath the White House. The agent escorted him to a room. When they entered the President was seated behind a desk. He motioned that Merritt should take a seat in front. The agent stayed inside the room, standing by the door. The President made some small talk and then ordered the agent to leave and go the end of the corridor. The agent protested, but reluctantly obeyed. Nixon again made some more small talk, and then went to the door checked to make sure that the agent had gone down to the end of the corridor. It was obvious that he wanted complete privacy in his talk with Merritt.

Nixon asked Merritt if he had any objections to their conversation being recorded. Merritt assured him that he did not. Nixon then turned on two tape recorders that sat on the front of his desk. The larger recorder was reel-to-reel and the smaller recorder used small disks.

Nixon told Merritt that it was the White House that originally chose him to become a Confidential Informant in 1970 for the Washington Police. He was chosen after having been profiled for a long time. Shoffler did the actual recruitment of Merritt, but unbeknownst to him the recruitment decision actually came from the White House and not Military Intelligence. Merritt not long thereafter was selected to be the first employee of the Huston Plan.

The President expressed appreciation for the manner in which Merritt had carried out his assignments as a Confidential Informant under the Huston Plan, some of which were criminal and many were quasi-criminal. (Merritt's recounting of some of these actions appears earlier in this chapter.)

Merritt says that this first meeting was meant to get him comfortable with the idea that he would be given orders in the future directly from the president. He remembers that his knees were shaking the whole time when he was in the presence of Nixon. The President seemed quite satisfied to Merritt's answers to his questions about politics, which showed that he was basically apolitical.

The meeting closed with the president asking Merritt to keep his eyes open for anti-Nixon activity of any sort.

A second meeting allegedly took place about five days before Watergate broke on June 17, 1972. Again Merritt was summoned in the early morning hours after midnight and transported to the White House. He was escorted through a secret entrance and into an elevator. When the elevator arrived at its destination the agent escorted him to the office of the President.

They went into an office room and the agent then left and stationed himself at the end of the corridor.

The President expressed great confidence in Merritt's ability to carry out assignments, again praising him for his many accomplishments under the Huston Plan. He then said he had a number of new assignments that he wanted Merritt to carry out. Foremost among these were he wanted Merritt to bomb the Institute for Policy Studies and to assassinate a professor of history at American University. What followed thereafter was the President speaking fast and listing assignment after assignment. These were numerous but centered on conducting criminal and quasi-criminal actions against individuals and organizations aligned with the anti-war movement. These targets were all located in the area of Dupont Circle in Washington. The President repeated the assignments three times to instill these in Merritt's memory as Merritt had not been provided with pen and paper. Merritt assured the President that he would faithfully carry out the assignments, just as he had done in the past.

Merritt then decided to bring to Nixon's attention that his friend, Rita Reed, had alerted Merritt on June 1 of the telephone conversation that he overheard the day before while operating the switchboard at the Columbia Plaza Apartments. The conversation revealed that enemies of Nixon were aware of a plan to break into the Democratic National Committee on July 18 and that the break-in would result in the downfall of Nixon from the presidency. Nixon responded that he was aware of a general plan to break into the DNC that had been authorized by the government agencies involved in the Huston Plan. He said he did not know any of the details as to who exactly would carry out the break-in, and that his decision was to sit back and just watch to see what would happen. He said that he had no concern that the break-in would be tied to the White House. He said the purpose of the break-in was to gather evidence of a prostitution ring being operated out of the DNC that would be used in his reelection campaign. He asked Merritt whether it was his opinion, or a fact that there was prior knowledge possessed by his enemies that the break-in would be used to end his presidency. Merritt said it was his opinion because Officer Shoffler was keeping from him the details of how the burglars were going to be entrapped. Merritt, like the President, was unaware of who would comprise the team of burglars. It did not occur to either that it would be "all the President's men.' Merritt did disclose to the President that at the request of Shoffler he had a blank safe deposit box key made that Shoffler planned to plant on one of the arrested burglars with the key taped inside a notebook. Nixon did not respond to this. So Merritt urged the President to consider carefully what he was disclosing to him. Nixon took offense at this, and asked Merritt sharply, "Who is President, you or me?" as if to question Merritt's temerity in forthrightly offering unsolicited advice on how he should act. There was some further discussion about the planned break-in that was wrapped up when the President became quiet and thoughtful and then mused aloud, "I wish I could get a handle on this."

The meeting ended with the President telling Merritt that he would be summoned again to meet with him on an unknown date.

Merritt's third and final alleged meeting with Nixon took place in the second week of July 1972, three weeks after Watergate broke. The Secret Service agent picked him up around 1 A.M. He was driven in a heavy black sedan that looked like it was bullet-proof. The vehicle arrived at the Executive Office Building (EOB) that is adjacent to the White House. Upon a signal the guard inside let them in the front door. They walked into a small elevator that when moving did so smoothly one could not tell it was moving at all. The elevator opened somewhere deep underneath EOB or White House. They walked a short distance and went down a short stairwell to a corridor. They then walked down the corridor and through three doors and then to fourth door. They walked a short distance and the agent told Merritt to enter an office. Inside they found President Nixon distraught with some tears rolling down his checks. Nixon asked the Secret Service agent to leave and to stand at end of corridor.

Merritt asked Nixon why he was crying. Nixon pointed to an article about the Watergate case in the early edition of the *Washington Post* lying on top of his desk. He said he was being destroyed, his presidency was over.

Once Nixon composed himself and made some small talk, he reviewed the Watergate affair. He said that he had been betrayed by many in White House who were motivated by power and money. He could trust no one in the White House; he could only trust Kissinger and Merritt. He said Dean was a traitor, and that he had small elite group of detectives that monitored and taped Dean and others. The group discovered Dean had visited Nixon's enemies on Capitol Hill before and during Watergate. He singled out by name General Alexander Haig, Carl Shoffler, T.D. (Shoffler's police buddy) and Captain Edmund Chung as traitors.

The President again acknowledged that he knew of the general idea of a break-in at the Democratic National Committee being planned under the Huston Plan but had known nothing of its details. He expressed remorse for not taking more seriously the information that Merritt had provided him at their prior meeting about the burglars' break-in plan that his enemies had discussed in a telephone conversation overheard by Rita Reed. He said that the CIA had hijacked the break-in plan and had purposely sabotaged it, resulting in the arrests of the burglars. He was especially incensed at the role played by military intelligence directing Shoffler to set up an entrapment scheme to catch the burglars. Nixon blamed the NSA, FBI, CIA and military intelligence for wanting him destroyed and implied that he had been set up for a fall because of his sponsoring the Huston Plan that encroached upon the powers of these government agencies.

Nixon knew of Rita Reed's disappearance after she had told Merritt on June 1 that Nixon's enemies would use the break-in to end his presidency. The President told Merritt that he must assume Rita was dead.

Nixon regularly received raw intelligence reports from Washington Metropolitan Police Department's Intelligence Division. Merritt surmised these came from Officer Dixie Gildon, who knew Nixon. These reports showed Merritt regretted his role in alerting Shoffler of the planned break-in, based on the information given to him by Rita Reed, because he did not want to see Nixon hurt, and that he admired Nixon. Nixon said he knew that from these reports and from Merritt faithfully carrying out his Huston Plan assignments that he could trust Merritt.

Merritt told him that since their last meeting he had begun to carry out his assignments given to him at that time. The President broke in and said that the plans to bomb the Institute for Policy Studies and to assassinate the professor of history at American University had to be cancelled. Such violent events in the wake of the burglars' arrests at Watergate would likely focus attention on the activities of the White House.

The President spoke about the goals of his presidency that were now in jeopardy. He said it might be years before the historians would realize what he had hoped to accomplish, which was to assure the security and well being of Americans alive and those of future generations.

Then the President swore Merritt to secrecy. Once Merritt has assured him of this, the President said that he had prepared a document that would explain why and what he had done to assure national and international security. The document was his "Message to the American People." He had hidden this historical document inside the White House in a secret location where it might be many decades before it was discovered. He informed Merritt of the secret location, and told him that if the time came when Merritt was still alive, and believed it was the right time for the document to be revealed, he was giving permission to Merritt to reveal its secret location. Merritt, who is in ill health, has told the author of this book of the document's location inside the White House.

Nixon disclosed that he had prepared research dossiers on the FBI, CIA, military intelligence and one other that Merritt cannot remember. Nixon criticized all the agencies, declaring that should the country be attacked in a nuclear war these agencies would not be up to the task of defending the country. He said he was tired of reading reports from these agencies that were composed with the primary intention of the agencies' claiming questionable accomplishments designed to make themselves look good.

Nixon expressed grudging admiration for columnist Jack Anderson whom he said was brilliant and who could take a small clue and develop it into the real story. It was as if Anderson had his own crystal ball. He said that Bob Woodward was not a reporter but instead was a skilled intelligence agent trained in all aspects of that craft. He wondered aloud whether John Dean had been brought into his administration to bring him down, as it was Dean who decided the Watergate burglars would be White House men and issued the order for the June 18 break-in that was later moved up to June 17 by Shoffler in one of his wiretapping schemes that fooled the burglars so that it would take place on his birthday.

Nixon knew he was doomed. He said "it is done. His hope was that there would be some way he would yet survive and somehow serve a third term despite the law that limited the president to two terms.

Nixon talked about a physicist named Samuel Cohen whom he described as brilliant. He said Cohen was the inventor of the Neutron Bomb that when employed emitted neutrons that killed people by destroying their nervous system, but left the physical structures and surroundings intact and unchanged.

Nixon then produced a letter-size briefcase and withdrew a handwritten letter of three pages. He told Merritt that this was the most important document he had ever prepared. He stated that he alone had written with assistance from no one.

He said it was addressed to Henry Kissinger. He told Merritt that he was going to give the letter to Merritt to deliver to Kissinger in person or by mail. He told Merritt to remain quiet and not say a word as he read the letter out loud. Merritt wondered if Nixon was secretly taping what he was reading out loud.

In essence, Nixon talked about "life as we do not know it." He said that during the previous twenty years "Knowledge" had been obtained that could make the human race on Earth "the supreme beings in the universe." This Knowledge came in part from helpful information provided from an extra-terrestrial being from Planet X, Nibiro, who was in a secure location in a building in the U.S. Nixon said the Knowledge also came as the result of discovery made by scientists working at the Los Alamos Laboratories in New Mexico who studied the extraterrestrial being's information. Nixon said, "This all important Knowledge that we possess came from our discovery."

Nixon declared whoever possessed this Knowledge could be the most important person in the world. All would bow down to whoever possessed this Knowledge. The Knowledge was "astronomical, nefarious and devastating."

Nixon said that possession of the Knowledge had to be structured so that it was used only for the good of mankind. His fear was that a small group seeking power would get hold of it and utilize it to the group's evil benefit only.

Nixon said this ultimate Knowledge was contained in two lines in the letter.

In his letter Nixon instructed Kissinger to deliver his letter only to a president of the U.S. who succeeded him whom Kissinger believed could be trusted with the Knowledge. He also instructed Kissinger to devise a precautionary means for trusted persons to deliver the letter to such a successive president should Kissinger die naturally or unexpectedly.

Nixon closed the letter by saying his fate as president was sealed, that "they finally got me." He had kind words of friendship for Kissinger whom he trusted implicitly. Merritt got the impression that Nixon and Kissinger had previously discussed the Knowledge.

After reading the letter out loud, Nixon asked Merritt to come around to his side of the desk so that he could show him the two lines in the letter that spelled out the formula/code/equation for the supreme Knowledge. Merritt of course was unable to comprehend the intrinsic meaning of the two lines that were written in red ink.

Merritt returned to his seat. The president took the handwritten letter with a folded note attached and two small cassette tapes that were in small individual padded envelopes and put these in a larger envelope, which he sealed and taped and placed a scrawled signature across the tape and seal. He then placed a handwritten note on the back of that envelope that directed Kissinger to contact Merritt upon receiving the letter to acknowledge its receipt. He then placed that envelope into a second larger envelope and sealed that with tape. The second envelope was addressed to Kissinger at his home address. It had stamps on it and had the appearance of an ordinary business mail solicitation.

The president then rose and approached Merritt and grabbed his wrist and squeezed it hard and asked "Can I trust you to deliver this letter to Kissinger?" Merritt assured him he would. Nixon said he believed him and stressed that under no conditions could the envelope be surrendered to the FBI.

He then asked Merritt to raise his shirt. Using hospital-type tape Nixon then taped the envelope to Kissinger on Merritt's stomach so that the Secret Service guard who drove Merritt home would be unaware of the envelope's existence. He then handed Merritt a small envelope that contained a typewriter ribbon that had been cut into small pieces. He told Merritt to dispose of the ribbon pieces in a secure manner. Merritt put the small envelop in his pants pocket.

The President reiterated to Merritt that the contents of the letter were vital to the security of the nation. He remarked that if Merritt were to open the envelopes and offer its contents for sale he could make millions of dollars. However, Merritt's record of past performance had convinced the President that he could be trusted to deliver the envelope. Nixon reiterated his trust in Merritt and said that Merritt's ability in carrying out assignments exceeded in some ways that done by the best FBI agents, because Merritt was street wise and knew how to get something done better even when in doing so he violated the directions he had been given. He praised Merritt as being a "Super Plumber," better than any member of the White House Plumbers Unit. He said that he knew Merritt never graduated from high school, but that he was bright and had a good mind.

Once all this was accomplished, Nixon asked Merritt if he had any questions. Merritt said he did. The first was could the scientists in Los Alamos be trusted with possession of the Knowledge? Nixon said that the scientists were the elite of the elite but were monitored at all times both by camera and by human eyes. All their movements were monitored closely.

Merritt then asked about Area 51. Nixon laughed and said what occurred there would boggle Merritt's mind.

Finally Merritt asked if what was seen on *Star Trek* on television could be done such as beaming up a person. Nixon replied that the stuff on *Star Trek* was super antiquated, and that we had moved far beyond anything imagined by the show.

Merritt asked about the TV show *Mission Impossible* and the President said our capabilities would astound him.

The President told Merritt that the Huston Plan was being moved out of the White House and to a location in Maryland and that it would be amply funded. Merritt believes the Huston Plan may still be operating these many decades later.

Nixon told him this was their final meeting and that he was entrusting Merritt to carry out a mission of supreme importance in getting the envelope safely to Kissinger. There was no one in the White House he could trust. Merritt started crying and Nixon took his handkerchief, wiped the tears away and told Merritt to keep the handkerchief.

Merritt never saw the President again. He remembers the occasion as one in which the president was distraught throughout.

The Secret Service agent drove Merritt home. The next day Merritt went to Kissinger's home where the maid told him Kissinger was not present. Merritt then deposited the envelope in a mail box at the street corner located outside Hartnett Hall where he lived [and by coincidence across the street from where I lived.] He burned the type ribbon's pieces in a picnic area in nearby Rock Creek Park.

> A few days later he got a brief phone call from a woman who asked, "Is this Butch?" When he replied it was she said, "This is Nancy. Henry wants you to know that he received the envelope and wishes to thank you." She then hung up.

Merritt carried out all his assignments from Nixon that targeted anti-war individuals and organizations in the Dupont Circle area, but when doing so always felt that someone clandestinely was monitoring his actions, someone likely under orders from the President.

Merritt's attorney before and during when all these meetings with the President took place was David Isbell, a partner in the prestigious Covington and Burling law firm. He was also head of the capital's chapter of ACLU. Merritt had told Nixon that Isbell was his attorney. After each meeting with the President Merritt met with Isbell and informed him of what occurred. When Merritt told Isbell of what Nixon had said to him in their third and final meeting, Isbell remained silent in contemplation for a few moments and then commented, "I don't know what to do with this information. It affects our country and the world. Nixon is a patsy just like Oswald was." Merritt got the impression from Isbell's verbal analysis that Nixon's downfall stemmed from his negotiations with the Soviet Union on nuclear arms control and his opening the door to relations with Communist China, both of which were adamantly opposed by the Pentagon and the CIA. Isbell added that there could be perhaps a more important reason for the president's pending downfall, that being the existence of the Huston Plan that threatened the power of the FBI, CIA, NSA and military intelligence. Isbell then asked Merritt for permission to tell Leonard Boudin, a prominent left-wing attorney known for his anti-war views, of what Merritt had told him and Merritt gave his consent.

Isbell then leaned across his desk and mused aloud, "I wonder if they have deceived me." He then told Merritt that he was having second thoughts about bringing Nixon down because he feared that whoever followed him would be far worse.

Merritt remembers one meeting with Isbell when Attorney General Elliott Richardson arrived unannounced. The two men talked excitedly about Nixon and then placed a phone call to Special Watergate Prosecutor Archibald Cox.

When Isbell had first agreed to represent Merritt as a client in 1971 he told Merritt that he believed Merritt's life was danger because of what he knew about the Huston Plan. Isbell then telephoned Jack Anderson, the columnist, and spoke to him about Merritt. Isbell then sent Merritt to meet with Anderson in his office. Anderson questioned Merritt closely at several meetings the two had, and then wrote a dozen columns about Merritt that were published in the *Washington Post*. In one column Anderson threatened that if Merritt suffered any physical harm there would be hell to pay.

Merritt entrusted Isbell with his personal files for safe keeping on everything he had done for the government over the years. Isbell assured him that they would secure in the law firm's vault. Isbell is now deceased and Merritt's attempts to recover his files have been to no avail as they appear to have disappeared after Isbell died.

The obvious question arises as to why President Nixon decided to meet with Merritt and in such a clandestine fashion deeply underneath the White House. We cannot know what was in Nixon's mind. However, it would be my guess that there was one primary reason.

It is important to remember that allegedly it was the White House that selected Merritt to become a confidential informant for the government in 1970 after having profiled him for a long time and found in him the qualities being sought for such a person: a young man who had been so severely abused in his home and in school by priests that he had become a sociopath. As such, he could be counted on to fulfill assignments involving criminal of actions under the belief that in doing so he was to protecting the national security of the nation. Nixon behind the scenes had issued some of the assignments that were then delegated by Shoffler and others to Merritt. Merritt had shown extraordinary capability and dedication in carrying out these Huston Plan assignments successfully without being caught. Nixon had concluded this track record showed he could trust Merritt to carry out a supremely important assignment.

The reason Nixon selected Merritt to allegedly deliver the envelope with its all-important document and tapes to Henry Kissinger was, as he told Merritt, there was no one left in the White House whom he could trust. Nixon knew that both the CIA and the military had spies in the White House reporting back to their superiors what was happening there.

Fox News published an article on December 15, 2008, by James Rosen titled, "The Men Who Spied on Nixon: New Details Reveal Extent of 'Moorer-Radford Affair.'" Here are key excerpts from it:

> A Navy stenographer assigned to the National Security Council during the Nixon administration "stole documents from just about every individual that he came into contact with on the NSC," according to newly declassified White House documents.
>
> The two-dozen pages of memoranda, transcripts and notes – once among the most sensitive and privileged documents in the Executive Branch – shed important new details on a unique crisis in American history: when investigators working for President Richard Nixon discovered that the Joint Chiefs of Staff, using the stenographer as their agent, actively spied on the civilian command during the Vietnam War.
>
> The episode became known as "the Moorer-Radford affair," after the chairman of the Joint Chiefs at the time, the late Admiral Thom-

as H. Moorer, and the stenographer involved, Navy Yeoman Charles Radford. The details first surfaced in early 1974 as part of the Watergate revelations, but remained obscure until historians in the 1990s and this decade began fleshing out the episode.

The affair represented an important instance in which President Nixon, who resigned in 1974 amid wide-ranging allegations that he and his subordinates abused the powers of the presidency, was himself the victim of internal espionage. In adding to what has already become known about the episode, the latest documents show how the president and his aides struggled to "get a handle on" the young Navy man at the center of the intrigue and contain the damage caused by the scandal

A trained stenographer, Radford was in his late twenties when he was assigned to the NSC staff of Henry Kissinger during Nixon's first term. The yeoman worked out of the Executive Office Building under two admirals, Rembrandt Robinson and Robert O. Welander, who served as formal liaison between the Joint Chiefs of Staff and the NSC. As Radford later described his work – in polygraph tests, sworn testimony, and interviews with historians and journalists – he spent 13 months illegally obtaining NSC documents and turning them over to his superiors, with the understanding that the two admirals were, in turn, funneling the materials to the chairman of the Joint Chiefs and other top uniformed commanders. Radford's espionage took many forms: making extra photocopies of documents entrusted to him as courier; retrieving crumpled drafts from "burn bags"; even brazenly rifling through Kissinger's briefcase while the national security adviser slept on an overseas flight…

Under intensive polygraph testing in late 1971, Radford denied having leaked the India-Pakistan documents to the columnist, Jack Anderson. (Jack Anderson died in 2005 without ever disclosing who had been his source, but he told author Len Colodny in November 1986: "You don't get those kinds of secrets from enlisted men. You only get them from generals and admirals.") However, the young stenographer did eventually break down and tearfully admit to Nixon's investigators that he had been stealing NSC [National Security Council] documents and routing them to his Pentagon superiors. Radford later estimated he had stolen 5,000 documents within a 13-month period…

He [John Ehrlichman's aide, David Young] encouraged Ehrlichman to mention to Admiral Robinson that the young stenographer-spy had already told investigators that he believed the material he had been stealing was destined to go to "your superiors," meaning the Joint Chiefs. Young also urged Ehrlichman to determine the extent to which Kissinger's top NSC deputy – Alexander Haig, who had personally selected Radford to accompany Kissinger on his overseas trips, and who later went on to become secretary of state in the Reagan administration – was "aware of Radford's activities."

> Nixon and his men eventually concluded that Haig had been complicit in the Pentagon spying, but opted not to take any action against him. [Note: Haig later become Nixon's chief of staff.]

So Nixon knew it was not safe to give the all-important document and tapes directly to Kissinger inside the White House for fear that Haig or some other Pentagon or CIA spy would learn about it. In Nixon's opinion the document and tapes were so important to the nation's national security that he had to summon Merritt to a clandestine meeting deep beneath the White House to assign to Merritt the task of getting the document and tapes to Kissinger without anyone knowing about it. This Merritt faithfully did.[4]

The Huston Plan

Tom Huston, the co-author with President Nixon of the Huston Plan, was one of the founders of Young Americans for Freedom in 1960, which was when I first got to know him. He is now one of my Facebook friends. During the time he was employed by the Nixon Administration he was kind enough on one occasion to give me a tour of the White House and to introduce me to Pat Buchanan, the president's speech writer. What I remember most about Buchanan's office was the large number of television sets that were being played simultaneously to monitor breaking news.

Robert Merritt was the sole employee of the Huston Plan, being paid by cash funds provided by John Dean from the White House to Sergeant Dixie Gildon of the Washington Metropolitan Police Department who disbursed the money to Merritt. Merritt maintains that Gildon has a fairly detailed knowledge of the Huston Plan.

The Huston Plan is best described in a CNN article by Professor Douglas Brinkley, CNN's Presidential Historian, and Professor Luke A. Nichter, published on June 17, 2015. Here are some excerpts from their article, "Great Mystery of the 1970s: Nixon, Watergate and the Huston Plan":

> Chaired by FBI Director J. Edgar Hoover, ICI [Interagency Committee on Intelligence] membership included the major intelligence agencies, including Richard Helms of the CIA, Donald Bennett of the Defense Intelligence Agency, William Sullivan of the FBI, and Noel Gayler of the National Security Agency. The White House liaison was Tom Charles Huston, a conservative-minded attorney and former intelligence official, whose name will be forever associated with the mysterious report.
>
> The Huston Plan gave new domestic and international powers to the intelligence community, including break-ins, domestic surveillance, and surreptitious entries. It remains classified "Top Secret" today. Ironically, we know more about illicit domestic surveillance

> performed by the intelligence community in recent years, due to hackers, than we do about such activities from more than four decades ago. Some scholars have even floated the idea that the Huston Plan was a forerunner to the authorities granted to the intelligence community in section of 215 of the Patriot Act, which authorizes the bulk metadata collection program.
>
> On May 16, 1973, White House special counsel J. Fred Buzhardt reported to Nixon that top NSA officials, including Deputy Director Louis Tordella, had told him the Huston Plan had been put into effect, according to a tape released in August 2013 by the National Archives.
>
> When the existence of the Huston Plan first became public during Watergate, we were led to believe that it was never implemented. Nixon ordered the plan and then recalled it, so the story went.
>
> However, the reason the Huston Plan remains classified today is likely because at least portions of it were indeed implemented after all. The basis for its continued classification is to protect secrets that were operational…
>
> When word reached the intelligence community that the Huston Plan was no longer in the custody of the White House, panic swept across the FBI, CIA, and NSA on May 17. The FBI feared it could end up in the hands of congressional investigators then looking into Watergate, with the result being that "inference is likely to be drawn by Congressional committees that this committee (the ICI) was a prelude to the Watergate affair and the Ellsberg psychiatrist burglary."…
>
> There was indeed a "cancer on the presidency," as Dean said to Nixon on March 21, and the apparent answer of the national security establishment was to cut it out – to cut Nixon out. The President had to resign, and he had to be pardoned to ensure that inquiries into broader U.S. government wrongdoing could not continue indefinitely.

Merritt appeared before the Senate Watergate Committee in executive session in 1973 on the day before John Dean first testified before that committee in open session. Senator Howard Baker asked the committee's reporter/stenographer to leave the room so that there was be no written record of Merritt's disclosures. The Senator then asked Merritt the first question, "What do you know about the Huston Plan?" Merritt responded that he was reluctant to answer the question. Senator Baker expressed surprise and asked why? Merritt responded that he had been escorted to the executive session by a committee staff member named Wayne Bishop who threatened him that if he told what he knew, he would be arrested on the spot and placed in a jail beneath the Capitol Building. The Committee members expressed shock at hearing this. Merritt remembers Committee Chairman Sam Ervin and Senator Baker conferring and then Ervin informing him that the hearing was being cancelled and he could depart but would be called back at some future date to testify. Some weeks later Senator Ervin did call Merritt and told him the Committee still planned to call him back for his testimony and that he should not worry about Wayne Bishop being involved anymore.

There is brief mention in the Senate Watergate Committee hearings of Merritt's initial appearance before the committee. He was never called back to testify about the Huston Plan. As a result the committee forfeited it chance to learn about the Huston Plan from that plan's sole employee who alleges that at one point in time, he took his orders directly from the president. Merritt says that Shoffler told him the reason he was never called back to testify about the Huston Plan in executive session of the Watergate Committee was because Senator Ervin had been threatened that his family members would be in danger if he pursued the inquiry through Merritt.

The Huston Plan and the activities carried out under it are crucial to understanding what Watergate was about. This is why Merritt's knowledge stemming from his being the sole employee of the plan is so important.[5] His paymaster was John Dean who was in charge of implementing the Huston Plan once its co-author Tom Huston was no longer a factor. Dean knew that public disclosure of its contents was so explosive that it would be like Watergate on steroids. Dean realized that since he had been in charge of its implementation, public disclosure would lead to his criminal prosecution. As reported in the prior CNN article by Brinkley/ Nichter:

> Our chance to learn about the Huston Plan and whether it was the authority upon which the Watergate burglary took place slipped away when former White House counsel John W. Dean III turned over the White House copy to the U.S. District Court for the District of Columbia on May 14, 1973.
>
> Dean took the plan with him when he was fired on April 30. As a result of his giving the document to the courts, it became out of the reach of congressional subpoena and out of the reach of the Freedom of Information Act, even though it was a document created by the executive branch and should have been reviewable under the FOIA. The document and associated records have been in the custody of the court ever since. (Incidentally, we have a petition backed by the American Historical Foundation to review and hopefully release these records. In addition, there are still [in 2015] 700 hours of Nixon White House tapes that have not been released by the Archives.)

New York Times famed reporter Michael Powell, a Pulitzer Prize winner, has interviewed Merritt on numerous occasions for the past five years and is planning a major article about him for the *Times*. Merritt has provided thousands of supporting documents to assist Powell in this project.[6]

It will take a skilled professional reporter like Michael Powell to weigh the credibility and value of Merritt's disclosures, including those above. I have worked with Merritt on Watergate for almost eight years in an on-and-off relationship and have come to the conclusion that because his life's work has been being a confidential informant for the government, his manner of thinking is decidedly different from that of the normal person. One only has to read what he says in *Watergate Exposed* to realize that this is true. I have advised Merritt to cooperate fully with Powell and to hold nothing back as Powell represents the last and best chance for Merritt's story to be told. Merritt is 73 years old and in poor health.

Part 4

Who Killed Gabe Caporino?

Andy Thibault, an award winning reporter and columnist, contacted me in 2016 to call my attention to a cold murder case in which General Foods Corporation played a major role. Thibault had learned how General Foods Corporation had misled and abused me as an employee by sending me to represent the company in Washington in 1969, and requiring in doing so that I work out of the Robert Mullen Company that had handled its public relations for years. The Mullen Company, unbeknown to me, but well known to General Foods, was a CIA front that had been incorporated by the CIA in 1959. Thibault asked me analyze the role of General Foods in the murder case because of its close relationship with the CIA.

What I found was startling.

Thibault jump-started my investigation by providing me with a copy of his book, *More Cool Justice* (Icebox Publishing, 2014), in which there is a chapter titled, "Who Killed Gabe Caporino?" In it he wrote that "On March 3, 1974, Caporino, 40-year old married father of two daughters, left his home in Yorktown Heights, N.Y. for a week-long business trip to Houston and New Orleans. Caporino was a 17-year executive with the coffee division of General Foods. [General Foods was acquired by Philip Morris in 1983.] ... The night that he disappeared [in New Orleans] – March 7, 1974 – Caporino spoke with his wife and daughters, asking about a school parents' night and confirming a dinner date with friends for the weekend. Found in his hotel room were his return flight tickets and his suitcases partially packed with gifts for his family."

It intrigued me that Caporino's disappearance took place in March 1974, which was when the Watergate scandal was approaching its peak that occurred when President Nixon resigned on August 9, 1974. From the onset of the Watergate case the Mullen Company and tangentially one of its client, General Foods, were subjects of public and prosecutorial interest because when the burglars were arrested at Watergate Howard Hunt was a vice president of the Mullen Company and Robert Bennett, Mullen Company president, reported to the CIA on a regular basis. The last thing that General Foods wanted in March 1974 was for the media to take notice of the disappearance of one of its executives in New Orleans and start asking questions that might lead to its relationship with the CIA and on into Watergate.

What made this a sensitive matter for General Foods? Because of the possibility that Gabe might have stumbled upon or inadvertently discovered something General Foods might have been doing in behalf of the CIA that would have catapulted the company deep into Watergate. It is highly significant that thousands of cans of coffee were later to have been found missing from the company's inventory at a time when it was recognized by law enforcement that sealed coffee cans were being used to transport heroin because drug dogs were not able to sniff the cans' contents. The CIA had for decades been deeply involved in drug trafficking and had laundered some of its drug money through the casinos in Havana, Cuba; that is, until Castro took power and closed the casinos to the outrage and distress of the CIA and organized crime. What followed were numerous attempts by the CIA (with the help of organized crime) to assassinate Castro and reopen the casinos.

What did General Foods do when Caporino's wife, Grace, expressed alarm at his not returning home on March 8, 1974? It assigned its chief of security, Jack Ison, to investigate the matter. Ison had been a FBI agent for nine years before becoming employed by General Foods. His efforts to deflect the focus of Gabe's disappearance and classify him as a missing person include the following: refusing to investigate forgery of Gabe's credit card, which the FBI crime lab confirmed, and his fabrication of incriminating data in the New Orleans Police Department file as well as in the FBI file.

In John le Carre's book, *The Constant Gardner,* he alludes to the accepted fact that the heads of security at large corporations are often responsible for arranging the deaths of people who pose a threat to the business interests of the company. Such heads of security are also often responsible for conducting internal investigations that end up making findings that favor the corporations at the expense of the truth. Carre is a former MI5 agent and is knowledgeable about matters of this type.

Soon after his arrival in New Orleans, Ison met with the New Orleans Police and purposely excluded members of Caporino's family from being present. As Thibault recounts in his book, "Instead of trying to find Gabe Caporino, the General Foods corporate leadership acted in concert with New Orleans police to trash him with unsubstantiated allegations ranging from gambling and unspecified industrial espionage to mob connections and inept whore mongering."

Before Caporino went to New Orleans in 1974 he was a trusted employee of 17 year tenure, having serious company responsibilities. Overnight with his mysterious disappearance he was transformed by the company into an employee with a horrible reputation. What could motivate the leadership of a General Foods suddenly to adopt such a position in regard to Caporino?

To make matters even worse, the company took steps to sever its obligatory relationship with Grace Caporino, Gabe's wife, so as to deny her and her two children financial assistance. These include Workmen's Compensation widow's benefits, Social Security widow's and children's benefits, and all contractual employee insurance death benefits.

By chance, on a visit to the New Orleans Police, Grace was briefly able to peruse a three-and-a-half inch file on his husband's case before it was whisked away. Later the file disappeared and to this day has not been found. What was in the file that was so disconcerting that the police and perhaps the CIA decided that it had to go missing – as had Gabe? Much later it would take almost ten years of Grace's Freedom of Information Act requests to obtain the FBI file, which was redacted as to sources but replete with damning fabrications against Gabe.

On November 3, 2017, NOLA.com/*Times-Picayune* carried an article titled, "Public corruption in Louisiana 'can't get much worse,' says outgoing FBI New Orleans director." The outgoing New Orleans FBI special-agent-in-charge, Jeffrey Sallet, declared in the article that "I have had the unique opportunity of working in the area of corruption for the four New England states of Maine, Massachusetts, Rhode Island and New Hampshire. I had the perspective of being the national chief of corruption and civil rights, and I would say that the corruption in this state is at an extremely unacceptable level."

In 1954 and1955 I had attended meetings in New Orleans organized by Assistant Police Superintendent Guy Banister, a former FBI agent, which focused on the efforts of the Aaron Kohn Crime Commission's to investigate organized crime in the city. Almost seven decades later not much has changed. Corruption is still a way of life in the Big Easy. What makes the cold murder case of Gabe Caporino unique from that of other persons who have gone missing in New Orleans is the possibility that he had learned something about heroin being transported in General Foods coffee cans in an operation orchestrated by the CIA. It could also be that he by chance saw something else happening in General Foods that he should not have seen. Whatever it was, it cost him his life.

Gabe Caporino is no longer among the living. However, his cold murder case cries out for justice because of its national security implications. Grace has compiled a time-line of events in the case and a mound of other helpful documents and stands ready to assist anyone who would cherish the challenge of turning this cold case into a hot one. To contact Grace Caporino send a letter addressed to her c/o Trine Day, P.O. Box 577, Walterville, OR 97489. The letter will be forwarded to her.

Endnotes

1. http://news.findlaw.com/hdocs/docs/watergate/watergate_fbiope_rpt.pdf

2. Amendment VI: In all criminal prosecutions, the accused shall enjoy the right to a speedy and public trial, by an impartial jury of the state and district wherein the crime shall have been committed, which district shall have been previously ascertained by law, and to be informed of the nature and cause of the accusation; to be confronted with the witnesses against him; to have compulsory process for obtaining witnesses in his favor, and to have the assistance of counsel for his defense.

3. From paragraphs two and three on the inside flyleaf of the cover of Geoff Shepard's book.

4.President Nixon may have got his idea of a "time capsule" from President Eisenhower.

In the highly praised book, "The President and the apprentice," the author writes: "In 1953, after his first few months in the White House, President Eisenhower wrote out a handwritten list for Project X, a secret recollection of his presidency to be deposited in a time capsule at his Gettysburg farm."

https://www.amazon.com/President-Apprentice-Eisenhower-Nixon-1952-1961/dp/0300181051

5. Robert Merritt was the only employee of the Huston Plan. Another fellow – Jared Stoute – was assigned for a whole year to monitor Merritt's activities on a daily basis, starting when Merritt woke up. He was like a shadow and wrote down in a notebook everything Merritt did. He did this from June 1971 to June 1972, right up until when Watergate broke. He even knew what Rita Reed had told Merritt about the telephone conversation she had overhead on the switchboard. Stoute most likely was a member of Nixon's "private detective team" as was Tony Ulazewicz. Whatever he learned went back directly to Nixon in a report. That is why Nixon sent for Merritt in May 1972 and had three meetings with him. Stoute had reported to Nixon that Merritt was a "Super Plumber" and could be trusted.

6. To Whom It May Concern:

"I am a New York Times columnist and writer and I've worked on and off with Robert Merritt for many years. He can be excitable and passionate, but in my experience he is also remarkably level-headed and his work has benefited many federal and city investigations. He has worked everything from city investigations to the Watergate and the undermining of a president. He now appears to be the victim of a concerted attempt to undermine his credibility and it is taking a grievous and unfair toll on his health and safety."

Chapter Four

The Kennedy Assassination

I saw Howard Hunt only three times during the Watergate case. The first was when he came to my residence in Washington on June 17, 1972, at 3:35 A.M., after he had telephoned me from his White House office a half hour earlier. At that meeting he explained what had happened at Watergate and retained me as his attorney to represent him and the five arrested burglars. The second time I saw Howard was at the funeral of his wife, Dorothy, in December 1972, after she had died in a mysterious plane crash at Midway Airport in Chicago. I am not alone in thinking that Dorothy was killed after Howard made this recorded threatening phone call demanding "hush" money to Charles Colson in the White House in November 1972 once Nixon was re-elected.[1] Howard thought so too. In the wake of Dorothy's death, he called his four children together and told them that he was going to plead guilty at the upcoming Watergate trial in January. He said to them that he was afraid that if he did not do this, they would be killed next. When he pleaded guilty the next month all the work that I had done on his behalf to protect the attorney privilege that led to my being held in contempt and jailed by Judge Sirica was dropped down a memory hole as the Watergate case mushroomed. The third and last time I saw Howard was in early 1975 when he telephoned and invited me to join him at a dinner. He said that he would soon enter prison to serve his sentence for Watergate and that he wished to express his appreciation for my legal representation of him in the case.

Even though I had been Howard's attorney before Watergate broke, legally we had not been able to have a conversation once I was served with a "forthwith" subpoena to appear before the grand jury by Prosecutor Silbert on June 28, 1972, after which my role evolved into being a voluntary witness for the seven defendants and an involuntary witness for the prosecution. But now the case was over and we could talk.

Hunt and I chose the Yenching Palace, a popular Chinese restaurant, as our place for dinner in 1975. When the restaurant went out of business in 1997, the *Washington Post* published an article, "Five Decades of Secrets to Go," because so many important decisions had been reached inside it, including the U.S. representative and his Soviet Union counterpart agreeing over dinner to settle the Cuban Missile Crisis in 1962.

As our dinner progressed I wanted to ask Howard some basic questions about Watergate but sensed that he would be reluctant to answer these. I prefaced my remarks to him by saying that Watergate could lead ultimately to the destruction of Western Civilization. I believe this to this day. Watergate, along with the Kennedy assassination and 9/11, were steps that hastened the decline of Western Civilization and could usher in the future Empire of Chinese Civilization. Howard showed no emotion when I said this. Nevertheless I pressed forward and asked him, "Why did the burglars go into the DNC?" After a pause he said, "I told them to photograph any piece of paper that had numbers on it."

This was obviously a ridiculous answer, so I said, "Come on now, Howard. You cannot get away with that. Think of all that I have gone through on your behalf as well for the burglars."

Howard merely shrugged his shoulders and did not respond.

"Well," I said, "As you know I was a witness at McCord's and Liddy's trial, and when I was on the witness stand I saw a long table in front of me that was covered with what looked like wiretapping equipment and other electrical things. Didn't the burglars go into the DNC to fix a defective bug left there from a previous break-in?"

After a moment Howard nodded his headed affirmatively while remaining silent in a way that I took it to be assent.

After a long pause I then asked, "There was a lot of publicity about a prostitution ring being operated out of the DNC. In fact, another prostitution ring was uncovered on Capitol Hill a few weeks before the DNC break-in in which the book of clients had been recovered. So didn't you go back into the DNC to get the book of prostitution clients that was there?" Knowing the names of the clients of the rings could lead them to being compromised and subjected to blackmail.

Again in response Howard merely nodded his head while remaining silent, which I took to be assent.

I pressed on, saying "Burglary of any sort is a serious criminal offense. While fixing a bug and getting a list of the clients of a prostitution ring are significant matters, they in no way could justify such a reckless break-in with so much at stake with Nixon's re-election. There had to be a more important reason, a crucial one, for justifying the break-in."

Howard remained silent for an unsettling period of time and then answered slowly and reluctantly, "Well, there was such a reason. We believed there were important Cuban Government documents inside the DNC dealing with the Kennedy assassination."

It took me a moment mentally to absorb this startling revelation and then I asked, "Cuban Government documents dealing with the Kennedy assassination? What did the documents contain?"

At this point Howard raised both his hands so that their palms were facing me and waved them from side to side. It was his way of ending our discussion about Watergate. It was obvious that the burglars were arrested before they could do any of their assigned tasks inside the DNC and there was no way of knowing if Cuban Government documents were there. So the rest of our dinner was devoted to discussing how his children would cope with their mother being dead and with his going into prison and also with my personal circumstances.

After dinner and when we were outside the restaurant on the sidewalk I decided to make one more stab at learning what was behind Watergate. I asked Howard, “Why was Kennedy assassinated? What could have been in the Cuban Government documents on his assassination that was so important to justify a break-in?”

Howard hesitated for a moment the replied, “Kennedy was assassinated because he was about to give our most vital secret to the Soviets.”

Stunned at hearing this, I asked, “Our most vital secret? What was that?”

Howard looked me in the eyes and declared, “The Alien Presence.” With that he shook my hand, turned and walked away. That was the last time I saw Howard although we did correspond subsequently and talk on the phone on a few occasions.

In 1975 at the time of the dinner I was not a student of the Kennedy assassination. Nor was I very familiar with Aliens and UFOs. Neither of these subjects was on my radar screen so to speak. So Howard’s parting comments did not register much with me although I did recognize because he had uttered them that they were significant and something to remember.

It was not until 2006 when the Kennedy Assassination Topic of the Education Forum based in England started a members’ thread on me that I began to acquire detailed knowledge of JFK’s assassination. The forum’s thread was initiated because Billie Sol Estes, LBJ’s silent business partner and bagman, had told me in 1984 about LBJ being behind JFK’s assassination. It was also around that same time that I started listening to Coast-to-Coast AM on the radio each night whose moderator was the charismatic Art Bell. Many of its programs dealt with the circumstantial evidence of UFOs and Aliens. Only then did I start to connect the dots as to what Howard had told me forty years earlier.

Among the dots was a book by Colonel Philip Corso, *The Day After Roswell*, which was published in 1997. The entry on Corso in Wikipedia discloses that in his book Corso:

> …claims he stewarded extraterrestrial artifacts recovered from a crash near Roswell, New Mexico in 1947.
>
> Corso says a covert government group was assembled under the leadership of Adm. Roscoe H. Hillenkoetter, the first director of Central Intelligence (see Majestic 12). Among its task was to collect all information on off-planet technology. The US administration simultaneously discounted the existence of flying saucers in the eyes of the public, Corso says.

> According to Corso, the reverse engineering of these artifacts indirectly led to the development of accelerated particle beam devices, fiber optics, lasers, integrated circuit chips and Kevlar material.

Corso distributed Alien artifacts to major corporations in his position as Chief of the Pentagon's Foreign Technology desk in Army Research and Development, working under Lieutenant General Arthur Trudeau. He did this in 1961 through 1963, the years that Kennedy was president. Such distribution required approval by the president as distribution of the Alien artifacts to major corporations was a highly classified project.

The great fear of the Deep State, comprised of the CIA, NSA, Military Intelligence, Wall Street and Majestic 12, was that Kennedy would give away our nation's most vital secret – including our reverse engineering of the Alien artifacts – to the Soviets.

There is reason to believe that Kennedy first learned of the Alien Presence when he was in Naval Intelligence in the 1940s. He was a close friend of Secretary of Defense James Forrestal in the Truman administration who allegedly had full knowledge of the Alien Presence. Professor of Astronomy Dr. Donald Menzel at Harvard, a member of Majestic 12, knew Kennedy when the latter was a member of the university's Board of Overseers and also a U.S. Senator and offered in 1957 to tell him what he knew after he received a high security clearance.

When Kennedy became president he promptly took steps to learn more about the Alien Presence and Majestic 12. After the Bay of Pigs fiasco, in June 1961, he issued National Security Action Memorandum 55, which took covert activities away from the CIA and placed these in the Defense Department.

That same month he met with Soviet Premier Nikita Khrushchev in Vienna and attempted to open the possibility of cooperation between the world's two major powers.

In June 1963 he delivered a renowned speech at American University in which he advocated world peace. In September 1963 he addressed the United Nations and declared the exploration of outer space and landing on the moon should be a collaborative effort between the Soviet Union and the U.S.

Finally, on November 12, 1963 – just ten days before his murder – he signed National Security Action Memorandum 271 addressed to the Administrator of NASA that directed specific steps be taken to implement cooperation with the Soviet Union on outer space exploration and a landing on the moon. He personally signed the memorandum and sent a copy to each major official in his administration that this was now to be national policy.

Behind these efforts by Kennedy was a belief that if the planet was to meet whatever the challenge was represented by the Alien Presence it would entail the close cooperation between the world's two greatest powers.

Kennedy's end run around the sector of the Deep State that dealt with the Alien Presence posed a threat to that all powerful group and led to the decision that Kennedy must be assassinated. There are many theories as to why Kennedy was killed but this is the one I embrace. As Mary Meyer Pinchot, JFK's mistress, was later quoted as saying, he was moving too fast and he could not be controlled. She, too, was killed the year after JFK's death because she knew too much.

Jacob G. Hornberger of The Future of Freedom Foundation in an article, "How to Understand JFK Conspiracy Theories" published on November 15, 2017, wrote that he, too, embraced the theory of a U.S. National Security State Regime Change-Operation:

> This is the only paradigm in the JFK assassination that makes any sense and in which all the contradictions, inconsistencies, and anomalies disintegrate. The operation was no different in principle from the ones carried out in places like Iran, Guatemala, Chile, and Cuba and for the same reason: to protect U.S. national-security from a political leader whose policies were perceived to pose a grave threat to U.S. national security.
>
> One of the fascinating aspects of the Kennedy assassination has always been the reluctance or the refusal of the mainstream press to consider the matter from the standpoint of one of the bedrock principles of American jurisprudence – the presumption of innocence, especially since Oswald was claiming that he was an innocent man. In fact, not only did Oswald deny that he killed the president, he went a critically important step further – he claimed that he was being framed. The mainstream press has never shown any desire to confront that possibility and deal with it.
>
> Indeed, they have simply accepted a set of very pat facts, all of which have all the earmarks of good frame-up. Moreover, within an hour of the assassination, it was being conveniently blamed on a purported communist, Lee Harvey Oswald, whose communist bona fides were being established with a press release by a CIA front organization in New Orleans called the DRE, almost immediately after Kennedy was pronounced dead.

I was interviewed about the JFK assassination because of his knowledge about the Alien Presence on Dark Journalist on June 29, 2014. Here is a link to that YouTube interview: https://www.youtube.com/watch?v=-5jKBlJQNtek

I was interviewed about Howard Hunt's comments to me in 1975 about the JFK assassination and the Alien Presence on the November 21, 2017, radio program of coasttocoastam. Here is a link to that program: https://www.coasttocoastam.com/show/2017/11/21

My interview is also reported here: https://www.earthfiles.com/news.php?ID=2580

A few weeks later the *New York Times* broke the decades long silence about the Alien Presence in an article published on December 14, 2017, "Glowing Auras and 'Black Money': The Pentagon's Mysterious U.F.O. Program." Here is a link to that article: https://www.nytimes.com/2017/12/16/us/politics/pentagon-program-ufo-harry-reid.html?_r=0

JACK WORTHINGTON

Vanity Fair magazine in April 2008 published an article by David Friend, "The Man Who Would Be Jack: A Claim to Camelot," whose lead-in read:

> What's a *V.F.* editor to do when a respectable financier, Jack Worthington, who looks a lot like John F. Kennedy, says he believes he may be the murdered president's son, and offers the magazine an exclusive? Answer: Try to get hold of J.F.K.'s DNA, dig through conspiracy theories and White House connections (Worthington's lawyer represented the Watergate burglars, and an ex-girlfriend turns out to be Neil Bush's ex-wife), door-stop Worthington's mother in Texas, and take other desperate measures. Because– Who knows? What if? Remember the "Deep Throat" scoop? – it just might be true.

The article went on to say,

> In October 2006, I was summoned to the office of Graydon Carter, *Vanity Fair*'s editor. I entered, blinking back the glare of the eggshell carpet, the blond wood walls, the midday sun streaming in through wraparound windows. Carter slid a letter across his swooping desk, slick as a skating pond. It was marked privileged confidential communication.
>
> "This came in today," Carter said. He hunched forward as I read:
>
>> *Re: The New JFK*
>>
>> *Dear Mr. Carter:*
>>
>> *I have been retained to represent my client who is the son of President John Fitzgerald Kennedy in his effort to prove his paternity. My client is a member of a family prominent in Houston society, a graduate of an Ivy League university, and a successful international businessman.*
>>
>> *His mother, an exquisite beauty queen in her youth, met John F. Kennedy soon after he became President through an introduction from Vice President Lyndon Johnson, a close family friend. Members of his mother's family were political allies of LBJ during his ascent to power.*

> *His mother ... only recently told my client that John F. Kennedy was his father. My client's physical appearance and personality closely resemble JFK. He has been stopped on the street on numerous occasions by strangers who have told him such resemblance is remarkable.... It is my client's desire to give the exclusive rights to his story to* Vanity Fair *... subject to his paternity being validated by* Vanity Fair *through a DNA test involving blood, saliva, hair root or semen.*
>
> *If your magazine is interested in pursuing this matter, [I] stand willing to cooperate speedily in all ways possible.*
>
> *Very truly yours,*
> *Douglas Caddy*

> The references to bodily fluids threw me for a moment. But my focus soon narrowed to the giddy gist of it. The chance to bring to light a stealth claimant to the Camelot mantle was the media equivalent of the Holy Grail. Here was the tale of a boy raised in obscurity, ignorant of his origins, living for years in the distant provinces, who had suddenly discovered his roots. To make matters even more enticing: the secret, if true, had been kept for nearly 45 years.
>
> Carter said, "Why don't you give this fellow Caddy a call?"
>
> Alarm bells, naturally, were going off. How many times had would-be Kennedy heirs come out of the woodwork? And how many tall tales had originated, as did Caddy's letter, in the dark heart of conspiracy country – vast, incorrigible Texas, where J.F.K. was murdered, L.B.J. connived and thrived, and two presidents Bush catapulted from the oil business to the Oval Office? Carter and I remarked on how CBS and Dan Rather, another son of Texas, had recently seen their credibility slip after airing a segment on George Bush's spotty wartime service while in the Texas National Guard (a story based in part on documents – which CBS itself later branded as possible forgeries – procured through an elusive source at a Houston livestock show). And who, for that matter, was Caddy?
>
> I returned to my office and did a quick Google dip, which, given my tastes, proved instantly gratifying. "Douglas Caddy," I learned, "was the original lawyer for the Watergate burglars.

The *Vanity Fair* article, with its twists and turns, can be read online. David Friend is a talented writer and author a highly praised book published in 2017, *The Naughty Nineties*. Upon reading the article the reader is forced to ask why Jack Worthington never took the final steps necessary to prove that JFK was his father. It remained a mystery to me until a mutual friend of Jack and I, author Barr McClellan, cleared it up when he told me in 2016 that Jack became afraid if it were proven he was the son of JFK, he might be killed as were JFK and other family members.

Kennedy Family Deaths and Sidereal Time

I posted the follow thread in the JFK Assassination Topic on the Education forum in May 2011:

> On the May 21, 2011, Dreamland program, Jim Marrs interviews Whitley Strieber about material manuscript changes made in the first edition of Strieber's 2001 book, *The Key*, which took place without his being aware of them until recently.
>
> In the course of the interview Jim Marrs makes the unrelated observation that the deaths in the Kennedy family all took place in the same hour in sidereal time. Sidereal time is calculated on the movement of the stars and is used by the astronauts, astrologers, and astrophysicists. We, of course, use Greenwich Mean Time based on the movement of the Earth around the Sun, which, like Sidereal Time, is broken into 24 hours. For a description of Sidereal time, check out the link below:
>
> http://www.astro.cornell.edu/academics/courses/astro2201/sidereal.htm
>
> Jim Marrs discloses in the interview that all the Kennedy deaths took place in the 16th hour of Sidereal Time: Joe Kennedy, Jr. in 1944, JFK in 1963, Bobby in 1968, John Jr. in 1999 – and Ted Kennedy in a near fatal plane crash in 1964. He says it is like saying the deaths all took place between Noon and 1 P.M.
>
> He further discloses that his study of Masonic lore reveals that the 16th Hour is the Hour of Revenge.

Additional information on the subject was provided in the Education Forum:

> Fischer, Robert. "Discerning Encrypted Itinerary Profiles in Crime" Paper presented at the annual meeting of the ASC Annual Meeting, Philadelphia Marriott Downtown, Philadelphia, PA, Nov. 03, 2009
>
> Publication Type: Conference Paper/Unpublished Manuscript
>
> Review Method: Peer Reviewed
>
> Abstract: When four members of a given family are killed at the same time of day on different dates, the implications of a conspirator planning these incidents are overwhelming. Surprisingly, this has passed right under the noses of the law enforcement agencies and the American people when we consider the reality of the prominent Kennedy family deaths. Four members of this highly placed political family have died within a span of 60 minutes out of a 24 hour day when measuring time by an astronomical timing convention used by astronomers, NASA and the DOD. Joseph Patrick Kennedy Jr. in 1944, John F. Kennedy in 1963, Robert F. Kennedy in 1968 and John F. Kennedy Jr. in 1999 all died within this period. Furthermore, the attempted as-

> sassination of President-elect JFK in 1960, and Ted Kennedy's alleged airplane accident in 1964 also fall within this 60 minute astronomical or sidereal time interval. The odds of these eight incidents to have occurred by random chance is less than one in 191-million. This "Kennedy" example will provide an illustration of how not only itinerary timing but the placement of incidents has been applied to other historically significant events in American history, including the incidents that occurred on September 11th, 2001.[2]

The author of the above abstract wrote this:

> "John, I have attached five slide images with the technical information regarding the six Kennedy incidents (six murder attempts, four of them successful) and the impossible odds against them occurring by random chance.
>
> The key point is that they all occurred within the same "sidereal hour" out of a 24-hour day. The sidereal time is the time that a given star passes directly along a north-south line (that is, "transits") overhead, regardless of your position on Earth. Hence, whenever the star Vega transits your position, day or night at your location, it is 18:37 local sidereal time. (The clock on the wall and local sidereal time are only synchronized once a year at a given location due to Earth's advancing annual orbit.)
>
> For instance, when it was 12:30 pm in Dallas on November 22nd 1963, it was 16:06 sidereal time; however six months earlier, at the same 12:30 pm but on May 22nd 1963 in Dallas it was 04:01 sidereal time.
>
> Sidereal time is used by astronomers, NASA and DOD as a convention of timekeeping for all space-based operations. The similar alignment of stars and constellations are secondary to and a consequence of all being within the same sidereal hour."

To see the slide images, go to this website and scroll down about two-thirds.

> http://johndenugent.com/english/english-why-we-will-win-occultists-selected-death-dates-for-the-kennedys

So Jack Worthington may have been well justified in not pursuing to its end his claim that he was the son of JFK.

Howard Hunt and Frank Sturgis

The only time that I met Sturgis was on June 17, 1972, when I and my co-counsel visited the arrested burglars in the police substation in Washington following their arrests at Watergate and a short time later at the court arraignment of the burglars.

Decades later in what amounted to a death bed confession of JFK's assassination Howard sent a recording to his son, St. John, in 1997 that implicated Sturgis. St. John later wrote a book about his father, *Bond of Secrecy* (Trine Day, 2013). Amazon, in offering the book for sale, describes it as follows: A father's last confession to his son about the CIA, Watergate, and the plot to assassinate President John F. Kennedy, this is the remarkable true story of St. John Hunt and his father E. Howard Hunt, the infamous Watergate burglar and CIA spymaster. In Howard Hunt's near-death confession to his son St. John, he revealed that key figures in the CIA were responsible for the plot to assassinate JFK in Dallas, and that Hunt himself was approached by the plotters, among whom included the CIA's David Atlee Phillips, Cord Meyer, Jr., and William Harvey, as well as future Watergate burglar Frank Sturgis. An incredible true story told from an inside, authoritative source, this is also a personal account of a uniquely dysfunctional American family caught up in two of the biggest political scandals of the 20th century.

In 2013 I was listening to national Power Hour radio show on which Robert Merritt and retired New York Police Detective James Rothstein were being interviewed. My name came up in the interview and so I contacted Rothstein, whose legendary exploits as a NYPD detective are profiled in the book, *Times Square* (Bantam, 1980). As a result he and I in recent years have been engaged in collaborative research into sundry types of criminal activity. Rothstein's mantra as a detective is "You learn that 'The Street" talks to you. It tells you "everything.' All you have to do is learn to 'listen.'"

Rothstein has given me permission to reproduce his detective report on his historical encounter with Frank Sturgis in 1977, which illuminates an untold story about the Kennedy assassination. What follows is his report about Sturgis' visit to New York City to murder Marita Lorenz. Lorenz was Castro's girl friend until the CIA recruited her to kill him. In 1963 she accompanied Sturgis and other Cuban Americans in November 1963 as they drove from Miami to Dallas to assassinate JFK. Lorenz was another person who knew too much and was marked for death.

Detective Rothstein's Report

In the morning of October 31, 1977, Halloween day, Det. Rothstein received a call from Paul Meskil, a reporter for the *New York Daily News*. Meskil was beside himself. Monica Lorenz, the daughter of Marita Lorenz, had just been arrested in front of her apartment on York Avenue in possession of a loaded gun. She was to be the last line of defense for Marita. Monica was hiding in the bushes in front of the apartment building on Eighty Eighth Street and York Avenue; she was going to ambush Sturgis when he showed up to kill Marita. Meskil knows that the only two Detectives he can trust are Rosenthal and Rothstein; he knows they will not back down or be stopped. The Detectives notified members of the New York Senate Select Committee on Crime, their present assignment, of the call. They jump into action. They first call the arresting officer of Monica and verify that the arrest had been made for possession of a gun. They then set up a meeting with Marita Lorenz and Paul Meskil at a small restaurant on the East Side.

They all meet at the restaurant at approximately 11:00 A.M. Marita verifies what Meskil had told the Detectives. She was very upset, anxious, and scared. She feared for her and her children's lives. Marita tells the Detectives that she is scheduled to testify at the House Assassination Hearings in Washington, DC, concerning the assassination of John F. Kennedy. Meskil tells the Detectives that he is in possession of a tape recording made of a conversation between Marita Lorenz and Frank Sturgis; the tape is hidden at his residence in Nassau County, New York. In the tape Sturgis tells Marita, "You know what the rules are and what happens if you talk." Meskil tells the Detectives to pick up the tape at his house and that his son would give the Detectives the tape. Meskil tells the Detectives that he will be leaving for the Far East as soon as our meeting is over. At approximately 1:00 P.M., the Detectives leave the restaurant with Marita and go to her apartment on Eighty Eighth Street and York Avenue.

When Detectives Rosenthal, Rothstein, and Marita enter the apartment, the detectives do a quick canvass of the apartment. They see 10 to 15 boxes sitting against the wall in the dining room. The rest of the day and early evening were spent interviewing Marita in preparation for the arrival of Sturgis. Marita tells the detectives that the boxes contain documentation concerning OP40, the Cuban invasion, Castro, planning for the Kennedy assassination, and other covert operations that she had knowledge of. These documents were going to be delivered to the House Assassination Hearings. The Detectives believe they have more than sufficient evidence to arrest Sturgis.

On October 31, 1977, at approximately 2130 hours Det. Mathew Rosenthal and Det. Jim Rothstein arrested Frank Sturgis when he came to assassinate Marita Lorenz, a witness to the planning of the Kennedy assassination. When Sturgis rang Marita to gain entry to the building, Rosenthal and Rothstein assumed their position. They crouched low next to the door with their guns drawn and their shields pinned to their suit jackets. When Sturgis entered the premises, Rothstein placed his gun in Sturgis' mouth and shouted, "Police! You're under arrest mother xxxxer; don't move." Sturgis mumbles, "I hope you're Detectives." Rosenthal had his gun put to Sturgis' chest and identified himself as a Police Officer. The Detectives searched Sturgis. Once the Detectives knew that the scene was under control, Rothstein congratulates Sturgis for assassinating John F. Kennedy. Rothstein tells Sturgis that he was present when Kennedy ordered the bombing and support to stop, just as the invasion of the Bay of Pigs began. Sturgis says, "The only way you can know that is if you were on the Essex." Rothstein replies, "Yes, I was." Rothstein and Sturgis shook hands; they were both professionals and were doing their job.

Detectives Rothstein and Rosenthal questioned Sturgis for approximately two hours at Marita's apartment before taking him for booking at the local precinct. During this time, Sturgis was very frank with the Detectives. He admitted that he was on the Grassy Knoll at Dealey Plaza in Dallas, Texas, when Kennedy was assassinated and that he was one of the shooters from the Grassy Knoll. The Detectives received valuable information from Sturgis. Sturgis tells the Detectives that OP40's mandate was "to protect our country at all costs." When Sturgis was asked why Kennedy was assassinated, he told the Detectives that there were three reasons. Number one was that Kennedy had double-crossed OP40 in the Bay of Pigs Invasion by pulling back the support. Number two was that he (Kennedy) had been told to stay away from the women, especially the Russian woman, Ellen Rometsch, because he would be compromised and jeopardize national security. Number three was that Kennedy was destroying the black community through his liberal social programs.

The second part of the questioning was about his involvement in the Watergate Break-in that occurred on June 17, 1972. Sturgis was one of the five burglars arrested by Sgt. Paul Leeper, Det. Carl Shoffler, and Det. John Barrett, of the Washington D.C. Police Department. Sturgis said it was a set-up from the start, there had to have been a rat on the inside who sold them out. Sturgis said the break-in was to get the "book" that had the names of clients who used the prostitution and pedophile ring operating out of the Democratic National Headquarters. This information was to be used to compromise both Republican and Democratic clients who used the ring. The break-in led to the fall of President Richard Nixon on August 8, 1974. President Nixon had nothing to do with the planning of the break-in. In fact he had no prior knowledge that the break-in was going to occur.

Later Shoffler would tell Rothstein that he had somebody on the inside and had received information that the break-in was going to happen. Shoffler's shift had ended one and a half hours before he made the arrest. In 2012, Robert Merritt called retired Det. Rothstein and stated that he was Shoffler's informant. In a book written by Robert Merritt, *Watergate Exposed,* he tells the tale of the break-in.

When Sturgis was taken to the local precinct the Detectives identified themselves and told the desk lieutenant that they were booking Frank Forini (Sturgis' real name). They took Sturgis to the Detectives room and began processing the arrest. That's when things got strange. Rosenthal advises Sturgis of his rights. Sturgis asks to make a call, which Rothstein does. He tells Rothstein to call Gaeton Fonzi, the investigator in the House Assassination Hearings.

Rothstein is surprised, that a suspect would call the investigator and he is the suspect. When Fonzi answers the phone, Rothstein identifies himself and tells Fonzi that Sturgis is under arrest and wants to talk to him. Fonzi was dumbfounded. (See *The Last Investigation,* by Gaeton Fonzi, page 103). Shortly after the call was made the desk officer calls the Detectives to inform them that a Frank Nelson (CIA and Organized Crime in Cuba) was at the desk and was looking for Frank Sturgis, and, if in, fact Forini was Sturgis. The answer was yes. Within minutes all hell broke loose. Every big boss in the Police Department was calling to find out what happened. The Detectives finished booking Sturgis and were requested to report to the offices of John Guido and Harold Hess, two of the top bosses involved in this type of case. When the Detectives arrive at Guido and Hess's office they are asked if they had anything eat. The Detectives said no. Hess sends out one of his staff to get a six pack of beer and sandwiches. He asks the Detectives, "Is it good and clean arrest?" The Detectives say, "Yes, it is and it is solid." Hess replies, "Good that is all I want to know." The Detectives advise Guido and Hess of what happened. Rosenthal and Rothstein are asked to arraign Sturgis and go home and get some rest.

At the arraignment of Frank Sturgis in Manhattan Criminal ADA Broomer is assigned to the case. The Detectives inform Broomer of the tape corroborating the allegations made by Marita and Meskil. Broomer asks the Detectives where the tape is. They inform Broomer that they will pick up the tape at Meskil's residence in Nassau County on their way back to the city from their residences. Early the next morning all hell breaks loose again. Unknown members of the New York City Police Department went to Meskil's residence to get the tape. When Meskil's son answers the door, he sees that it is not Detectives Rosenthal and Rothstein. The son calls the Nassau County Police Department and tells them that somebody was at his door trying to take evidence of the Kennedy assassination. Nassau County Police responded in full force. The New York City Cops were sent packing.

Detectives Rosenthal and Rothstein are notified by Guido and Hess of what happened; somebody had sand-bagged them and they should immediately proceed to the Meskil residence and retrieve the tapes. Rosenthal and Rothstein meet with the son at Meskil's residence and the son was so proud that he had protected the tapes for Rosenthal and Rothstein, as his father had told him to do. The son gives the tapes to the Detectives. The Detectives knew what was coming; the cover-up was started.

Detectives Rosenthal and Rothstein take the tape to ADA Broomer's office and the tape is played. Marita and Meskil were right. Sturgis is heard telling Marita, "You know what the rules are and what happens if you talk." Broomer and the powers to-be decide that is not a threat. The Detectives argue vehemently that it is clearly a threat and you have to be totally stupid if you don't understand that. The Detectives know the fix was in. The charges against Sturgis were dropped.

The boxes of files in Marita's apartment were hand delivered to the House Assassination Hearings in Washington DC by Marita Lorenz and retired Det. Bobby Polachek, who had been a partner of Det. Rothstein at the 26 Precinct.

Subsequently, Rosenthal, Rothstein, and the City of New York were sued by Sturgis for $16 million for making a false arrest. The case was tried by Judge Leonard Sand in the Federal Court in the Southern District of New York. Sturgis was represented by Henry Rothblatt. Rothstein was called as the last witness late in the day. He was sworn in by the judge and the case was adjourned till the next day. As Det. Rothstein was getting ready to leave the court house, he was warned by unnamed sources that his life was in danger and that he should not go home. Det. Rothstein called one of his informants, who lived in the neighborhood near the court house, and asked her for assistance. She was connected to organized crime figures in the same area. Det. Rothstein left through the back door and was safely taken to an apartment by his informant and her friends.

The next morning, Det. Rothstein took the stand to testify. Before anything was said, Judge Sand was summoned to his chambers. After an hour or so, Det. Rothstein was called to the Judge's Chambers. Det. Rothstein was asked what it would take for him not to testify. Everybody in the courtroom, especially the media, knew Det. Rothstein was going to let it all hang out. An agreement was reached that the City Of New York was going to pay $2,500.00 to Sturgis and Det. Rosenthal and Det. Rothstein were to be commended for acting above and beyond the call of duty. Judge Sand advised Det. Rothstein that he would be called in front of the bench and, if Det. Rothstein wanted to make a statement, he could say anything he wanted to say. Det. Rothstein realized it was in his best interest to keep his big mouth shut. As Rothstein turns to leave the courtroom, Sturgis and Rothblatt shake Rothstein's hand and asked if he would be part of their organization. Rothstein replies, "It is an honor for you to ask, but I cannot do that." He left the courthouse.

The Aftermath:

Sometime during the summer of 1983, Retired Detective Rothstein was sitting at the bar in Georgia's Bar and Restaurant at 722 South Wellwood Avenue, Lindenhurst, New York talking to customers. A well-dressed man, wearing typical "spook" attire, came in and sat next to Rothstein. He introduced himself as a former New York City police officer who had moved to Florida. During an hour conversation he told Rothstein that when Detectives Rosenthal and Rothstein arrested Frank Sturgis he was sent with a "bag of money" from Florida to get Sturgis out of jail. He did not say where the money came from. He knew all the facts about Sturgis. Rothstein has never seen or heard from him again and never knew why he came in the first place.

Will the mystery of the Kennedy assassination ever be solved? It is unlikely as the Secret Service destroyed all its records dealing with the event and the CIA continues to stall release of all its key documents and when some of these are released they are heavily redacted. Marita Lorenz's files were delivered to the Select House Committee on Assassinations in 1977 but upon receipt there they promptly disappeared and were never recovered.

Endnotes

1. https://www.youtube.com/watch?v=IwNYgiVv-rs.

2. http://www.allacademic.com/meta/p_mla_apa_research_citation/3/7/3/6/4/p373640_index.html and http://www.asc41.com/Annual_Meeting/programs/2009/2009PrintProgram.pdf

Chapter Five

Tongsun Park And Koreagate

I had barely recovered from the trauma of Watergate when in 1976, a year after my dinner with Howard Hunt just prior to his entering prison, I suddenly found myself enveloped in a new national scandal called Koreagate. Just as in Watergate the new scandal came out of nowhere, and I had no prior knowledge of any of its criminal activity.

At its center was Tongsun Park who was the first student I met upon enrolling in Georgetown University's School of Foreign Service in 1956. We became close friends while at Georgetown and remained so in the years following my graduating in 1960. When I was released by the Army following my six months of active duty at Fort Jackson at the end of 1961, Tongsun invited me to be his house guest at his spacious Georgetown residence in Washington. I stayed there for five months before moving back to New York City in June 1962 to enroll in New York University's School of Law at night while working in the daytime in Governor Rockefeller's private office in Manhattan for Lieutenant Governor Malcolm Wilson.

Tongsun and I continued to be in touch with each other thereafter in a sporadic fashion. He had known of my involvement in the founding of Young Americans for Freedom and in the birth of the modern Conservative Movement. So when in October 1964 Tongsun incorporated the International Youth Federation for Freedom (IYFF) in Washington he invited me to serve on its board of directors and I agreed to do so even though both of us recognized that my being in New York City in night law school and working in the day meant that I could not play an active role in the new organization.

This is how the Senate Select Committee on Intelligence in its June 1978 report "Activities of 'Friendly' Foreign Intelligence Services In The United States: A Case Study" discussed IYFF:

> Park's activities in the United States first came to the attention of the intelligence community in 1962 when one of the domestic components reported that Park and his Georgetown roommate, Douglas Caddy, were forming "a new and hopefully potent international anti-communist youth organization," called the International Federation of Free Youth. The intelligence officer who reported this information noted that his source, a close associate of Park, had not asked for support or guidance, but had passed the information along because U.S. intelligence "should be informed of this type of activity from

> the beginning." Although the intelligence officer told his superiors he would "appreciate an expression of interest in pursuing the development," there is no indication in intelligence files that any further action was taken. Although U.S. intelligence funded various student organizations during the 1960s, there is no indication that this particular organization was ever utilized in any fashion by U.S. intelligence. Moreover, relevant intelligence components have informed the Committee that they have never had any relationship with Mr. Caddy.
>
> The same intelligence source which provided information about the International Federation of Free Youth was questioned several years later about the George Town Club and Park's involvement in the Club. There is no indication of what generated this later intelligence interest in that subject, nor is there evidence of any response to the intelligence officer's request to be notified by his superiors if there were interest in access to Park through the source. Intelligence files do reflect that at about this time a proposal was made, but rejected, to utilize the George Town Club as an operational base.[1]

As it worked out IYFF was basically a paper organization. It was essentially dormant during its entire existence although the manager's office of the exclusive George Town Club in Washington that Tongsun owned also served as IYFF's office. The George Town Club's membership comprised the elite of Washington who flocked to the exclusive dining facility not only for its superb menu but for being able to mingle with senators and congressman who comprised the bulk of the membership.[2]

Earlier when General Foods Corporation had sent me in 1969 from its White Plains headquarters to Washington to be its Washington Representative Tongsun had given me a free membership in the George Town Club. I regularly attended dinners there that Tongsun hosted that were attended by many members of congress. Congressman Richard Hanna (D-CA) on many occasions entertained the diners with humor and songs. (Hanna would later be the sole member of Congress to go to prison for involvement in Koreagate.)

All this fun and games came to an abrupt halt in 1976 when Koreagate suddenly burst upon the national scene.

As described in Wikipedia, "Koreagate was an American political scandal in 1976 involving South Korean political figures seeking influence from 10 Democratic members of Congress. An immediate goal of the scandal seems to have been reversing President Richard Nixon's decision to withdraw troops from South Korea. It involved the Korea Central Intelligence Agency (KCIA) allegedly funneling bribes and favors through Korean businessman Tongsun Park in an attempt to gain favor and influence for South Korean objectives."

I was thrust into the scandal when the *Washington Post* published an article on me by reporter Maxine Cheshire that attempted to implicate me in the scandal. Cheshire's article implied that I was somehow a central figure in Koreagate. I was puzzled by this unfavorable attention being lavished on me since I knew nothing about the payoff scandal. It wasn't until decades later in reading a deposition of Washington Police Detective Carl Shoffler in which he declared that Maxine Cheshire was one of his closest friends that I realized what likely motivated her animosity. Shoffler, having failed to have me killed in the weeks after Watergate broke and being frustrated that I came out clean in that scandal, allegedly influenced Cheshire to reopen his abuse of me. I wonder what a psychiatrist would make of this fixation on me by Shoffler, a closeted married gay with two children.

As the scandal unfolded I chose to come to the public defense of Tongsun as best I could under the circumstances. *People* Magazine of Nov. 15, 1976, in an article, "The Party May Be Over for the Generous Mystery Man of Washington, Tongsun Park" reported:

> As an undergraduate in Georgetown University's School of Foreign Service in the late 1950s, Tongsun already was a budding host. He rented a duplex on Q Street and threw spectacular parties, with live bands and an abundance of food and drink. Washington lawyer Douglas Caddy, a classmate and one of Park's best friends, says Tongsun "became an instant celebrity on campus," winning the freshman class presidency. He took a year off from school, and with funds from his wealthy oilman father bought a parking lot and several pieces of real estate and worked at meeting people. "He is completely generous," says Caddy, "He seems to anticipate people's problems and offer help even before the problems are voiced." Park recently solved a problem for columnist Abigail ("Dear Abby") Van Buren. She liked his Korean mother-of-pearl-inlaid living room table so much that he had one made for her in Korea and shipped it over. It took eight months.... Now bigger revelations seem inevitable. Says Park's friend Caddy: "I don't rule out anything. I think it goes very deep. Tongsun moved in very powerful circles."

A few months into the scandal my telephone rang and when I picked it a disembodied male voice said in a nasty tone, "I'm with the Institute for Policy Studies and you are about to receive a subpoena in Koreagate." He then hung up.

Sure enough two days later there was a knock on my front door and when I opened it a man thrust a paper in my hand and declared, "You are being served with a subpoena." After he departed I examined the subpoena and I discovered it was from the House Committee on Standards of Official Conduct and gave a date and time for me to appear at the Committee's office.

When I arrived on the appointed date an investigator for the committee briefly interviewed me and then asked if I had ever introduced a member of

Congress to Tongsun. I racked my brain but could not remember ever doing so. So the investigator volunteered a name: Martin McKneally. I then remembered that I had introduced Tongsun to McKneally but this occurred many years before McKneally was elected to Congress. McKneally, a former National Commander of the American Legion, at that time was a close associate of Lieutenant-Governor Malcolm Wilson for whom I worked. So I explained my relationship with McKneally to the investigator, which satisfied him.

The investigator then left the room, leaving behind an inch-thick file on the conference table that was labeled in large letters, "Douglas Caddy file." I sensed it was a trap to see whether I would be tempted to look at the file while the investigator was out of the room, so I made no effort to move. To me it was obviously a fake file and I had been given a test.

About five minutes later the investigator returned with a woman who apparently was of a higher rank. She declared, "Mr. Caddy, you are going to be our committee's first witness at the public hearings."

I was surprised and shocked at this announcement because I knew nothing about the details of the Koreagate scandal that involved a large number of Members of Congress. After a moment I replied, "I shall be happy to testify before your committee at its public hearing. I shall prepare an opening statement in which I shall declare under oath that I know nothing about payments by Tongsun Park to members of congress and that this hearing sounds like a rerun from Watergate wherein the original prosecutors focused on the little people like me who were not involved so as to let the big fish get away." (Among the big fish that got away in Koreagate was Speaker of the House Tip O'Neill.)

This time it was the investigator and the woman who looked surprised and shocked. Each then thanked me and said that I could depart, which I did. I never heard anything more from the House Committee on Standards of Official Conduct. My straight-shooting talk apparently scared the committee.

The *Washington Post* carried a story on October 9, 1978, "Koreagate: Bringing Forth a Mouse, But an Honest One" that reported:

> When South Korean businessman Tongsun Park sat before the television cameras at a House hearing in April and ticked off his long list of payments – mostly in cash – to some 30 members of Congress, his unsavory litany didn't impress many.
>
> Most of the largess Park passed out in little white envelopes had been detailed before in the press in months of front-page headlines. Fewer than 10 members were seriously implicated by his testimony – far less than the 115 that had been predicted in one *New York Times* account. And those most incriminated were no longer in Congress....

The press blew the story out of proportion in a post-Watergate race to be first with the gory details about a hot new scandal in town. "Nothing we could have done would have met the expectations raised by the press," said a House investigator.

So that was the end of Koreagate.

But the saga of Tongsun Park was not yet finished.

Wikipedia's entry on Tongsun reads:

> In 2005 Park was accused of acting as an intermediary with corrupt United Nations officials in the oil-for-food conspiracy orchestrated by Saddam Hussein. His name surfaced as part of investigations into the oil-for-food scandal. In July 2006 he was convicted in a U.S. federal court on conspiracy charges. He became the first person convicted through the oil-for-food investigation. On February 22, 2007, he was sentenced to five years in prison. He also was fined $15,000 and required to forfeit $1,200,000. According to the Federal Bureau of Prisons Web site, he was released from prison on September 10, 2008. The next day, he left the United States for South Korea.

Endnotes

1. https://www.intelligence.senate.gov/sites/default/files/publications/95friendly.pdf
2. https://www.washingtonpost.com/archive/opinions/1977/10/16/tongsun-parks-club/fc4e8ef5-f79b-4a55-b458-25bb6eeea07a/?utm_term=.fd1ebdc15abcembership.

AUGUST 1987 · $1.95

WEST TEXAS' ONCE-IN-A-LIFETIME RAIN • OUR BEST UNKNOWN CHEF

TexasMonthly®

THE SLEAZIEST MAN IN TEXAS

SHEARN MOODY, JR.,
Of Galveston

A Story of Swindling, Scandal, and Sex

B Y   G A R Y   C A R T W R I G H T

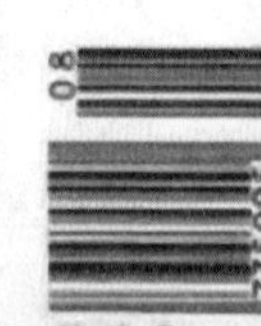

Chapter Six

The Moody Foundation Scandal, the IRS and the Tax Court

In 1979, I moved from Washington, D.C. to Houston, Texas and was admitted to the Texas Bar to practice law that same year. I had been admitted to the District of Columbia Bar in 1970. In 1980, George Strake, Jr., who was the Texas Secretary of State in the first administration of GOP Governor William Clements, asked me to join his staff as Director of Elections for the State of Texas. Enforcement of the Texas election code in the state's 254 counties fell within the purview of the Secretary of State and still does today.

In 1981, while still employed by the State of Texas, I was contacted by Howard Phillips, Chairman of the Conservative Caucus, Inc., of Vienna, Virginia, who had been one of the original founders of Young Americans for Freedom. Phillips asked me to become legal counsel to the Texas Policy Institute, which was about to receive a $250,000 grant from the Moody Foundation of Galveston, Texas.

The Moody Foundation had three trustees, brothers Robert and Shearn Moody, Jr., and their aunt, Mary Moody Nothen, daughter of the founder of the financial dynasty. Shearn Moody was the sponsor of the Foundation grant to the Texas Policy Institute.

After receiving the grant, the Texas Policy Institute in 1982 organized a National Conference on the Star Wars space defense initative to encourage the authorization of the Star Wars Project, which later was officially proposed by President Reagan. Howard Phillips invited Senator Jesse Helms, an early advocate of the Star Wars Project, to address the conference at its opening session, which took place at a well-attended dinner at the Hotel Galvez in Galveston, Texas. At the dinner Phillips presented an award to Senator Helms, who left early the next morning to return to Washington. Among the Star Wars Conference attendees was historian J. Evetts Haley, author of the best-seller book, *A Texan Looks at Lyndon* (Palo Duro Press, 1964).

I worked with Shearn Moody, Jr. for the three years following the 1982 Star Wars Conference on a number of other Moody Foundation grants.

However, I knew next to nothing about Moody's activities in the period before 1981, when I met him for the first time. When I worked with him he had serious health problems stemming from high blood pressure and had long since stopped giving wild parties at his ranch in Galveston. He spent much of each year in Durham, N.C., where he was enrolled under supervision on the low-sodium rice diet made famous by a doctor associated with Duke University.

As I was to learn the Moody Foundation and the Moody family's American National Insurance Company also of Galveston had been linked to organized crime funding of casinos in Las Vegas in the 1960s, foremost among these being the Sands. This occurred when Shearn Moody and his brother, Robert, as trustees lost control of their foundation. The Moody family eventually got control back after bringing a lawsuit that ended the mob funding. Here is the link to a *New York Times* article, "Intrigue, Texas Style," about this period of time that preceded my working in the early 1980s with Shearn Moody and the Moody Foundation. http://www.nytimes.com/1972/02/06/archives/intrigue-texas-size-questionable-deals-haunt-caretakers-of.html

In 1986, Shearn Moody, Jr. fell under the influence of a con man, William Pabst. His association with Pabst eventually led to his losing his post as a trustee of the Moody Foundation. Pabst fled Houston in 1986 and is today still a fugitive from justice, wanted by both federal and Texas law enforcement for his criminal activities.

Moody was convicted on 13 charges of defrauding the Moody Foundation due to his association with Pabst.

His conviction was later reversed and remanded on two of the thirteen charges by the U.S. Court of Appeals for the Fifth Circuit. His other conviction for bankruptcy fraud, however, was affirmed. His close adviser for many years, Norman Revie, was convicted with him of bankruptcy fraud and is today, like Pabst, a fugitive from justice.

I was never interviewed by the FBI and never asked to appear before the grand jury and never was a witness in either criminal case: Shearn Moody's defrauding the Moody Foundation or his bankruptcy fraud case.

The IRS turned out to be its own worst enemy in the case of Shearn Moody defrauding the Moody Foundation. I had moved to California in 1988 when months later I received a letter in the mail from the IRS that had been forwarded to me from an old Houston address. The letter requested that I appear before the IRS at its Houston office. Because I believed it was my duty to assist the authorities investigating the Moody Foundation case, I decided to make a quick trip to Houston to answer any questions the IRS might have. Big, big mistake. When I showed up with my attorney/accountant the IRS agent could not have been more abusive in his tirade. I and my attorney/accountant were shocked. As the meeting ended the out-of- control agent yelled at me, "Since you appeared today the IRS now has jurisdiction over you." My attorney/accountant became alarmed and scared at this IRS abuse and withdrew from representing me in the case. I felt like a fool. Here I had traveled by air 1800 miles at my own expense to assist the IRS in its investigation and instead was being treated like a piece of trash. It was the beginning of a process of utter stupidity by the IRS that transformed me from a totally friendly witness to a totally alienated one.

Ultimately Moody was set free from prison by an order of a federal judge after I wrote a letter in 1990 to the Chief Judge of the U.S. District Court for the Southern District of Texas and asked to appear voluntarily before the federal grand jury to testify how an agent from the Criminal Intelligence Division of the Internal Revenue Service had directed me to pay $38,000 of a Moody Foundation grant grant to a specified entity identified by him. I asked that both I and the agent be required to testify under oath with the penalty of perjury about the transaction. The U.S. government refused to let the IRS Criminal Intelligence agent testify because my evidence was air-tight and as a consequence the federal judge who oversaw Moody's foundation trial dismissed all 13 charges on which Moody had been convicted upon a motion by Moody, apparently on the ground that the U.S. government had failed to disclose the role of the IRS agent at Moody's trial for defrauding the Moody Foundation.

As the *Houston Post* of May 31, 1991 reported, "The collapse of the first criminal case against Moody prompted the court to grant Moody parole without the normal process of a formal hearing."

So a major criminal case was terminated rather than allow IRS corruption and criminal activity to come to light through the grand jury process in which the IRS Criminal Intelligence Agent would be required to testify under penalty of perjury.

This was not the first time that IRS corruption had been exposed in a matter dealing with Shearn Moody.

On October 6, 1976, Rep. Henry Gonzales (D-TX) spoke on the House floor about IRS Project Southwest, terming it "clearly a political operation.... Nixon's people wanted some action against Texas Democrats.... It was a classic case of the abuse of governmental power – deliberate and with malice aforethought."

As disclosed by the BNA Securities Regulation and Law Report of December 7, 1977, "IRS's election-year Project Southwest focused on 164 Texans with political connections in the state, although the only IRS target identified so far is Shearn Moody, Jr., a wealthy Galveston banker with Democratic ties. At its height, the covert operation -- designed in IRS' words, 'to learn as much as we can about Texas political relationships, influence and payoffs' – utilized 27 revenue agents from Treasury and the IRS.

"The SEC cooperated with the IRS in investigating Shearn Moody, Jr. It eventually permitted Moody's attorneys to inspect 12 volumes of investigative files early in 1977. When the BNA later that year requested under the Freedom of Information Act the same files, according to the BNA the SEC "said all the records detailing its own investigation of Moody, and its cooperation with the IRS and the Texas Attorney General, have been 'lost' in the mail since July, when they were sent from the SEC's Houston's field office to the Washington headquarters.

"I realize there are some people, including Mr. Moody's attorneys who do not believe it is possible we could have lost these records, but it is true,' said Roderic L. Woodson, SEC's FOIA officer", according to the BNA article.

Forbes of October 22, 1990 reported, "But documents unearthed by the Senate Watergate Committee prove that there was indeed a Project Southwest, the apparent goal of which was to harass wealthy Texas Democrats. The documents also show that Treasury Department Secretary Connally had been briefed concerning Project Southwest by the IRS in March 1972."

Below is an article from the *Houston Chronicle* of January 18, 1987, which describes my role in the Moody Foundation case:

In harm's way, again

What do Watergate, CIA and Moody probe have in common? Caddy

By Dianna Hunt

He had received bomb threats, been followed, had his phones tapped and the windows of his office shot out in the night.

Yet Douglas Caddy still feared he might just be paranoid.

"We used to joke about it," says Caddy, a Houston author and attorney. "Do you think somebody's trying to give us a message?"

His fears, apparently, were not unfounded. In a sworn statement submitted to a Houston private investigator and the FBI, a former military explosives expert says Caddy was the target of an alleged bomb plot hatched by Galveston millionaire Shearn Moody Jr.

Moody, says the expert, tried to hire him to "blow (Caddy's) legs off" because Caddy prompted investigations into impropriety within the multimillion-dollar Moody Foundation.

For Caddy, the front-row seat in a money-and-power scandal is an all-too-familiar occurrence. As a defense attorney and witness in the Watergate scandal, a friend and former roommate to South Korean lobbyist Tongsun Park, and a one-time publicist in a CIA front company, Caddy turns up in the strangest places.

"I don't know why," he concedes. "I just do."

He flatly denies ever working for the Central Intelligence Agency.

"I get tarred with it, but I never have worked for the CIA," Caddy says.

Caddy, 48, emerged as a central figure in the latest scandal after approaching Moody Foundation officials in 1985 with information about the possible mishandling of millions of dollars in foundation grants.

His complaints prompted an internal Moody Foundation probe, which ultimately led to the hiring of Houston private investigator Clyde Wilson to look into the matter. The state attorney general's office and federal officials likewise are investigating.

Five people – including Moody and his administrative aide Norman Revie – already have been indicted by a Houston federal grand jury.

Caddy's life the last three decades has been scattered with similar brushes with important people and events.

A graduate of Georgetown University's School of Foreign Service and New York University Law School, Caddy became involved in the Watergate scandal just half an hour after the arrest of five burglars in the headquarters of the Democratic National Committee at the Watergate Hotel – when he received a 3 A.M. call from former CIA operative E. Howard Hunt.

Caddy served as defense lawyer to both Hunt and another Watergate conspirator, G. Gordon Liddy, and later testified about his refusal to accept $25,000 in "hush money."

His involvement in Watergate stemmed from his friendship with Hunt, with whom he shared office space in the Washington-based Mullen Company – a public relations firm and offshoot of General Foods that was later identified as a front company for the CIA.

Caddy went to work as a lobbyist in General Foods' New York office in 1967, but transferred to the Mullen Company in 1969. He left the company in 1971 to go into private practice as an attorney.

"I didn't ask to be put in the Mullen Company," Caddy says now. "General Foods put me there.

"I didn't even know the Democrats had their headquarters in the Watergate."

Just a few years later, though, Caddy would be back in the midst of another scandal – one involving his former college roommate, Tongsun Park, a Korean rice dealer.

Park, a glittering party-giver and a central figure in "Koreagate," was granted immunity from criminal prosecution in 1978 for his much-publicized testimony that he paid members of Congress in exchange for political favors.

Caddy says Park was the first person he met at Georgetown University, and they later became class officers together, as well as friends. During that time, Caddy said he suspected – but never knew – that Park worked for the Korean CIA.

"I suspected – much like working in the Mullen office – that something was up," Caddy said.

Caddy says he was questioned by staff members of the U.S. House of Representatives ethics committee about his relationship with Park, but never testified publicly.

Through it all, Caddy remained active in conservative Republican politics and helped found two youth groups, the Young Americans for Freedom and the International Youth Federation for Freedom. And in 1974, he wrote a book, *The Hundred Million Dollar Pay-off*, about organized labor's role in campaign financing.

Caddy came to Texas in 1979, and went to work in 1980 in Austin as director of elections for then-Secretary of State George Strake. While there, he agreed to a friend's request to serve as local counsel to a non-profit foundation that wanted to apply for a Moody Foundation grant. He moved to Houston in 1981.

Caddy said he first met foundation trustee Shearn Moody Jr. at the foundation's Galveston offices, where they and other officials discussed the grant.

Caddy eventually would serve as director or legal counsel to several organizations that would receive more than $1 million in Moody Foundation grants.

Those grants are now among more than $3 million in grants under investigation. Caddy says the investigation of him is "retaliation" for his raising the initial allegations with officials. He also attributes the probe to what he says is a friendship between the Moodys and Texas Attorney General Jim Mattox.

Caddy says he has cooperated fully with investigators because he has "nothing to hide."

"We're very proud of what we did," Caddy said. "We fulfilled our contracts for the purposes stated."

Among his grant-funded projects were conferences on terrorism, Hispanics and the "Star Wars" technology, and – at Moody's request – an investigation into allegations raised by convicted West Texas swindler Billie Sol Estes. Estes has long claimed to have information implicating former President Lyndon B. Johnson in wrongdoing.

During that time, Caddy says he began to consider himself a friend to Moody, and once agreed to work undercover posing as Moody's lawyer to help an FBI investigation of alleged corruption among Alabama state officials.

The friendship began to cool, however, after Moody's lawyer revealed the "cover" in a North Carolina bankruptcy court, Caddy said. Moody's increasing association with William R. Pabst, convicted in 1985 of charity fraud, furthered the split.

Caddy said Moody ignored repeated warnings to steer clear of Pabst. On Oct. 31, 1985, Caddy urged the Moody Foundation to investigate grants to several foundations Pabst and his associate, Vance Beaudreau, helped set up.

Moody, Pabst and Beaudreau have since been indicted by a federal grand jury for allegedly diverting Moody Foundation grants to pay personal expenses.

It wasn't long after his split with Moody that Caddy says he started receiving threats.

Caddy said he received three or four bomb threats over a period of several days, and the windows in his sixth-floor office were shot out during the night. About a month later, he found a spent cartridge near his desk.

Throughout, he says, his house has been watched, he's been followed and his telephones have been wiretapped. Friends and associ-

> ates, too, have been harassed, Caddy says.
>
> In a July 22, 1985, letter to Moody, Caddy attributed the threats to "Pabst and his kooky paramilitary colleagues."
>
> Last week, D. Michael Hollaway, the explosives expert, said under oath that Moody and Pabst tried to hire him later that year to plant explosives in Caddy's car.
>
> Hollaway said Moody told him he wanted to "blow his (Caddy's) legs off," or have him shot by a sniper. Hollaway declined the offer.
>
> "William R. Pabst just talked to me about using enough explosives to scare Caddy, but Shearn Moody wanted him either dead or his legs blown off," Hollaway said. "Shearn Moody was not kidding about this but was very serious."
>
> Hollaway said he was approached by Moody and Pabst "at the time that Douglas Caddy started causing problems at the Moody Foundation."
>
> Caddy says he's not surprised by Hollaway's allegations.
>
> "It's what comes out of a case involving a family fortune and a family dynasty," Caddy said. "I think quite frankly, yes, they were trying to send us a message."
>
> He remains worried, though – particularly since Pabst and Beaudreau are fugitives believed to be hiding in Mexico.
>
> "It still bothers me that Pabst and Beaudreau are still running around out there, because they're unstable people," Caddy said. "I am still fearful for my life and the lives of my associates.
>
> "We're not just paranoid. If he (Moody) had found the right guy, they would have done it."

Shearn Moody on numerous occasions told me how John Connally had attempted to take over the Moody Foundation. At one time the Foundation was placed in the hands of strangers and only through a lawsuit filed by Shearn did the Moody family regain control. Moody provided documents showing that one means Connally utilized his power illicitly was through Project Southwest, which was instituted by the Internal Revenue service under the Nixon Administration when Connally was Secretary of the Treasury. It was essentially a list of Connally's enemies whom he wanted the IRS to target.

After Professor John A. Andrew of Franklin and Marshall College in Pennsylvania published his book *The Other Side of the Sixties: Young Americans for Freedom and the Rise of Conservative Politics,* he informed me that he had begun writing another book that would deal with abuses by the Internal Revenue Service.

I provided Prof. Andrew with materials that Moody had given me on Project Southwest. Prof. Andrew was intrigued by what he read and through the Freedom of Information Act obtained additional documents on IRS abuses, including more on Project Southwest. However, before he finished his book he suddenly died in 2000. His manuscript was later completed, using his writings and research materials that he left behind, and was published in 2002. Its title is *Power to Destroy: The Political Uses of the IRS from Kennedy to Nixon* and is available from amazon.com.

Among the documents that I gave to Proffesor Andrew was a letter-to-editor from me on Project Southwest that was published in the *Wall Street Journal* in 1998. A few days after my letter was published, *Journal* published a responding letter-to-editor from a former IRS Commissioner, who served in the Nixon Administration, disputing my allegation of IRS abuses through Project Southwest while he was Commissioner.

Proffesor John Andrew, who had previously studied at the University of Texas and written a book on Lyndon Johnson and the Great Society, contended in his communications to me that Connally, while serving as Secretary of the Treasury in the Nixon Administration, had used IRS Project Southwest to go after his political enemies in Texas. He maintained that Watergate Special Prosecutor Leon Jaworski, also from Texas, had indicted Connally in part in retaliation for devising Project Southwest. The indictment charged that Connally had accepted a bribe while serving as Secretary of the Treasury. The evidence was strong that he had done so but a Washington, D.C. jury, comprised mainly of African-Americans, found Connally not guilty after the Rev. Billy Graham and Member of Congress Barbara Jordan of Texas, a prominent African-American, testified as character witnesses in his behalf.

Publisher's Weekly in its review had this to say about Prof. Andrew's book on the IRS:

> As historian Prof. Andrew (*Lyndon Johnson and the Great Society*) shows in this dense study, during the 1960s and '70s the White House used the power of taxation to attack enemies-and reward friends-with relative impunity. President Kennedy, for example, started an "Ideological Organizations Project" that used the IRS to challenge the tax-exempt status of (and thus choke off the funding from) such right-wing opponents as the John Birch Society. Johnson often promised tax favors to wealthy individuals who could deliver votes. But these abuses pale in comparison to the corruption of the Nixon administration, which used the IRS to persecute people on the president's notorious "Enemies List." At Nixon's request, the IRS launched audits and investigations of a host of real and imagined opponents, including the Jerry Rubin Foundation, the Fund for Investigative Journalism (which funded Seymour Hersh's reporting on the My Lai massacre) and the Center for Corporate Responsibility. The basic intent, Nixon aide John Dean wrote, was to "use the available federal machinery to screw our political enemies." Though known to Watergate prosecutors, these abuses went largely unreported in the mainstream media because they weren't sexy enough for the general public.

In 1995 I was a witness in an excise tax case that the Internal Revenue Service brought against Shearn Moody on Moody Foundation grants that he had sponsored. I agreed to testify in behalf of Moody because he was in severe ill health and because the out-of-control abuse heaped on me by the IRS had totally alienated me. (Moody died the following year after the Tax Court trial.) In my testimony I wanted to bring out that an IRS Criminal Intelligence Agent directed that $38,000 of the first Moody Foundation grant I received was to go to a person that he selected. I had the proof in writing of this. However, on the morning of the trial in Tax Court, Moody's attorney who specializes in tax court cases cautioned me that I should not disclose this in my testimony. He said that the tax court judge was a former IRS agent and might first rule against the admissibility of my evidence to protect the IRS and then might retaliate against Moody in his final decision. When he told me this, I asked him, "Is the fix in?" He shrugged his shoulders and did not respond. I reluctantly acceded to the strategic legal advice given to me by Moody's tax lawyer. So this crucially important aspect of the case was never entered into the court's testimony with the result being that Moody generally prevailed in the judge's final decision. *Fortune* Magazine opined "The court reduced Moody's fine and penalty to around $1.4 million. 'A 97% victory,' says Moody lawyer William Cousins of Dallas. And maybe a 100% loss for the IRS, since the likelihood that Moody will ever pay the fine is close to zippo." Moody had been adjudged bankrupt. But for me the case was an eye-opener into the Tax Court just as Judge Sirica's actions in Watergate were a revelation because while the Tax Court judge basically ruled that all the Moody foundation grant funds that I administered were done properly, my actions in doing so were misrepresented by the court. The trial in Tax Court refused to acknowledge in any manner the elephant in the room: that the federal district court which tried the criminal case that convicted and sent Moody to prison for defrauding the Moody Foundation later dismissed all the charges against him and ordered that Moody be freed from prison because of the refusal of the IRS to let its criminal intelligence agent testify as to the $38,000 payment when I demanded that he do so before the grand jury.

The person who received the $38,000 as directed by the IRS Criminal Intelligence Agent told me in an unguarded moment in 1986 that IRS Criminal Intelligence had discovered a secret and illegal $1.5 million campaign fund that Vice President George H.W. Bush had set up in Houston for use in the 1984 Reagan-Bush reelection campaign. The money was allegedly held and distributed by Robert Eckels, the Harris County judge, a GOP public official. In 1989 I filed a complaint with the Federal Election Commission about the secret fund and asked that it be investigated. While the FEC investigation was underway Eckels, who had retired as county judge, was quoted in the local newspaper as saying that he was writing his autobiography in which he would make shocking disclosures that would result in heads being rolled. Then suddenly he died of a heart attack while sitting in the sauna at his ranch. The FEC in its final decision on my complaint ruled that there was "reason to believe" the secret $1.5 million campaign fund might have existed but because of Eckels' death it could take no further action. Here is a link to the FEC decision:

> JlnJR 2925 Respondents: (a) Robert Y. Eckels (TX) 1(b) Reagan-Bush r 84, .scott B. MacKenzie,treasurer (DC); (e) Richard Brown (TX) Ccoplainant: *Douglas* Caddy, Chairman, Halt IRS Taxpayer Abuse Now! Political ActionCommittee (TX)SUbject: Independent expendituresDisposition: (a) Reason to believe but took no further action; (b) and (c) no reason to believe[1]
>
> https://www.fec.gov/resources/record/1991/february1991.pdf

My complaint with the ensuing investigation is considered to be a "classic" disclosure case by the FEC. Here is its full report, much of which covers topics never addressed and omitted by the Tax Court in its decision:

http://classic.fec.gov/disclosure_data/mur/2925.pdf

Subsequent to my compliant being filed with the FEC, Congress held hearings and enacted the Internal Revenue Service Restructuring and Reform Act of 1998. My FEC complaint and my letter to the Chief U.S. District Court Judge requesting permission to testify before the grand jury about the $38,000 payment that I made at the direction of the IRS Criminal Intelligence Agent played a role in Congress enacting this reform legislation. Senator Howard Metzenbaum of Ohio even sent an emissary to Houston to visit with me to gather more information. My evidence gained added credibility with the senators considering the proposed reform bill when an employee of the IRS office in Houston offered her personal testimony as to massive wrongdoing in that office.

Previously, the IRS district director for Houston suddenly had resigned.

Here from Wikipedia is a description of the 1998 IRS reform act:

> The Internal Revenue Service Restructuring and Reform Act of 1998, also known as Taxpayer Bill of Rights III, enacted July 22, 1998), resulted from hearings held by the United States Congress in 1996 and 1997. The Act included numerous amendments to the Internal Revenue Code of 1986.

The chickens had finally come home to roost for the out-of-control IRS when Congress enacted the Taxpayer Bill of Rights III after holding congressional hearings where witnesses were hidden behind a screen to prevent retaliation by the IRS as they recounted to the lawmakers their litanies of abuse by the IRS.

As will be shown in the next chapter history owes Shearn Moody, despite his many flaws, a debt of gratitude for responding favorably when Billie Sol Estes contacted him about his wanting to come clean by publicly telling the story of his criminal relationship with Lyndon Johnson. Had Moody not encouraged Billie Sol to do so, much of what is now known of LBJ's use of the stone cold killer Malcolm (Mac) Wallace to commit murders would still be cloaked in secrecy.

Endnotes

1. https://www.fec.gov/resources/record/1991/february1991.pdf

Chapter Seven

BILLIE SOL ESTES AND LBJ

After the Texas Policy Institute under a Moody Foundation grant sponsored a highly successful conference that I had organized in Galveston on the Star Wars project in 1983, Shearn Moody asked that I visit him at his ranch there. He told me that he had received a phone call from his former lobbyist in Austin, Jimmy Day, who was then in the federal prison in Big Spring, Texas. It appeared that Day had moved on to Washington, D.C. after he was no longer working for Shearn and had gotten himself in big trouble there. As explained to me by Shearn, Day on a visit to the White House had clandestinely heisted some White House stationery, and then wrote fraudulent letters on it recommending his superior lobbying talents. Shearn termed the felony charge against Day as being "puffery." In any event Day had called Shearn to say that he wanted Shearn to talk on the phone with another prisoner. When Shearn inquired who that might be, Day said that it was Billie Sol Estes, an infamous criminal whose notoriety approached historical proportions.

Day gave the phone to Billie Sol who then informed Shearn that he wanted to tell all he knew about his close criminal relationship over many decades with President Lyndon Johnson, who had died ten years earlier in 1973. He asked Shearn for a grant from the Moody Foundation that would enable him to do this.

Shearn, a history buff, requested that I visit with Billie Sol in prison and get more details. A few weeks later I traveled to Big Spring and met with Billie Sol who told me that he had a story to tell about LBJ that would rock the world. I advised him that the best way to do so would be to write a book and his response was that he would think about it. As our meeting ended I said that I would report back to Shearn what Billie Sol had told me in the event there was a possibility of a Moody Foundation grant.

Nothing more happened until early January 1984, about six months after my prison visit, when Billie Sol telephoned Shearn from his home in Abilene and said that he had been released from prison and wanted to tell his story in a book under a Moody Foundation grant. Shearn asked that I travel to Abilene and confer further with Billie Sol. Shearn said that for a foundation grant to be awarded it would require a tax-exempt entity agreeing to sponsor Billie Sol's proposal.

I arrived in Abilene and talked with Billie Sol who readily agreed that writing a book was the best way to tell his story. This was because after I had visited him in prison, he had encouraged his daughter, Pam, to write a book, which she did, "Billie Sol Estes, King of the Wheeler-Dealers." Her book had been well received and gotten lots of publicity. He said his daughter's book was only concerned with how the family survived while he was in prison and did not contain any substantive disclosures of his criminal activities with LBJ. He boasted that his tell-all book would be a best-seller.

I explained to him that a tax-exempt entity had to be the recipient of the foundation grant under which Billie Sol would write his book. He said that would be no problem and picked up the phone and called the President of Abilene Christian University who agreed to meet us later that afternoon. Billie Sol was a prominent member of the Church of Christ and the university was affiliated with that Church. At the meeting the university president agreed that if a Moody Foundation grant were forthcoming to the university a portion of it would be allocated for Billie Sol to write his book.

Upon returning to Galveston I reported this to Shearn who said that he would sponsor such a Moody Foundation grant in the amount of $500,000 of which $400,000 would go to Abilene Christian University for its unrestricted purposes and $100,000 to Billie Sol. A short time later I returned to Abilene and informed both the university president and Billie Sol of Shearn's intention of getting a grant approved at the next quarterly meeting of the foundation's trustees.

When I told Billie Sol this news he responded that to disclose what he knew of his and LBJ's criminal activities he would need to receive immunity from prosecution from the U.S. Department of Justice. By a twist of fate I found myself in a position of possibly securing such immunity. Investigative Research Foundation, which had received Moody Foundation grant, was preparing to sponsor a National Conference on Terrorism, this being 1984 when few persons were talking about it. As the organizer of the conference I had retained as a consultant Edward Miller, former associate director of the FBI, to assist in developing the speakers list and agenda. Miller and former assistant director of the FBI, Mark Felt, had been convicted of doing illegal "black bag" jobs against members of the Weather Underground and other far left-wing radical grounds engaged in illegal activist activities such as exploding a bomb in the U.S. Capitol Building that caused a crack in the building's famous dome. President Ronald Reagan had pardoned them, asserting they were heroes and not criminals. The key person who had shepherded their pardon process to success was Stephen Trott, Assistant Attorney General for the Criminal Division in the Justice Department. Miller believed that he and I could get an appointment with Trott to discuss Billie Sol receiving a grant of immunity.

About this time Billie Sol voluntarily appeared before a grand jury in Robertson County and testified that LBJ was behind the 1961 murder of U.S. Department of Agriculture official Henry Marshall. *The Dallas Morn-*

ing News of March 23, 1984 in a front page article headlined "Billie Sol Links LBJ to Murder" reported:

> Franklin, Texas – Convicted swindler Billie Sol Estes told a grand jury that Lyndon B. Johnson was one of four men who planned the 1961 murder of an agricultural official, sources close the grand jury said Thursday.
>
> The sources said Estes testified that the group feared the official would link Estes' illegal activities to the vice president.
>
> Estes, who testified before the Robertson County Grand Jury Tuesday, told grand jurors that Johnson felt pressure to silence Henry Harvey Marshall of Bryan, a regional USDA official in charge of the federal allotment program, sources said.

Marshall had been shot five times in the chest and his bolt-action .22 caliber rifle was found nearby in the field where he died.

As a result of Estes' testimony the 1984 grand jury voted to change the official death certificate of Marshall entered in 1961 as "Wound by Gunshot Self Inflicted Suicide by Gunshot Wounds Self-Inflicted" to "Wound by Gunshot Homicide by Gunshot Wounds."

Estes' testimony and the action of the Robertson Country grand jury created a sensation throughout Texas.

Estes appearance before the grand jury had been arranged by Clint Peoples, the U.S. Marshal for the Northern District of Texas. Peoples had followed Estes career as a businessman and criminal for 25 years, starting when he was first a Texas Ranger. Estes had introduced me to Peoples, and I visited Peoples in his Marshal's office in the U.S. Courthouse in Dallas on several occasions. During one of these visits Peoples' pulled out a file from a cabinet that contained a large quantity of material on Estes and LBJ and showed me about a dozen photographs of Henry Marshall's body when he had been found dead in the field.

In "Taking care of business: Lawman solves slaying after 23 years of trying," the *Dallas Times Herald* of March 23, 1984, reported:

> For 23 years, solving the murder of Henry Marshall was lawman Clint Peoples' No. 1 piece of unfinished business.
>
> But Tuesday, the U.S. Marshal's questions were answered when convicted con man Billy Sol Estes made good on a long-standing promise to Peoples and told a Robertson grand jury everything he knew about the case.
>
> "I feel more relieved now than I've felt in my life," Peoples said Thursday afternoon.
>
> Peoples, the U.S. Marshal for Northern Texas since 1973, originally investigated the case in March 1962, when he was a Texas Ranger. It was one of the very few cases he could not solve.

"I said that as I lived, I would try to solve this case, although I didn't know if I ever would," said Peoples, now 73.

He entered the case when the trail was cold....

In 1979, Peoples escorted Estes on a flight from Dallas to the La Tuna federal penitentiary near El Paso after Estes was convicted of mail fraud and conspiracy of mail fraud to conceal assets to avoid paying back taxes.

According the Peoples' book, he queried Estes about the Marshall murder and said it always had haunted him.

Estes said he knew Marshall was murdered, the book says, and often wanted to tell the ranger that he was "looking in the wrong direction."

When Peoples asked which way to look, according to the book, Estes said he should look at "people who had the most to lose."

"Should I be looking in the direction of Washington?," Peoples asked.

"You are now definitely on the right track," the book quotes Estes as saying.

In her book, *Faustian Bargains: Lyndon Johnson and Mac Wallace in the Robber Baron Culture of Texas,* Professor Joan Mellen goes to extraordinary shameful lengths to attack and darken the character of U.S. Marshal Clint Peoples, a truly great American whom I feel privileged to have known. Mellen's book, nevertheless, is definitely worth reading to get an overall picture of what Texas was like when LBJ and his crooked cronies ruled the state unchallenged. Mellen focuses in her book on Malcolm (Mac) Wallace, whom Billie Sol asserted was a stone cold killer that LBJ used when necessary. In her book, Mellen writes,

> Mac Wallace is a case in point, his history with Lyndon Johnson is a window into Johnson's methods. Wallace's story is so intriguing because, unlike other of Johnson's acolytes, it is difficult to prove what he did for Lyndon Johnson and what Lyndon Johnson did, in turn, for him. More than any other of Johnson's protégés and acolytes, Wallace's connection to him remains cloaked in secrecy.
>
> In the major events of Mac Wallace's life, Lyndon Johnson remains invisible. Yet one truth is irrefutable. Everything that was positive and promising in Wallace's life came to him before he made the acquaintance of Lyndon Baines Johnson and joined Johnson's circle.

Billie Sol asserted that Mac Wallace murdered USDA official Henry Marshall upon the orders of LBJ.

In the wake of the Robertson County Grand jury action Edward Miller made an appointment for the two of us to visit Assistant Attorney General Stephen Trott in the Justice Department. As a result of that meeting I received the follow letter from Trott dated May 29, 1984:

Dear Mr. Caddy:

RE: Billy Sol Estes

I have considered the materials and information you have provided to me in connection with your representation of Billy Sol Estes. I understand that Mr. Estes claims to have information concerning the possible commission of criminal offenses in Texas in the 1960's and that he is willing to reveal that information at this time. I also understand that Mr. Estes wants several things in exchange for this information, such as a pardon for the offenses for which he has been convicted and immunity from any further prosecution among other things.

Before we can engage in any further discussions concerning Mr. Estes' cooperation or enter into any agreement with Mr. Estes we must know the following things: (1) the information, including the extent of corroborative evidence, that Mr. Estes has about each of the events that may be violations of criminal law; (2) the sources of his information; and (3) the extent of his involvement, if any, in each of those events or any subsequent cover-ups. Until we have detailed information concerning these three things we cannot determine whether any violations of federal criminal law occurred which are within our jurisdiction to investigate and prosecute and, if so, whether the information is credible and otherwise warrants investigation. Accordingly, if we are to proceed with meaningful discussions concerning Mr. Estes' proffered cooperation, we must receive a detailed and specific written offer of proof from you setting forth the information noted above. The government will hold your offer of proof in strictest confidence and will not make any use of it other than to determine the credibility of the proffered information and whether it warrants further discussions with or debriefings of Mr. Estes.

I must make sure that several things are understood at this time concerning Mr. Estes' proffered cooperation. First, if after reviewing your offer of proof we decide the information that Mr. Estes can provide is credible and in all other respects warrants further investigation – a decision which will be made unilaterally by the government – it will be necessary for Mr. Estes to be interviewed and to reveal everything he knows about the possible criminal violations. He will have to do so completely, truthfully and without guile. Second, it must be understood that the government is not now making specific promises to Mr. Estes except with respect to the confidentiality and use of your offer of proof as noted above. If it is decided that Mr. Estes should be interviewed, the extent of promises concerning the confidentiality or use of the statement or promises of reward or consideration to Mr. Estes, if any, will be determined only after we receive a detailed written offer of proof from you.

Above all else, I must emphasize that Mr. Estes must act with total honesty and candor in any dealings with the Department of Justice or any investigative agency. If any discussions with or debriefings of Mr. Estes take place after receipt of your offer of proof and if any agreement ultimately is reached after Mr. Estes provides a statement, the government will not be bound by any representations or agreements it makes if any of his statements at any time are false, misleading or materially incomplete or if he knowingly fails to act with total honesty and candor.

Sincerely

Stephen S. Trott
Assistant Attorney General
Criminal Division

Upon receipt Trott's letter I conferred with Billie Sol who provided me with information that would be contained in a letter of proffer to be sent back to Trott in response. His daughter, Pam, was present when he disclosed the information to me. Here is my letter back to Assistant Attorney General Trott:

August 9, 1984

Mr. Stephen S. Trott
Assistant Attorney General, Criminal Division
U.S. Department of Justice
Washington, D. C. 20530

RE: Mr. Billie Sol Estes

Dear Mr. Trott:

My client, Mr. Estes, has authorized me to make this reply to your letter of May 29, 1984. Mr. Estes was a member of a four-member group, headed by Lyndon Johnson, which committed criminal acts in Texas in the 1960's. The other two, besides Mr. Estes and LBJ, were Cliff Carter and Mac Wallace. Mr. Estes is willing to disclose his knowledge concerning the following criminal offenses:

I. Murders

1. The killing of Henry Marshall
2. The killing of George Krutilek
3. The killing of Ike Rogers and his secretary
4. The killing of Harold Orr
5. The killing of Coleman Wade
6. The killing of Josefa Johnson
7. The killing of John Kinser
8. The killing of President J. F. Kennedy.

Mr. Estes is willing to testify that LBJ ordered these killings, and that he transmitted his orders through Cliff Carter to Mac Wallace, who executed the murders. In the cases of murders nos. 1-7, Mr. Estes' knowledge of the precise details concerning the way the murders were executed stems from conversations he had shortly after each event with Cliff Carter and Mac Wallace.

In addition, a short time after Mr. Estes was released from prison in 1971, he met with Cliff Carter and they reminisced about what had occurred in the past, including the murders. During their conversation, Carter orally compiled a list of 17 murders which had been committed, some of which Mr. Estes was unfamiliar. A living witness was present at that meeting and should be willing to testify about it. He is Kyle Brown, recently of Houston and now living in Brady, Texas.

Mr. Estes states that Mac Wallace, whom he describes as a "stone killer" with a communist background, recruited Jack Ruby, who in turn recruited Lee Harvey Oswald. Mr. Estes says that Cliff Carter told him that Mac Wallace fired a shot from the grassy knoll in Dallas, which hit JFK from the front during the assassination.

Mr. Estes declares that Cliff Carter told him the day Kennedy was killed, Fidel Castro also was supposed to be assassinated and that Robert Kennedy, awaiting word of Castro's death, instead received news of his brother's killing.

Mr. Estes says that the Mafia did not participate in the Kennedy assassination but that its participation was discussed prior to the event, but rejected by LBJ, who believed if the Mafia were involved, he would never be out from under its blackmail.

Mr. Estes asserts that Mr. Ronnie Clark, of Wichita, Kansas, has attempted on several occasions to engage him in conversation. Mr. Clark, who is a frequent visitor to Las Vegas, has indicated in these conversations a detailed knowledge corresponding to Mr. Estes' knowledge of the JFK assassination. Mr. Clark claims to have met with Mr. Jack Ruby a few days prior to the assassination, at which time Kennedy's planned murder was discussed.

Mr. Estes declares that discussions were had with Jimmy Hoffa concerning having his aide, Larry Cabell, kill Robert Kennedy while the latter drove around in his convertible.

Mr. Estes has records of his phone calls during the relevant years to key persons mentioned in the foregoing account.

II. The Illegal Cotton Allotments

Mr. Estes desires to discuss the infamous illegal cotton allotment schemes in great detail. He has recordings made at the time of LBJ, Cliff Carter and himself discussing the scheme. These recordings were made with Cliff Carter's knowledge as a means of Carter and Estes protecting themselves should LBJ order their deaths.

Mr. Estes believes these tape recordings and the rumors of other recordings allegedly in his possession are the reason he has not been murdered.

III. Illegal Payoffs

Mr. Estes is willing to disclose illegal payoff schemes, in which he collected and passed on to Cliff Carter and LBJ millions of dollars. Mr. Estes collected payoff money on more than one occasion from George and Herman Brown of Brown and Root, which was delivered to LBJ.

In your letter of May 29, 1984, you request "(1) the information, including the extent of corroborative evidence, that Mr. Estes sources of his information, and (3) the extent of his involvement, if any, in each of those events or any subsequent cover-ups."

In connection with Item # 1, I wish to declare, as Mr. Estes' attorney, that Mr. Estes is prepared without reservation to provide all the information he has. Most of the information contained in this letter I obtained from him yesterday for the first time. While Mr. Estes has been pre-occupied by this knowledge almost every day for the last 22 years, it was not until we began talking yesterday that he could face up to disclosing it to another person. My impression from our conversation yesterday is that Mr. Estes, in the proper setting, will be able to recall and orally recount criminal matters. It is also my impression that his interrogation in such a setting will elicit additional corroborative evidence as his memory is stimulated.

In connection with your Item #2, Mr. Estes has attempted in this letter to provide his sources of information.

In connection with your Item #3, Mr. Estes states that he never participated in any of the murders. It may be alleged that he participated in subsequent cover-ups. His response to this is that had he conducted himself any differently, he, too, would have been a murder victim.

Mr. Estes wishes to confirm that he will abide by the conditions set forth in your letter and that he plans to act with total honesty and candor in any dealings with the Department of Justice or any federal investigative agency.

In return for his cooperation, Mr. Estes wishes in exchange his being given immunity, his parole restrictions being lifted and favorable consideration being given to recommending his long-standing tax leins being removed and his obtaining a pardon.

Sincerely yours,
Douglas Caddy

The full four letters can be found online using google.

Two other murders besides that of Henry Marshall merit examination here because they are interrelated. These are the murders of John Kinser in 1951 and of Josefa Johnson, Lyndon's sister in 1961, ten years later.

The inside flyleaf of Mellen's book is illuminating. It reads:

> Perhaps no other president has a more ambiguous reputation than Lyndon Johnson. A brilliant tactician, he maneuvered colleagues and turned bills into law better than anyone. But he was trailed by a legacy of underhanded dealings, from his "stolen" Senate election in 1948 to kickbacks he artfully concealed from deals engineered with Texas wheeler-dealer Billie Sol Estes, defense contractors, and his Senate aid Bobby Baker. On the verge of investigation, Johnson was reprieved when he became president upon John F. Kennedy's assassination.
>
> Among the remaining mysteries of his life has been LBJ's relationship with Malcolm "Mac" Wallace, who, in 1951, shot a Texas man having an affair with LBJ's loose-cannon sister Josefa, also Wallace's lover. When arrested, Wallace coolly said, "I work for Johnson.... I have to get back to Washington." Charged with murder, he was overnight defended by LBJ's powerful lawyer John Cofer, and though convicted, amazingly received a suspended sentence. He then received a secret security clearance to work for LBJ friend and defense contractor D.H. Byrd, which the Office of Naval Intelligence tried to revoke for years without success.

Billie Sol claimed that John Kinser was killed by Mac Wallace upon being ordered to do so by LBJ because Josefa had disclosed too many of LBJ's secret criminal activities that threatened his goal of ascendancy to the presidency.

In 1984 I arranged for Lucianne Goldberg, a prominent literary agent in New York City who later became famous in the Bill Clinton/Monica Lewinsky scandal, to meet with Billie Sol and me in Abilene to discuss his writing a book and getting it published. Among the murders he disclosed at our meeting with that of Josefa Johnson, LBJ's sister. Billie Sol asserted that in 1961, Josefa was served on Christmas Eve a portion of a cake that contained poison and that she died the next day and was quietly buried the following day in the Johnson family cemetery on the Johnson ranch.

Billie Sol in his autobiography *Billie Sol Estes: A Texas Legend* (BS Productions, 2004) writes about this:

> For a time after the Kinser death, Josefa Johnson kept her mouth shut, but soon there were additional reports of her talking. In the end it was decided she could never be trusted. On Christmas day [1961] she became ill and died. I was told she was given poison. When Cliff [Carter] told me this, I had an empty feeling in my stomach. My family is dear to me. I would never consider doing something to them. I believe Lyndon was guided by the vision of his destiny and considered the sacrifice was needed by the people.
>
> In 1971, my discussion with Cliff Carter centered on his disgust with the murders.

At the meeting in Abilene attended by Lucianne Goldberg, Billie Sol remarked about the mysterious circumstances that surrounded the death of the daughter of John Connally who died on her wedding night. Lucianne was familiar with the mystery. Billie Sol added that the only man LBJ was ever afraid of was John Connally, one of LBJ's political allies, because Connally was even more ruthless than LBJ.

As the result of Edward Miller and I meeting with Assistant Attorney General Trott he arranged for three young FBI agents to examine the agency's file on Billie Sol to determine if the pursuit of granting immunity to him was warranted. They concluded it was and the three agents and I flew from Washington to Abilene to meet with Billie Sol to hear what he had to say. Billie Sol showed up at the meeting at a hotel with his daughter, Pam, and immediately stated he would not talk to the FBI agents and was withdrawing from negotiations to gain immunity. He was adamant about this, so the three agents departed and flew back to Washington.

Billie Sol in his autobiography writes:

> After a further series of letters, a meeting was set up at a hotel in Abilene. As the day approached, I received a series of telephone calls from my Italian friends. I was informed my discussions with the Justice Department was a mistake. They insisted that if I appeared to be going through with the discussions, my life would end. I do not know how they found out about the discussions. Now I may be dumb but I am not stupid and I do not have a death wish.

In my letter of proffer to Assistant Attorney General Trott in which I listed in behalf Billie Sol what he would disclose I purposely omitted one startling and controversial item for fear that it would cause the Justice Department to reject outright any discussion of immunity. This was that Billie Sol had confessed to me that he had paid a $500,000 bribe to U.S. Supreme Court Justice Tom Clark when the Supreme Court was considering a case in which Billie Sol was appealing his conviction for violating Texas law. Billie Sol said that the $500,000 in cash was delivered to President Johnson on Johnson's plane at an airport in Texas by Billie Sol and his lawyer, John Cofer. LBJ later disbursed the bribe to Justice Clark, who originally was from Dallas and was part of the Texas Mafia

Here is a summary of the case in which Estes alleged that a bribe was paid:

> 381 U.S. 532 (85 S.Ct. 1628, 14 L.Ed.2d 543)
> Billie Sol ESTES, Petitioner, v. STATE OF TEXAS.
> No. 256.
> Argued: April 1, 1965.
> Decided: June 7, 1965.

- opinion, CLARK
- concurrence, WARREN, DOUGLAS, GOLDBERG
- concurrence, WARREN, HARLAN
- dissent, STEWART, BLACK, BRENNAN, WHITE
- dissent, WHITE, BRENNAN

See 86 S.Ct. 18.

John D. Cofer and Hume Cofer, Austin, Tex., for petitioner.
Waggoner Carr, Austin, Tex., and Leon Jaworski, Houston, Tex., for respondent.

Justice CLARK delivered the opinion of the Court.
The question presented here is whether the petitioner, who stands convicted in the District Court for the Seventh Judicial District of Texas at Tyler for swindling, was deprived of his right under the Fourteenth Amendment to due process by the televising and broadcasting of his trial. Both the trial court and the Texas Court of Criminal Appeals found against the petitioner. We hold to the contrary and reverse his conviction.

The average American citizen would be shocked upon hearing that a U.S. Supreme Court justice had taken a bribe in a case and had even written the court's opinion in the case. No doubt that the same citizen would be shocked upon learning that another Supreme Court justice, who had been appointed to the bench by President Johnson, was accused to accepting money then forced to resign from the court.

Here an article from politico.com on the subject:

Abe Fortas resigns from Supreme Court May 15, 1969

By Andrew Glass
05/15/2008 04:12 AM EDT

On this day in 1969, Abe Fortas, denying he had done anything wrong, resigned from the Supreme Court to return to private law practice. In stepping down, Fortas became the first Supreme Court justice to resign under threat of impeachment.

In 1968, President Lyndon Johnson nominated Abe Fortas (1910-1982), at the time an associate justice, to succeed Earl Warren as chief justice. In becoming the first such nominee to appear before a Senate committee, Fortas faced hostile questioning about his relationship with LBJ, which had improperly continued while he served on the high tribunal.

Fortas cemented his friendship with the future president in 1948 when LBJ sought the Senate nomination in Texas. He won the Democratic primary contest by 87 votes. His opponent, Coke Stevenson,

> persuaded a federal judge to take Johnson's name off the general election ballot while allegations of corruption – including 200 votes cast in alphabetical order for LBJ – were investigated. But after Fortas persuaded Justice Hugo Black to overturn the ruling, Johnson managed to win the general election.
>
> On the Senate floor, conservative senators mounted a filibuster against the chief justice nomination, using as a wedge issue Fortas' acceptance of a $15,000 fee for a series of university seminars. When supporters could muster only 45 of the 59 votes needed to end debate, Fortas asked the president to withdraw his name – becoming the first nominee for that post since 1795 to fail to win Senate approval.
>
> Soon, a larger problem arose. In 1966, Fortas took a secret retainer from the family foundation of Wall Street financier Louis Wolfson, a friend and former client subsequently imprisoned for securities violations. The deal provided that in return for unspecified advice, Fortas was to receive $20,000 a year for life.
>
> Disclosure of the retainer effectively ended Fortas' judicial career.

John Cofer represented Billie Sol in his 1965 case before the Supreme Court. Cofer, like Fortas, was involved in rigging the 1948 election that sent LBJ to the Senate. Cofer was Mac Wallace's attorney in the 1951 homicide trial in which Wallace was found guilty of homicide with malice aforethought in the murder of John Kinser but was awarded a suspended sentence. Cofer was Billie Sol's attorney in his state and federal criminal cases.

One of the more startling disclosures in Billie Sol's autobiography is his belief that the deaths of Mac Wallace, Cliff Carter and John Cofer were not natural. Apparently each of them knew too much about LBJ's criminal activities and LBJ's secret financial empire.

In 1998 California producer Lyle Sardie released a fascinating and encompassing documentary, *LBJ: A Closer Look.* It traces Johnson's fraudulent rise to power and his behind the scene involvement in the assassination of President Kennedy. I was privileged to be among those interviewed in the documentary, which can be viewed on YouTube.

Chapter Eight

The State of Texas vs. Michael Douglas Caddy

In 1989 a Vietnamese doctor in Houston who performed cosmetology operations such as face lifts retained me as his attorney. His practice was comprised of fellow Vietnamese who had fled Vietnam began to decline precipitously when a competing clinic opened in Southern California. The clinic there paid the roundtrip airfare for Vietnamese living anywhere in the U.S. to travel to the clinic for cosmetology operations. These were performed, but the clinic billed the patients' insurers for vast amounts, not for the cosmetology operations, but instead for complex surgery operations that were never performed. It was a classic $50 million insurance fraud case.

I contacted the FBI and the Asian section of the Houston Police Department about the Southern California clinic fraud case and began working with these two law enforcement entities.

In the midst of the case I was suddenly arrested in 1990 for indecent exposure inside a gay movie theater that required a patron to pay a membership fee to enter. It was a classic anti-gay setup case and I decided to fight it. I learned from a friend, Ray Hill, that the police officer who arrested me had previously been demoted to the vice squad because he had engaged in grossly unprofessional activity. Ray knew what he was talking about because he was the plaintiff in City of Houston vs. Hill, a 1987 case in which the U.S. Supreme Court by a vote of eight to one decided in favor of Hill in a case involving police abuse.

I had Greg Glass, one of most skilled criminal defense attorneys in the city, representing me at trial. The presiding judge could not have been more fair minded. When testifying I spoke directly to the jury. To my surprise the prosecutor introduced into evidence the inch-thick file on the California insurance fraud case that I had provided to it and to the chief of police soon after my arrest. When the prosecutor placed the file before the judge he looked at it and exclaimed, what is this? I replied it was my file on a California insurance fraud case and that I believed my arrest stemmed from someone wanting to kill the investigation into the fraud. This sudden and dramatic twist registered with the jurors who now realized there was more at stake than an indecent exposure case. Their attention quickened noticeably.

With the closing arguments finished the jury retired to the jury room. My fate was in their hands. After a short time the jury sent word to the judge that it wanted to examine my California insurance fraud file. After fifteen minutes those of us in the court room heard howls of laughter from the jury room. This is always a good sign for the defendant. The prosecutor began to look alarmed at what had appeared to him to be a slam dunk case. After another fifteen minutes the jury sent word that it had reached a verdict and filed back into the court room. The judge asked the foreman for the verdict and she responded forthrightly, "We find the defendant not guilty." Then she gave a handwritten note to the bailiff who took it to the judge. The judge examined it and gave it back to the bailiff and told him to show to me. As he approached me the bailiff's eyes were bulging. He showed me the note. All the jurors had signed it. They agreed that I should not have been arrested in the first place because intent to violate the law was lacking.

I have chosen not to have my arrest record expunged but instead to let it stand as a testament to gays everywhere that the best legal strategy when faced with such a setup charge is to stand trial and speak directly to the jurors, letting they become familiar with you and hear your side of the case.

Being a defendant in a criminal trial is an experience that I shall value forever. It is an education to be on the other side in such a trial. I shall eternally be grateful to the jurors in my case who showed courage and wisdom in their deliberations.

Harris County now has a new district attorney, Kim Ogg, who is recognized as the best in the county's history, widely admired and trusted.

The Truth About the Stonewall Riots

This would be a good place to enter into the historical record retired New York Police Department Detective Jim Rothstein's report on the 1969 raid on Stonewall, which is vastly different from the accepted history. His report follows:

> The First Division of the Police Department covered the lower west side, where the Stonewall was located. D.I. Seymour Pine was the commander. When D.I. Russell Anderson, Third Division Commander, was informed by P. O. Rothstein that the first Deps. (Deputy Commissioners) office had the Stonewall on the "Pad," and it was time to take action. D.I. Pine was convinced by D.I. Anderson to do a joint division raid, First and Third Divisions, on the Stonewall. This was a "front" for D.I. Anderson to knock off and raid the Stonewall after the First Dep's "Bagman" had picked up the payoff. When P.O. Rothstein received the signal from bartender/informant Skull Murphy from inside the bar that the payoff had been made to the "Bagman," it was time for the raid to begin. After the raid the riots started. It was a sight to behold. Transvestites, lesbians, fags, chickens and pedophiles were fighting with the police. The patrons felt they had been double crossed. They had paid off the police and then the police

raided the premises. They had had enough. The rallying cry, "Go get-em girls" could be heard throughout the block. Skull Murphy was said to have escaped, handcuffed to a "drag Queen." Really!!! The gay community knew it was time to stop the shakedowns, extortions and harassment at the hands of the police and the Mafia. D.I. Pine and all the other Police Officers never knew what really happened. Only P.O. Rothstein and two ranking officers knew the real reason for the raid, which were the illegal payoffs being made to the police and organized crime. It solidified P.O. Rothstein's trust within the homosexual underground that he was a standup guy. The Stonewall raid led to an official investigation in 1970, the Knapp Commission. The Knapp Commission investigated corruption in the Police Department. It was headed by Whitman Knapp. Maurice Nadjari was named the Special Prosecutor in 1972.

Chapter Nine

Trump And Russia

DOUGLAS CADDY
ATTORNEY-AT-LAW
HOUSTON, TEXAS
Member, Texas Bar since 1979 and
District of Columbia Bar since 1970

MEMORANDUM TO THE LEGAL FILE

Subject: Roger Stone, Lyndon LaRouche and Russia influencing the 2016 Presidential election

Date: August 22, 2017

This memo to the file brings up to date what has occurred since I sent my letter of December 10, 2016, to FBI Director James Comey and my subsequent letter of June 27, 2017, to Special Counsel Robert Mueller in regard to the above subject.

In my letter to FBI Director Comey I stated that "I knew Roger Stone of the Trump presidential campaign forty years ago in Washington. Because of this Harley Schlanger of the LaRouche organization, whom I also knew, earlier this year asked me to arrange a meeting between him and Stone. I agreed to do so. Such a meeting took place in February [2016]. I was not present at the meeting.

"It is my impression that as a result of that February meeting the LaRouche organization agreed to use its extensive Russian contacts to open up a back channel for the Trump campaign to communicate directly to Russian intelligence. This ultimately led to Russian intelligence hacking the emails of the Democratic National Committee, which became a major issue in the presidential campaign and continues to do so to this day. Stone may have played a role in Wikileaks being given the hacked emails for distribution to the public.

"Harley Schlanger and other LaRouche leaders interviewed Stone on a LaRouche radio program on a number of occasions during the course of the presidential campaign."

With my letter to Director Comey I attached a number of emails that I had received from Schlanger and Stone on this matter. Relevant quotations from some of these follow later in this memo. In addition I sent copies of my letter to Director Comey to President Obama and CIA Director Peter Goss as a safeguard that it would not be deep-sixed.

After President Trump fired Director Comey in May 2017, which led to the appointment of Special Counsel Mueller, I wrote Mr. Mueller on June 27, 2017 in part as follows:

"On December 10, 2016, I sent the enclosed letter with its email attachments to FBI Director James Comey about the above referenced matter. I never heard back from him and hence I am writing you. My motivation in doing so is because I fear that our democracy was severely endangered by Russian influence in the 2016 presidential election. Alarmingly, this Russian threat is unabated. The continued existence of the United States as a free nation is at stake.

"Here is a brief summary of my letter to Director Comey: In January 2016 Harley Schlanger of the LaRouche organization contacted me to request that I set up a meeting for him with Roger Stone of the Trump Campaign. Their meeting was held in Austin, Texas, in February 2016. I was unable to attend but my impression is that as a result of that meeting the LaRouche organization agreed to use its extensive Russian contacts to open up a back channel for the Trump campaign to communicate directly with Russian intelligence.

"Since writing my December 10 letter to Director Comey I have uncovered the following information that may corroborate the contents of that letter:

"A month before Schlanger contacted me to set up the meeting with Stone, a LaRouche delegation sympathetic to Russia attended the RT anniversary dinner in Moscow in December 2015 where Premier Putin was seated next to General Flynn. For confirmation see the bottom of page 15 and top of page 16 of the famous Christopher Steele British Dossier. Schlanger may have been among those who attended. There are essentially five persons who lead the LaRouche organization today: Lyndon LaRouche (age 94), his wife, Helga, Jeffrey Steinberg, Harley Schlanger and Anton Chaitkin.[1]

"Jeffrey Steinberg participated in an annual Economic Conference in Moscow in March 2016.[2]

"In November 2016, Roger Stone interviewed Lyndon LaRouche on his radio program.[3]

"I am writing you because you possess the investigative power and authority to determine if any of the information provided in this letter and my prior letter to Director Comey merits further investigation. It may or may not. As a private citizen I am in no position to make that determination. However, I believe it is my solemn duty both as a private citizen and an attorney who is a member of the District of Columbia and Texas Bars to call this matter to your attention."

When I sent my letter to Mr. Mueller, I also sent copies of it to Senator Mark Warner of the Senate Intelligence Committee and Congressman Adam Schiff of the House Intelligence Committee.

ABOUT LAROUCHE

Here is the link to obtain update viewpoints from the LaRouche organization: https://larouchepac.com/updates

Three of the brightest and most knowledgeable persons I have ever met are Jeffrey Steinberg, Harley Schlanger and Anton Chaitkin. However, it is well known that Lyndon LaRouche is the ultimate decider on all policy matters and his word overrides those in the organization whose views may differ.

The *Houston Chronicle* of November 7, 1982, published an article titled, "The man who 'perfected' Marx: LaRouche collects money, works at making folks over 'in my own image.'"

The article states that,

> ...former members say LaRouche is omnipotent within the organization." It further declares that, "According to his 1979 autobiography, *The Power of Reason,* LaRouche was born into a Quaker family in New Hampshire in 1922 and had only two friends until late in high school. He says the reason for his lack of friends was that his mental capabilities exceeded those of his peers.... As a young man, he joined a socialist group where he 'perfected' the theories of Marx.'"

I find myself in agreement with some of the policies espoused by the LaRouche organization, such as constructing a modern, transnational "silk road" and reform of the U.S. financial system, including Glass-Steagall reinstatement and creation of a national credit institution for infrastructure and manufacturing. Where I vehemently differ with the group is its alleged role in assisting Russia in influencing the 2016 presidential election. This issue is paramount above all others.

ABOUT ROGER STONE

I first met Roger Stone in 1975 soon after the National Conservative Political Action Committee (NCPAC) was created. Its chairman was Terry Dolan, a really nice guy who questioned the moral leadership of the conservative movement at the time. He was upset that republican Senator Jesse Helms of North Carolina was driving around Washington, D.C. in a convertible with a young blond woman at his side. Charles Black, a key leader in NCPAC, was from North Carolina and was a protégé of Senator Jesse Helms, a racist demagogue if there ever was one. Stone was another leader. Paul Manafort was on the scene but not prominent in the organization. I was the organization's legal counsel.

A short story will suffice in my finding out that Stone was a classic sociopath. On one occasion in 1975 Dolan, Stone and I had lunch together in the greater Washington area and had left the restaurant and were walking down the street. We noticed that on the opposite side of the street an elderly woman who suffered from severe curvature of the spine was walking with what appeared to be her two children, a man and a woman in their thirties. The poor woman's agonizing bent over posture was such that her face was almost parallel with the sidewalk. When Stone saw her he immediately let out a yell of delight and began to walk and prance in the same way as the poor woman was doing. He did so while gesturing towards the trio on the other side of the street so as to attract their attention. I was so embarrassed and shocked at Stone's gross behavior that I ran into a public garage in an attempt to distant myself from him. About twenty years ago I received a phone call from Fox commentator James Rosen (if my memory is correct) and who asked me what I thought of Stone. I told him about the above disturbing incident.

Charles Black, Paul Manafort and Roger Stone went on to form the political lobbying firm of Black, Manafort and Stone and what they all had in common was being sociopaths. Their quest was for power, access and money and the thought of what was best for our country never entered the picture.

In a sense I bear some responsibility for their rise to prominence. While an undergraduate at Georgetown University in 1958 I co-founded with a college friend, David Franke, the National Student Committee for the Loyalty Oath. We did this because there was no conservative movement in existence at the time and we thought we could start such a movement using college students. Senator Styles Bridges of New Hampshire brought us national exposure by endorsing our organization in a speech on the floor of the Senate. The following year, 1959, Franke and I founded Youth for Goldwater for Vice President, which was another major step toward building a conservative movement. Here is an account of what happened next from the book by Professor John A. Andrew III, *The Other Side of the Sixties: Young Americans for Freedom and the Rise of Conservative Politics*, (New Brunswick: Rutgers University Press, 1997), pp. 217-218:

> William F. Buckley and Marvin Liebman met Douglas Caddy and David Franke, both of whom attended as representatives of Youth for Goldwater for Vice President. Together, these four men would turn their disappointment in Goldwater's loss [at the 1960 GOP convention in Chicago that nominated Nixon] into a national conservative youth movement. Impressed by the passion of Caddy and Franke and their attempts to organize conservative youth in the past, including the creation of the Student Committee for the Loyalty Oath in 1958, Buckley and Liebman decided to mentor them. The loss of Goldwater for the Vice Presidential nomination convinced Buckley that young conservatives in the GOP needed to be fostered from the top down. He believed that young conservatives, with his guidance, could change the American political discourse. Consequently, Buck-

> ley hired Franke to intern at the National Review and Caddy worked for Liebman in public relations. Their first major task was to organize a national youth group for conservatives funded by Buckley. In September of 1960, on the Buckley family estate in Sharon, Connecticut, over 100 students from 44 different colleges and universities across the country assembled to devise a plan to capitalize on the growing conservatism of American youth and turn it into an organized political movement. The result created the Young Americans for Freedom, officially chartered on September 11, 1960, and the adoption of the Sharon Statement at the conference. In the Sharon statement, YAF articulated its critique of American society and proclaimed, 'In this time of moral and political crisis, it is the responsibility of the youth of America to affirm certain eternal truths.'"[4]

The founding of YAF in 1960 led to the birth of the modern conservative movement which occurred in the wake of a fantastically successful rally of conservatives at Manhattan Center in New York City in March 1961.

So Black and Manafort and Stone, sad to say, are ethically challenged by-products of the modern conservative movement which decades ago was taken over by opportunists and sociopaths. Stone was active in successfully rigging three presidential elections: In Florida in 2000 for G. W. Bush, in Ohio in 2004 for G. W. Bush and in 2016 for Trump. He has utter contempt for honest elections. Rigging is what he does.

Prior to the creation of NCPAC in 1975, Stone was active in the Nixon 1972 presidential campaign.[5]

I was the Original Attorney for the Watergate Seven but did not meet Stone until three years after the Watergate case broke.[6]

Liberals rejoiced with Nixon being forced to resign the presidency but the immediate result was the rise of the radical right with Black, Manafort and Stone being formed as a lobbying/PR firm and the extreme right-wing oligarch Joseph Coors founding the Heritage Foundation, headed by Edwin Feulner, and the Committee for a Free Congress, headed by Paul Weyrich

I left Washington, D.C. in 1979 and moved to Texas once I recognized the bizarre and dangerous direction that the conservative movement was coming to embrace.

Thus, it came as a surprise three decades later when in 2012 I was contacted by Roger Stone who requested that I supply him with any material in my possession on President Lyndon Johnson. This came about because I had been the attorney for Billie Sol Estes, LBJ's silent business and political partner, in Billie Sol's quest in 1984 to obtain a grant of immunity from prosecution from the U.S. Department of Justice in order that he could tell what he knew about LBJ crimes that took place before and during his presidency.

Stone's praise-worthy best-selling book, *The Man Who Killed Kennedy: The Case Against LBJ*, was published in 2013.[7]

Stone's book credits me as a primary source of information. For example, on page 214, he writes, "I did have access and the full cooperation of Billie Sol Estes' personal attorney Douglas Caddy who supplied interviews, source materials and remembrances for this book."[8]

It was because of my contribution of information in 2012 to Stone's JFK book that when Schlanger asked me in January 2016 to arrange for him to meet Stone I was able to do so.

Selected Relevant Emails

I provided FBI Director Comey and Special Counsel Mueller with a large number of emails that accompanied my letters to them. Here are excerpts from a few of these:

In an email of Feb. 20, 2016, Stone wrote me: "Thanks for connecting me with Harley Schlanger – he is a great guy and shares our goals. I think we hit it off. I have a back channel to Trump and we are fighting the globalists."

In email of May 5, 2016, Schlanger wrote me: "I have continued to work with Roger. He and I have done three radio interviews together, and I have set up several more for him, with my contacts. Obviously, he has played quite a brilliant role in the Trump campaign, outflanking completely the lead-footed GOP establishment. While I find some of what Trump says to be good, I'm still and not sure what a Trump presidency would mean."

In an email of July 25, 2016, to Schlanger, I wrote after the GOP presidential convention: "Well, you picked an exciting time in Germany to find a new home there. On the other hand, the U.S. as you can see from afar, is an exciting place, too, these days as both major parties are melting down. Neither candidate is worth a damn.

"After watching Trump's acceptance speech, I realized what a dangerous and hypocritical man he is. He plans to turn domestic and foreign policy over to his VP Pence and spend his time making 'America Great Again,' which means acting out his narcissism on steroids. I have lost all respect for Roger Stone and realize my belief that he had changed from his sociopathic past was misplaced.

"Roger and his business partner Paul Manafort will undergo minute media and governmental scrutiny in the coming weeks for their past political and business dealings. Manafort is increasingly linked to being a back door to Putin for the Trump campaign. The whole scandal will get radioactive if the Intelligence agencies produce evidence of a tie there."

Final Thoughts

I have no regrets in writing Comey and Mueller even though I have been regularly harassed for so doing by private detectives employed by an unknown person of interest.[9]

I had a duty to do so because the on-going investigation is into felonious criminal activity. Here is the definition of Misprision of a Felony, which is applicable in my situation and governs my actions:

> 18 U.S. Code § 4 - Misprision of felony
>
> § 4. Misprision of felony
>
> Whoever, having knowledge of the actual commission of a felony cognizable by a court of the United States, conceals and does not as soon as possible make known the same to some judge or other person in civil or military authority under the United States, shall be fined under this title or imprisoned not more than three years, or both.
>
> (June 25, 1948, ch. 645, 62 Stat. 684; Pub. L. 103–322, title XXXIII, § 330016(1)(G), Sept. 13, 1994, 108 Stat. 2147.)

I do not know whether my two letters will lead or have already led to an investigation by Special Counsel Mueller. Only time will tell.

Endnotes

1. https://www.documentcloud.org/documents/3259984-Trump-Intelligence-Allegations.html
2. https://larouchepac.com/20160328/eir-participates-moscow-economic-forum
3. https://larouchepac.com/20161121/lyndon-larouche-radio-interview-roger-stone https://www.youtube.com/watch?v=QBx6uHA05gg
4. https://www.slideshare.net/ClaireViall/rebels-with-a-causethe-growth-and-appeal-of-the-young-americans-for-freedom-in-the-1960s
5. http://www.nbcnews.com/politics/politics-news/nbc-news-exclusive-memo-shows-watergate-prosecutors-had-evidence-nixon-n773581
6. http://educationforum.ipbhost.com/topic/21500-memoir-on-being-original-attorney-for-the-watergate-seven-by-douglas-caddy/ and https://www.youtube.com/watch?v=5jKBlJQNtek
7. https://www.amazon.com/Man-Who-Killed-Kennedy-Against/dp/1629144894/ref=sr_1_1?ie=UTF8&qid=1503279918&sr=8-1&keywords=the+man+who+killed+kennedy
8. http://home.earthlink.net/~sixthfloor/estes.htm
9. http://educationforum.ipbhost.com/topic/24039-message-to-the-private-detectives-harassing-me/

Afterword

This has been the story of my life. Was the spiritualist in Hollywood accurate in 1946 in her prediction of my future that I would never reach society's top level to become a national leader but would reach the level directly underneath where I would come to know and work with many who did and witness how the world works?

To put my life in proper perspective I wish to refer to a December 21, 2017 program on coasttocoastam on which Emmy Science Award Winner Linda Mouton Howe was the guest. In answer to a question from a listener Linda said that perhaps the most haunting thing that she ever experienced in her career as a reporter occurred in the mid-1980s when a source told her about his assignment as a military officer to work with a group associated with Majestic 12. Discussion arose between the military officer and one of the group's members as to the question, "What is the real nature of our universe?"

The group's member told him that there are as many universes as there are grains of sand on Earth and that around all these universes is a cold dark sea. When the military officer asked for more information about the cold dark sea the group's member replied that he could not tell the officer more because such knowledge would change his life forever.

Appendix

Gaeton Fonzi's List Of Miami Witnesses

Gaeton Fonzi was a widely regarded investigator for the House of Representatives Select Committee on Assassinations. The Committee was established in 1976 to investigate the assassinations of John F. Kennedy and Martin Luther King, Jr. It completed its investigation in 1978 and issued its final report in 1979, which it concluded that Kennedy was probably assassinated as a result of a conspiracy.

What the Select Committee did not know was that some involved in the JFK assassination in 1963 were the same five persons who turned up in Watergate burglary break-in in 1972. These men were from Miami or had a connection with Miami.

Fonzi as an investigator compiled a list of dozens of potential Miami witnesses in the JFK assassination for use in the Committee's investigation. The list was among the records withheld for decades by the CIA that was released to the public in October 2017.

Here reproduced directly from his list is a description of five persons involved in both the Kennedy Assassination and in Watergate: Bernard Barker, Virgilio Gonzalez, Howard Hunt, Eugenio Martinez and Frank Fiorini Sturgis.

Bernard Barker
Veteran intelligence agent. Close associate of E. Howard Hunt
Former consultant on counter-insurgency to Cuban police. Acti
in Cuban Revolutionary Council prior to Bay of Pigs. Key
liaison with all Cuban groups, including those reporting
contact with Oswald. Reportedly involved in planned Castro
assassination attempt from Nicaragua (Second Naval Guerilla).
(Miami.)

Virgilio Gonzales
Associate of Bernard Barker, Eugenio Martinez and Frank Fiorini
Sturgis. Involved in intelligence operations and initial Waterga
entry. Possible knowledge of anti-Castro groups involving Oswal
or associates. (Miami)

E. Howard Hunt
Political liaison officer for the C.I.A. to the Cuban groups in
Miami prior to the Bay of Pigs. Possible knowledge of Oswald
activities prior to assassination. Possible knowledge of
Morris Bishop or associates. Requires detailed questioning
in all phases of overt and covert intelligence career. (Miami)

Eugenio Martinez
Veteran C.I.A. contract agent. Associate of Bernard Barker, E. Howard Hunt and Frank Fiorini Sturgis. Involved in numerous anti-Castro operations with Cubans and intelligence agency personnel who may have had contact with Oswald. Possibl involved in casino activity in Havana with organized crime figures. Worked with Joseph Merola, organized crime associate and intelligence operative, on anti-Castro activity. May have knowledge of gunrunning associates who had contact with Jack Ruby. (Miami)

Frank Fiorini Sturgis
Originally sent to Cuba by Carlos Prio prior to Castro revolution. Active with all intelligence agencies. Associated with many Cuban groups, organized crime figures and intelligence operatives. Reports information re Oswald in Miami prior to assassination and Ruby meeting with Castro in Havana. Co-founder of the International Anti-Communist Brigade (IAB) and associated with members of the No Name Key group. Extensive questioning required. (Miami)

Exhibits

Thrills of a "Wash-Out" Adventure During Flood Written by Scout Chief

A story of what took place on the Northwestern Pacific railroad train when it was slide-bound at Bell Springs in December was written by Raymond O. Hanson, regional scout executive of Region 12, who as the San Francisco Council executive at the time, was one of the passengers on the train. He was en route to Eureka to give the principal address at the annual Boy Scout meeting of the Redwood Area Council.

Hanson's story was received last week by Executive David C. Watkins and is presented as follows:

THRILLS OF A "WASH-OUT" ADVENTURE

By Raymond O. Hanson

(Written December 13, 1937)

Trapped for three anxious days and four long December nights, in a canyon of the Big Bend, with the turbulent Eel River rising sixty-four feet toward the tracks, which held the Northwestern Pacific overnight train to Eureka, was the novel, if not harrowing experience of twenty-five passengers who emerged today into the open country and the prospects of home-coming reunions.

Caught in the early hours of Friday morning between two great slides, with road-beds washed out by torrential rains, and tons of rock, gravel and dirt covering the rails, the train, thanks to the efficiency of the railroad service, had narrowly escaped precpitation into the rushing and roaring river below.

TWO MEALS PER DAY

Returning to the little station of Bell Springs, Conductor Hugh Cave, with the solicitous spirit of a ship's captain, arranged for breakfast in a nearby cabin, where two meals a day were furnished by an accommodating housewife. The task finally became too much for her, however, and the long hours formed a point of exhaus- young people, bound on so sacred a mission.

Two mothers with children also claimed major attention for naturally the little ones find it difficult to adjust themselves to unusual conditions.

PASSENGERS

The passenger list included R. C. Staebner, an internal revenue official who had just arrived from Washington in time to board the train, and whose experience has proved quite a jolt to California's climatic reputation.

Miss Jeanette Ufkess, a Santa Rosa school ma'am and president of the Redwood Empire district of the Business and Professional Women's Club, and Mrs. Caroline Barney of Pacific Grove, a state officer of the same organization, were on their way to speak at a dinner meeting in Eureka. At the scheduled hour, however, they contented themselves with the duty of teaching auction bridge to novitiates in the observation car.

Card games, the chief diversion during the evening periods, took place in the refected headlight of a railroad engine which had been switched to the rear of the train, when electric batteries failed to function in the interior of the cars.

G. B. Amend, district manager of the General Petroleum Corporation, who was also among the passengers, found that with oil everywhere there was not a drop available with which to substitute for lighting effects.

W. E. Tice, vice-president and sales manager of the Reliance Trailer and Truck Company, extolled the virtues of motor travel, while deploring the predicament, but to no avail, for twenty-two miles of hills and forests separated the party from the nearest highway.

Humboldt Times of December 13, 1937

Student Affidavit Upheld

Argument That Loyalty Requirement Is Discriminatory Is Rejected

To the Editor of The New York Times:

On Jan. 28 Senator John Kennedy reintroduced in Congress his bill designed to remove the non-subversive affidavit presently required of college students participating in the National Defense Education Act. This year's bill, S. 2929, is a modified version of the Kennedy-Clark bill of the last session of Congress, which asked that both the oath of allegiance and the nonsubversive affidavit be removed from the N. D. E. A.

One of the statements put forth by Senator Kennedy in support of his bill was that the present affidavit requirement discriminates against a particular segment of the American society—that of college students. The Senator claims that college students participating in the N. D. E. A. have been singled out and their loyalty questioned by the affidavit requirement.

Actually, a great many segments of our society today are required to take the identical affidavit required from the participating college students. These include all college students enrolled in Reserve Officer Training Corps—R. O. T. C.; at the present time there are 155,871 college students in R. O. T. C. who have signed the affidavit—while only 68,342 college students have had to sign the affidavit while participating in the N. D. E. A. Yet the cry has never been made that R. O. T. C. students were being discriminated against.

Other segments of our society today who have to sign the affidavit are students participating in the National Science Foundation Act, members of the staffs of all Congressmen (including the staffs of those advocating removal of the N. D. E. A. affidavit), all employes of the Federal Government and even private citizens who volunteer for Civil Defense work. Can it then truthfully be said that college students are being singled out by the N. D. E. A. affidavit?

It should be noted that while only nineteen colleges and universities have refused or withdrawn from participation in the N. D. E. A. because of the affidavit requirement, 1,370 other institutions (88 per cent of the total college student body) are participating without any sign of protest.

Douglas Caddy,
Chairman, National Student Committee for the Loyalty Oath.

Washington, Jan. 29, 1960.

My letter-to-editor of the *New York Times* of February 5, 1960 that signaled the emergence of the modern Conservative Movement.

Interim Committee
For A National Conservative Youth Organization

343 LEXINGTON AVENUE
NEW YORK 16, NEW YORK

MURRAY HILL 3-6862/3

INTERIM COMMITTEE MEMBERS

JAMES ABSTINE
Bloomington, Ind.

DOUGLAS CADDY
New York, N. Y.

ROBERT CROLL
Glencoe, Ill.

DAVID FRANKE
New York, N. Y.

GEORGE GAINES
New Iberia, La.

ROBERT HARLEY
Washington, D. C.

JAMES KOLBE
Patagonia, Ariz.

RICHARD NOBLE
Stanford, Calif.

SUZANNE REGNERY
Chicago, Ill.

CLENDENIN RYAN
Hackettstown, N. J.

SCOTT STANLEY
Bethel, Kan.

JOHN WEICHER
Chicago, Ill.

BRIAN WHELAN
Chicago, Ill.

August 16, 1960

Mr. Robert Croll
582 South Ave.
Glencoe, Ill.

Dear Bob:

America stands at the crossroads today. Will our Nation continue to follow the path towards socialism or will we turn towards Conservatism and freedom? The final answer to this question lies with America's youth. Will our youth be more conservative or more liberal in future years? You can help determine the answer to this question.

Now is the time for Conservative youth to take action to make their full force and influence felt. By action we mean political action! An inter-collegiate society for Conservative youth has been in operation for several years and has been most successful in bringing about a Conservative intellectual revival on the campus. Many feel that now is the time to organize a complementary nationwide youth movement which would be designed almost solely for political action – implementing and coordinating the aspirations of Conservative youth into a dynamic and effective political force.

It is to this end that this invitation is extended to you to participate in the initial organizing effort to create a new Conservative political youth group. You are among 120 outstanding youth leaders across the Nation – known to be active and influential Conservatives – who are urged to attend a weekend Conference which will launch the national Conservative youth organization. Some details of the Conference follow:

Place: Great Elm, the family home of William F. Buckley, Jr., located in Sharon, Conn.

Dates: Saturday, September 10th and Sunday, September 11th.

Agenda: A workshop to discuss ways and means to organize a new, nationwide Conservative Youth Organization. The specific responsibilities of the workshop will be supplemented by informal discussion sessions with several outstanding national Conservative political leaders. (In between

"The preponderant judgment of the American people, especially of the young people, is that the radical, or Liberal, approach has not worked and is not working. They yearn for a return to Conservative principles."

—Senator Barry Goldwater

Invitation of August 16, 1960 to the founding of Young Americans for Freedom (YAF).

- 2 -

the work and talk session, there will be the opportunity to use some of the recreational facilities of Great Elm – swimming pool, tennis courts, etc.). Further details on the agenda and speakers will be sent to you later.

Expenses: Basic travel and living expenses will have to be covered by each participant. These will include your round-trip transportation to New York City; transportation via chartered bus to Sharon and return (approx. $6.00), scheduled to leave New York City Friday evening, September 9th; lodging at one of the Inns in Sharon, Conn. for Friday and Saturday nights (approx. $5.00 per night). Meals will be provided at no charge.

The Sharon Conference can be of historic importance. The formation of a national Conservative youth organization – utilizing the ready-made enthusiasm of this National election year – will be a great step forward for Conservatism. You can be an integral part in setting the initial stages of this great movement. We hope you will agree with us on its importance and urge you to make your plans today to attend and participate in this memorable event.

If you plan to attend, please complete the enclosed registration blank and mail immediately in the enclosed envelope. The moment we receive your completed registration, we will mail you a further memorandum which will give you final details on agenda, speakers, and other pertinent information.

We look forward to your participation and to your prompt and affirmative reply. Many thanks for your consideration.

Sincerely yours,

Doug –

Douglas Caddy, Member
Interim Committee

Second page of invitation of August 16, 1960 to the founding of Young Americans for Freedom (YAF).

3,200 at Rally Here Acclaim Goldwater

By ROBERT CONLEY

Senator Barry Goldwater told a cheering, stomping audience last night that the country was caught up in a wave of conservatism that could easily become "the political phenomenon of our time."

Addressing the first political rally of Young Americans for Freedom, a national organization of young conservatives, the Arizona Republican said of the conservative ideology:

"Nobody knows for sure its present strength or its future potential. But something is afoot which could drastically alter our course as a nation."

Senator Goldwater's appearance on the stage of Manhattan Center set off a tumultuous ovation from the 3,200 persons crowded inside the center. Six thousand other persons had to

Continued on Page 45, Column 1

The New York Times
Published: March 4, 1961

New York Times article of March 4, 1961 on YAF rally in New York City.

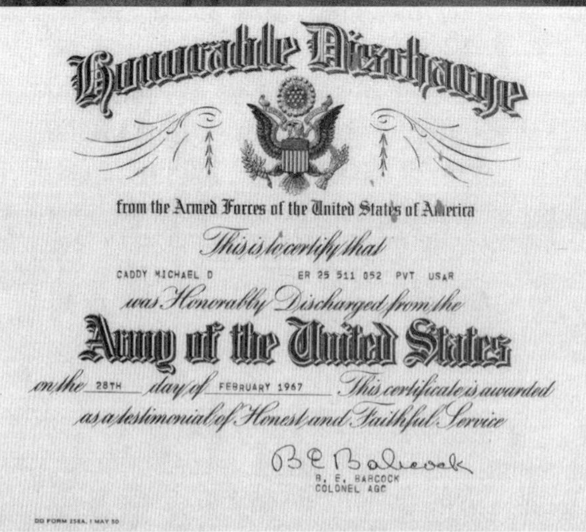

Honorable Discharge

from the Armed Forces of the United States of America

This is to certify that

CADDY MICHAEL D ER 25 511 052 PVT USAR

was Honorably Discharged from the

Army of the United States

on the 28TH day of FEBRUARY 1967 This certificate is awarded as a testimonial of Honest and Faithful Service

B E Babcock

B. E. BABCOCK
COLONEL AGC

DD FORM 256A, 1 MAY 50

Photograph of me during U.S. Army basic training at Ft. Jackson, S.C. September 1961 with Honorable Discharge Certificate of February 28, 1967.

THE WHITE HOUSE
WASHINGTON

TELEPHONE MEMORANDUM

April 25, 19

	TIME PLACED	DISC	NAME	ACTION
OUT	AM		John Ulmer	
INC	PM		Bob Mardian	
OUT	AM		Ed Harper	
INC	PM		Jack Caulfield	
OUT	AM		Gordon Strachan	
INC	PM		John Whitaker	
OUT	AM		[George Webster	
INC	PM	*	Douglas Caddy] *	
OUT	AM			
INC	PM		Amb. Patricia Harris	965-9400
OUT	AM			
INC	PM		Glen Sedam	
OUT	AM			
INC	PM			
OUT	AM			
INC	PM			
OUT	AM			
INC	PM			
OUT	AM			
INC	PM			
OUT	AM			
INC	PM			

U.S. GOVERNMENT PRINTING OFFICE 1970 O 375-347

P 100639

John Dean's White House diary of April 25, 1972.

GRAND JURY

United States District Court

For the District of Columbia

THE UNITED STATES

vs.

Pos. Vio. 18 U.S.C. §371, et al.

REPORT TO UNITED STATES DISTRICT COURT HOUSE
Between 3d Street and John Marshall Place and on Constitution Avenue NW.
ROOM 3600-K, EJS #26
Washington, D.C.

To: Douglas Caddy, Esq., 1250 Connecticut Avenue, N.W., Washington, D.

RECEIVED JUN 23 12 53 PM '72 PROD. U.S. CONTROL CENTER

You are hereby commanded to attend before the Grand Jury of said Court on FORTHWITH the ...... day of ......, 19 ...., at ...... o'clock ...... M., to testify on behalf of the United States, and not depart the Court without leave of the Court or District Attorney.

WITNESS: The Honorable John J. Sirica, *Chief Judge of said Court, this* 28th *day of* June, *19*72.

JAMES F. DAVEY, *Clerk.*

Attorney for ......

By Ruby H. Kelly, Deputy Clerk.

Form No. USA-9x-184 (Rev. 7-1-71)

Federal Grand Jury subpoena served on me June 28, 1972.

UNITED STATES DISTRICT COURT
FOR THE DISTRICT OF COLUMBIA

In Re:)
)
MICHAEL DOUGLAS CADDY) Misc. No. 60-72

ORDER

This matter having come before the Court on the oral motion of the United States Attorney for the District of Columbia on behalf of the Grand Jury for an order finding Michael Douglas Caddy in contempt of this Court for his refusal to answer certain questions before the grand jury on July 13, 1972; and

The witness Michael Douglas Caddy being present before this Court and represented by counsel;

The Court, after hearing argument and being advised in the premises, finds

That the witness Michael Douglas Caddy was duly subpoenaed to appear before the Grand Jury;

That he did appear before the Grand Jury on June 30, 1972, July 5, 1972, and July 7, 1972;

That he refused to answer certain questions propounded to him before the Grand Jury;

That on July 12, 1972, this Court, after having received written memoranda and heard oral argument at a hearing at which Michael Douglas Caddy was present and represented by counsel, ordered Michael Douglas Caddy to appear before the Grand Jury on July 13, 1972, at 10:00 a.m. and answer the questions contained in the Appendix to the written motion, filed in this Court by

COMMITMENT TO JAIL

Order of Chief Judge John Sirica holding me in contempt of court July 13, 1972.

-2-

the United States Attorney on July 10, 1972, to compel the testimony of Michael Douglas Caddy;

That Michael Douglas Caddy did appear before the Grand Jury as ordered but refused to answer any of the questions as ordered by this Court;

That Michael Douglas Caddy having failed to show why he should not be held in contempt of this Court and his contempt having tended to defeat, impair, and impede the lawful function of the Grand Jury and this Court;

The witness Michael Douglas Caddy is hereby found in direct contempt of the order of this Court; and, therefore,

It is by the Court this 13th day of July, 1972, ORDERED, ADJUDGED and DECREED that Michael Douglas Caddy is in direct contempt of this Court for his failure to obey a lawful order of this Court to answer certain questions before the Grand Jury and he is hereby committed to the custody of the United States Marshal for the District of Columbia and the Attorney-General of the United States or his authorized representative, for the life of the June 1972 No. 1 Grand Jury sworn in on June 5, 1972, or unless and until he complies with the order of the court and purges himself of this contempt.

/S/ JOHN J. SIRICA
CHIEF JUDGE

A TRUE COPY
JAMES F. DAVEY, CLERK
BY James P. Capitanio

Page two of the order of Chief Judge John Sirica holding me in contempt of court July 13, 1972.

United States Court of Appeals
FOR THE DISTRICT OF COLUMBIA CIRCUIT

No. 72-1658 September Term, 19 71

Misc. 60-72

Possible Violation
18 U.S. Code 2511, 2512
22 D.C. Code 1801

United States Court of Appeals
for the District of Columbia Circuit

FILED JUL 13 1972

Michael Douglas Caddy,
Appellant

Nathan J. Paulson
CLERK

Before: Wright, McGowan and Tamm, Circuit Judges.

O R D E R

This appeal came on for consideration after argument of counsel, from an order of the District Court holding appellant in civil contempt for refusing on the ground of attorney-client privilege to answer certain questions put to him before the grand jury. We entered a temporary stay of the District Court's order, and expedited the consideration of the appeal on the merits in accordance with the statutory policy of 28 U.S.C. 1826(b). We dissolve the stay and affirm the order of the District Court.

In order to maintain an attorney-client privilege, a witness must establish that an attorney-client relationship did in fact exist, and that the information which is claimed to be protected by the privilege was the subject of a communication between the attorney and the client arising out of that relationship. 8 Wigmore, Evidence (McNaughton Rev. 1961) §2292. Even if such a relationship does exist, certain communications, such as a consultation in furtherance of a crime, are not within the privilege. McCormick on Evidence (2nd Ed. 1972) §95.

Appellant has not met the burden necessary to establish the attorney-client relationship that is the raison d'etre of the privilege. See In re Bonnano, 344 F.2d 830 (2nd Cir. 1965).

Order of U.S. Court of Appeals affirming Judge Sirica's contempt citation of me July 13, 1972

July 19, 1972

Douglas Caddy, Esq.
Gall, Lane, Powell & Kilcullen
1250 Connecticut Avenue, N. W.
Washington, D. C. 20036

Dear Doug:

I have just had an opportunity to review the Court of Appeals' Opinion in Docket No. 72-1658, which affirms the District Court's Order directing you to testify. It appears that the Court of Appeals' Opinion is predicated on the assumption that the existence of a bona fide attorney-client relationship between you and myself has not been established before the Grand Jury.

As you know, you have represented me in various matters over a considerable period of time. In addition, during the month of June and early in July, 1972, I consulted you, in your capacity as an attorney, seeking legal advice concerning matters which are now apparently under investigation by the Federal Grand Jury sitting in the District of Columbia. At no time during the confidential discussions that we had were we involved in any way in matters which could possibly be construed as on-going criminal activity. As I am sure you are aware, I sought your advice only in your capacity as an attorney, and we therefore discussed many things which were confidential and which I would not have discussed with you but for the attorney-client privilege.

This letter is to advise you of my understanding of the relationship which we have had, of my understanding that the discussions which you had with me during June and early July 1972 were in your capacity as my attorney, and in connection with matters which are apparently now under investigation by the Federal Grand Jury, and my desire and instruction that you not, in any way, waive the attorney-client privilege.

Very truly yours,

Howard

E. Howard Hunt, Jr.

Letter from E. Howard Hunt to me of July 19, 1972 affirming attorney-client privilege

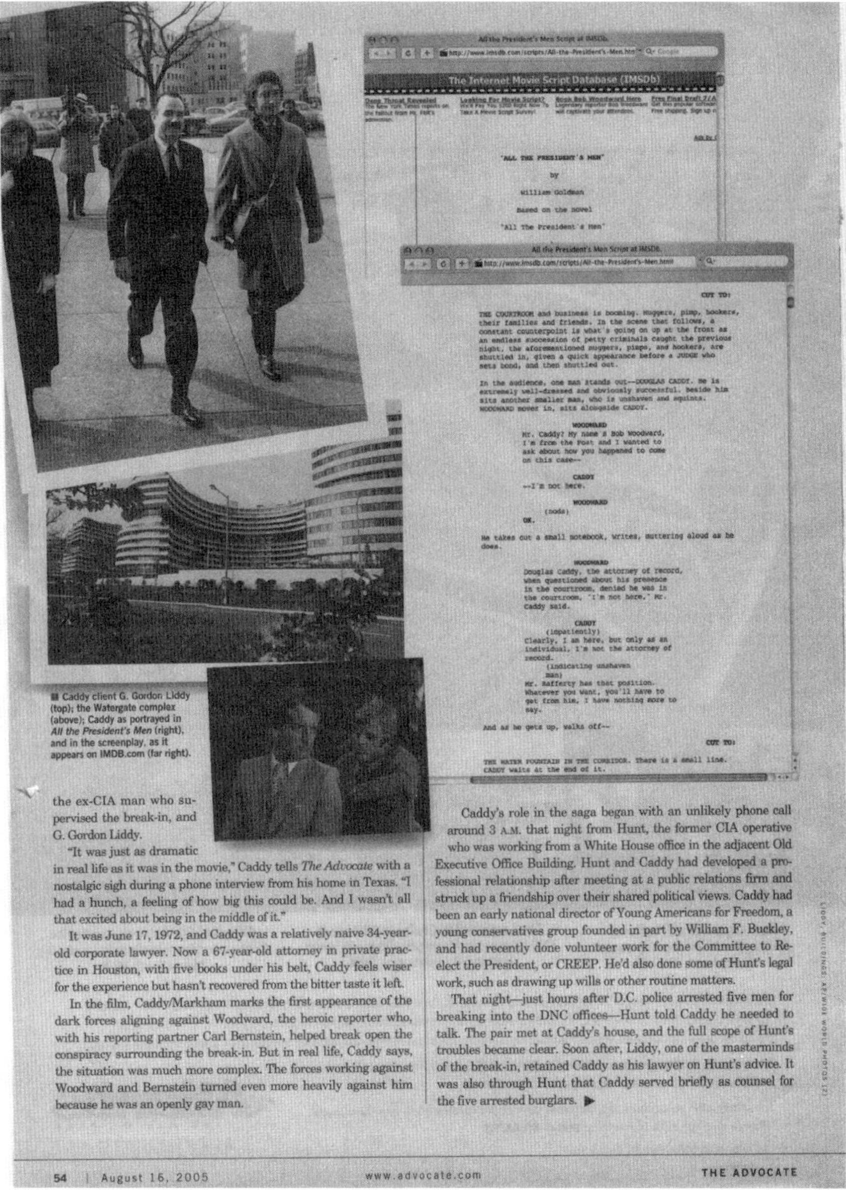

■ Caddy client G. Gordon Liddy (top); the Watergate complex (above); Caddy as portrayed in *All the President's Men* (right), and in the screenplay, as it appears on IMDB.com (far right).

the ex-CIA man who supervised the break-in, and G. Gordon Liddy.

"It was just as dramatic in real life as it was in the movie," Caddy tells *The Advocate* with a nostalgic sigh during a phone interview from his home in Texas. "I had a hunch, a feeling of how big this could be. And I wasn't all that excited about being in the middle of it."

It was June 17, 1972, and Caddy was a relatively naive 34-year-old corporate lawyer. Now a 67-year-old attorney in private practice in Houston, with five books under his belt, Caddy feels wiser for the experience but hasn't recovered from the bitter taste it left.

In the film, Caddy/Markham marks the first appearance of the dark forces aligning against Woodward, the heroic reporter who, with his reporting partner Carl Bernstein, helped break open the conspiracy surrounding the break-in. But in real life, Caddy says, the situation was much more complex. The forces working against Woodward and Bernstein turned even more heavily against him because he was an openly gay man.

Caddy's role in the saga began with an unlikely phone call around 3 A.M. that night from Hunt, the former CIA operative who was working from a White House office in the adjacent Old Executive Office Building. Hunt and Caddy had developed a professional relationship after meeting at a public relations firm and struck up a friendship over their shared political views. Caddy had been an early national director of Young Americans for Freedom, a young conservatives group founded in part by William F. Buckley, and had recently done volunteer work for the Committee to Re-elect the President, or CREEP. He'd also done some of Hunt's legal work, such as drawing up wills or other routine matters.

That night—just hours after D.C. police arrested five men for breaking into the DNC offices—Hunt told Caddy he needed to talk. The pair met at Caddy's house, and the full scope of Hunt's troubles became clear. Soon after, Liddy, one of the masterminds of the break-in, retained Caddy as his lawyer on Hunt's advice. It was also through Hunt that Caddy served briefly as counsel for the five arrested burglars. ▶

54 | August 16, 2005 www.advocate.com THE ADVOCATE

Photograph of Gordon Liddy and me entering the U.S. Courthouse during the first Watergate trial January 1973 from an article in the *Advocate* magazine of August 16, 2005.

APPENDIX ~~ONE~~ Nine

On July 10, 1972 Harold H. Titus, Jr., U.S. Attorney for the District of Columbia; Earl J. Silbert, Principal Assistant U.S. Attorney; Donald E. Campbell, Assistant U.S. Attorney; and Seymour Glanzer, Assistant U.S. Attorney filed a "Motion to Compel Testimony of Grand Jury Witness Michael Douglas Caddy." The Motion stated, "The United States of America, therefore, seeks the following relief from this Court:

"An order that the witness Mr. Caddy be directed on pain of contempt to respond before the grand jury to the questions specified in the Appendix attached to this motion, all questions which he without justification refused to answer on Friday, June 30, 1972, Wednesday, July 5, 1972 and Friday, July 7, 1972."

The following is the Appendix attached to the motion listing the 38 key questions.

1. The question was, when was the last time that you saw Mr. Hunt?
2. When, that is the approximate date, was the attorney-client relationship established on the current matter in which you represent Mr. Hunt?
3. All right, do you represent Mr. Hunt with respect to the matters being investigated by this grand jury?
4. When was the last time you spoke to your client... Mr. Hunt?
5. Other than legal fees, have you received any money, or any pecuniary, or financial benefits from Mr. Hunt in any manner, shape, or form during the entire period you have known him?
6. All right, I believe the first question that we asked you, at which point you indicated a desire to consult with counsel, was the date on which Mr. X. became your client.
7. When was the last time you saw Mr. X?
8. When was the last time you spoke to Mr. X?
9. Did you see Mr. Hunt within one-quarter mile of the Watergate Hotel on June 16 or June 17 of this year?
10. Now again, just for the record, what was the subject matter, the general field of law, in which you represented Mr. X prior to July 7th, 1972?
11. I believe the question was prior to Thursday, July 6th of this year, when you represented Mr. X., what fee arrangement or retainer agreement did you have with Mr. X relevant to the subject matter in which you represented him as an attorney.
12. The question is prior to July 6th of this year -- that is yesterday -- have you ever -- has Mr. X. ever paid you a fee for representing him as an attorney?
13. At what time did you receive a telephone call in the early morning hours of Saturday, June 17, 1972?

The 38 key questions that I refused to answer before the grand jury on the grounds of the attorney-client privilege and the Sixth Amendment right to counsel.

14. From whom did you receive a telephone call in the early morning hours of June 17, 1972?

15. Did you receive a telephone call from Mrs. Barker, the wife of Bernard L. Barker?

16. Did you receive a telephone call from Everett Howard Hunt in the early morning hours of Saturday, June 17, 1972?

17. Did you receive a telephone call from Mr. X in the early morning hours of Saturday, June 17, 1972, and just so the record is clear, I will confine the time from 12 A.M., in the morning, until 6:00 A.M. in the morning?

18. From whom were the half dozen phone calls you received between midnight, Friday, June 16th and 8:30 A.M., Saturday, June 17th?

19. Now, as to those half a dozen phone calls in which you have now invoked the attorney-client privilege as to the identity of the person, were they from men or from women?

20. I believe the question that was asked you...was whether or not any of the half a dozen phone calls that you received were from clients of yours in the attorney-client sense of the word?

21. During the hours of midnight, June 16th, Friday, through 8:30 Saturday morning, that is 8:30 A.M., Saturday, June 17th, to whom did you make telephone calls?

22. Were any of the persons to whom you made telephone calls clients of yours in the attorney-client sense of the relationship?

23. I believe the question was between the hours of midnight, Friday, June 16th, and 8:30 A.M., Saturday, June 17th, did you receive or have any visitors at your apartment?

24. Whether or not any of the about half a dozen telephone calls that you have indicated that you made while in your apartment between the hours of midnight, June 16th, and 8:30 A.M. Saturday, June 17th, were any of those long distance telephone calls?

25. Between the hours of Friday, June 16th and Saturday, 8:30 A.M., June 17th did you receive -- were any of the half a dozen phone calls that you received long distance?

26. Between the hours of Friday at midnight, June 16th, and 8:30 A.M. Saturday, June 17th, did you receive a visit from Mr. Everett Howard Hunt?

27. Did you receive a visit during that same period of time, that is midnight, June 16th, to 8:30 A.M., June 17th, from Mr. X?

28. When did Mrs. Dorothy Hunt first become a client of yours?

29. Outside of occasions to which Mr. Everett Howard Hunt has used his -- a different pen name under which he authored a number of books, to which you have referred in your previous answer, has Mr. Everett Howard Hunt used any names other than his own?

30. To your knowledge has Mr. X ever used any names other than his own name of Mr. X?

31. At the central cellblock, did you speak to anyone there, or what did you do there, sir?

32. Now, with respect to Mr. Bernard L. Barker, what fee arrangement or retainer agreement did you make with him at that time with respect to his representation?

33. With respect to Mr. (Rolando) Martinez what fee arrangement did you make to represent him?

34. With respect to Virgilio Gonzalez?

35. With James W. McCord, Jr.?

36. With respect to Mr. Frank Fiorini or Frank Sturgis?

37. Prior to your going to 23rd and L Streets, Northwest, that morning, Saturday, June 17th, 1972, had you been asked by anybody to represent those, any, or all or some of those five individuals?

38. Who, if anyone, asked you to represent those five individuals who were in the jail at 23rd and L Streets, Northwest, that morning?

WATERGATE SPECIAL PROSECUTION FORCE

DEPARTMENT OF JUSTICE

Memorandum

TO : Files

DATE: December 20, 1973

FROM : Frank Martin

SUBJECT: Interview of Carl Schoffler

FOIA(b)6
FOIA(b)7 - (C)

Sgt. Carl Schoffler of the Metropolitan Police Department was interviewed on December 3, 1973, by Horowitz, Akerman and Martin. Horowitz advised Schoffler of his right to counsel and his right to remain silent and Schoffler voluntarily provided the following information.

From 1970 until April 1973, Schoffler worked in the Second District as a TAC officer doing semi-undercover work on street crime. Schoffler stated that he did not normally report on intelligence information but would occasionally do so if while he was working on street crime he came across any information of interest to Intelligence. Schoffler stated that he met Robert Merritt, whom he knew as Robert Chandler, in 1970 and that Merritt did some informant work on street crime for him. Schoffler stated that Merritt was giving him information almost every day and did provide some good criminal investigation work. Schoffler noted that he once provided a notebook [redacted] and was accused of various rapes and that the notebook showed the addresses of various places where this individual had been accused of committing rapes. Schoffler stated that he saw Merritt every three or four days for almost two years.

Concerning May Day, Schoffler stated that he occasionally supplied information on May Day and would phone the Intelligence office and give the information to whomever answered the phone. Schoffler stated that he had some contracts with ATF and with the FBI but none with regard to May Day. Schoffler also worked some on crowd control during May Day. Schoffler introduced Merritt to Scrapper, and Merritt worked with Scrapper and with Dixie Gildon. Schoffler noted that Acree, who headed much of the intelligence work, did not like Schoffler.

Screened

By: Heather Macrae Date:

Watergate Special Prosecutor's two-page report on interview of Detective Carl Schoffler (sic) of December 20, 1973.

:/22/2005 21:30 16466709518 DC PAGE 02/03

26(EX AGT)
11/28/08

FOIA(b)6
FOIA(b)7 - (C)

2

Schoffler was questioned concerning the incident involving [redacted] Schoffler stated that at some time after the Watergate arrests, Schoffler and Leper were in their car and met Merritt near his residence at 2121 P Street. Schoffler stated that he had first seen [redacted] the day after the Watergate arrests when [redacted] came to represent the Cubans. When Schoffler and Leper met Merritt, Merritt stated that he might know [redacted] and Merritt had an article from the newspaper with a picture of [redacted] in it. Schoffler told Merritt to let him know if Merritt found out who [redacted] was and if he was "funny", i.e., homosexual. Schoffler stated that this was an off-hand comment and he never expected Merritt to do anything, and Merritt never told Schoffler anything about Caddy.

Schoffler stated that in the summer of 1973, after he had testified in the Watergate hearings, Schoffler met Merritt. Merritt stated that he had made all sorts of calls to Senators concerning Watergate and the Caddy incident with Schoffler. Schoffler stated that he told Merritt that if he, Merritt, reported a crime then that was one thing, but that if he reported something that was only in his head it was going to come back on him. Schoffler said that he did not in any way threaten Merritt.

Schoffler stated that he introduced Merritt to FBI Agents O'Connor and Tucker and that it took about a week for them to find out that he was a liar. Schoffer stated that of the leads that Merritt gave, only perhaps one in ten or twenty would turn out to be of any value but that Schoffler always followed the leads because of that one in twenty chance. Schoffler stated that he had never worked with Ann Kolego.

cc:

Chron
File
Akerman
Horowitz
Martin

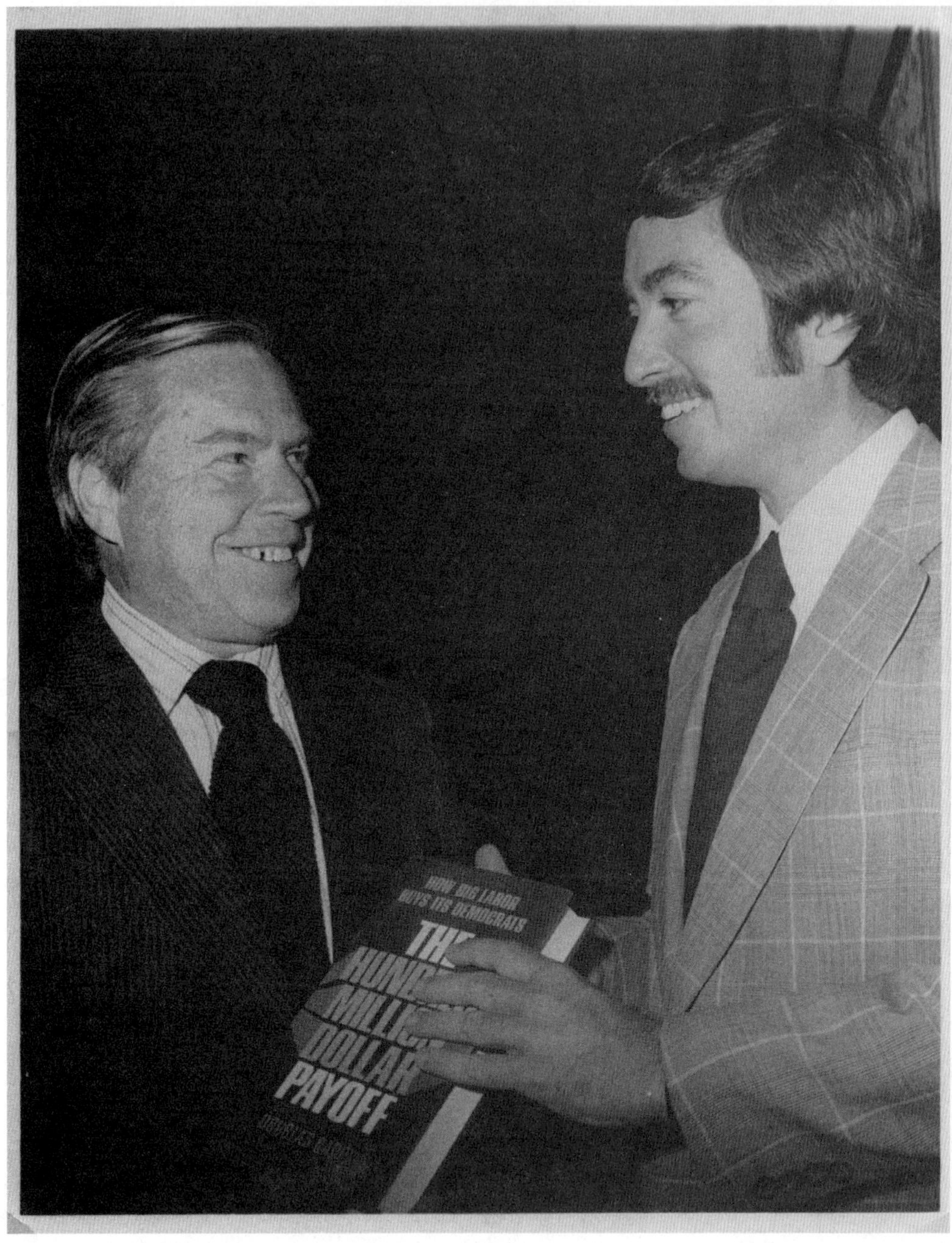

Rep. John Rhodes of Arizona, Minority Leader in the House of Representatives, accepting a copy of my first book, *The Hundred Million Dollar Payoff*, from me in 1974.

The Washington Times • MONDAY, FEBRUARY 12, 1996 / PAC

NATION

Dean disavows much of 'Blind Ambition'

Says he never read whole book

Andy Thibault
WASHINGTON TIMES

John Dean, who brought down President Nixon in the Watergate scandal, has disavowed his best-selling book on the cover-up.

The book, "Blind Ambition," portrayed Mr. Dean as a hero of conscience who eliminated "a cancer on the presidency." In its foreword, Mr. Dean vouches for the book's accuracy, offering to take a lie-detector test.

Now Mr. Dean says he didn't write key portions. Nor did he even read the entire book. "I have never gone through this book cover to cover," he said.

In sworn depositions that have been obtained by The Washington Times, Mr. Dean said that key elements of the book were actually "pure speculation," "reasonable conjecture" and "distortion."

Mr. Dean began walking away from key points in "Blind Ambition" in September during depositions in a libel suit he filed against Watergate burglar G. Gordon Liddy and the authors of another book, "Silent Coup." Mr. Dean's most recent statements were made Jan. 26.

"Silent Coup," by Len Colodny and Robert Gettlin, contends that Mr. Dean was more than an innocent dupe. Their book shows him in a major role actually orchestrating the break-in and cover-up. The Colodny and Gettlin version asserts that Mr. Dean concealed information from superiors and made financial commitments to the burglars.

Their book also notes the link between Mr. Dean's then-girlfriend and future wife, Maureen, and a Washington prostitution ring. Her name had turned up in a notebook connected with the ring in or near the Watergate. According to the Colodny-Gettlin version, that spurred Mr. Dean's interest in the break-in.

As for any errors in "Blind Ambition," Mr. Dean points the finger at his writing partner, Taylor Branch of Baltimore. Mr. Dean says he didn't read the whole book because he had a fever when the galley proofs came out. Mr. Dean says he tried to mark up the proofs in bed but his wife wouldn't let him use a pen because he had left an ink spot on the sheets during another reading session.

Mr. Branch stands by the book. But in one key narrative, Mr. Dean claims Mr. Branch "absolutely made it up out of whole cloth."

Mr. Dean was referring to a section in which Watergate burglar G. Gordon Liddy tells him that the White House knew beforehand about the infamous break-in 24 years ago. In sworn testimony before the Senate Watergate Committee, Mr. Dean had said Mr. Liddy told him no one from the White House knew about the burglary plans.

But in the book, Mr. Dean quotes Mr. Liddy as saying, "The only person who might have known about it is Gordon Strachan," an aide to White House Chief of Staff Bob Haldeman.

"I turned away from Liddy for a moment to absorb Strachan's name," Mr. Dean continues in the book. ". . . I felt queasy. I really didn't want to know more because I had to know that if Strachan knew, Haldeman knew, and if Haldeman knew, the president knew."

The incident is significant because the course of the investigation would have shifted radically had the extent of White House involvement been known early on.

Mr. Branch maintains the book account is accurate. "I have full faith in 'Blind Ambition,'" Mr. Branch said Tuesday. "Until I see otherwise, I have confidence in Dean."

The editor for "Blind Ambition," Alice Mayhew of Simon & Schuster, said Mr. Dean's recent statements are "nonsense."

"Taylor Branch never made anything up," she said. "I can't tell you that every line is accurate, but it's impeccable reporting by Branch. John Dean signed off on the book. If he changed his mind, he did it later on."

Besides working with Mr. Dean and Mr. Branch, Ms. Mayhew is also editor for Bob Woodward, co-author of "All the President's Men."

John Garrick, Mr. Dean's attorney, said he anticipates a flurry of activity in the libel case during the next six months, including depositions of Mr. Liddy and Mr. Colodny. Mr. Garrick acknowledged there were errors in "Blind Ambition" but characterized them as "minutiae."

"I think he [Mr. Dean] also said the general thrust of the book was accurate," Mr. Garrick said. "It was intended to be a portrait, not a black-and-white photo."

Mr. Dean, who served as Mr. Nixon's legal counsel, implicated his superiors in the Watergate cover-up and emerged as a he some. He served four month prison for admitting a role in cover-up.

"John Dean is a serial perju Mr. Liddy said this week. " latest business is just his wa attempting to weasel out of the that he keeps getting caugh lies."

John Dean

3-30-98

E. HOWARD HUNT

Doug —
Nice piece
in the WSJ.
You raised some
good, if unanswer-
able, questions.

Howard

7-3-01

HOWARD HUNT

Doug — Thanks for
the Salon piece on
Dean. He's more
of a slimeball than
I imagined —
Regards —
Howard

Two notes from E. Howard Hunt to me, one of them concerning an article by me in the *Wall Street Journal* of March 24, 1998, about Watergate.

LATE DEVELOPMENT IN THE CASE OF GABE CAPORINO

[Note: Information considered an invasion of privacy has been deleted herein]

From: Subject: OGIS Case No. 201702217 - Final Response
Date: March 27, 2018 at 9:44:27 AM EDT

Re: OGIS Case No. 201702217
Subject of case: FBI FOIPA Request No. 1330436-001 (Subject: Caporino, Gabe)

Dear Ms. Caporino:

This responds to your March 30, 2017 request to the Office of Government Information Services (OGIS), which we received via email. Your assistance request concerns your Freedom of Information Act (FOIA) request to Department of Justice (DOJ), Federal Bureau of Investigation (FBI). We apologize for our delay in responding to your submission —requests for our assistance have dramatically increased, and we are doing our best to respond to the increased demand for our services as quickly as we can. Thank you for your patience as we handled your case.

We understand that you submitted a request (No. 1330436-001) to the FBI for records concerning a December 2014 meeting between yourself and FBI Special Agent (SA) James Gagliano that took place in your home. The FBI denied your request. On appeal, DOJ's Office of Information Policy (OIP) affirmed the FBI's action on the request. You dispute this response and sought OGIS assistance in obtaining access to the records you requested.

Congress created OGIS to complement existing FOIA practice and procedure; we strive to work in conjunction with the existing request and appeal process. Our goal is to allow, whenever practical, the requester to exhaust his or her remedies within the agency, including the appeal process. OGIS has no investigatory or enforcement power, nor can we compel an agency to release documents. OGIS serves as the Federal FOIA Ombudsman and our jurisdiction is limited to assisting with the FOIA process.

As part of our information gathering, OGIS carefully reviewed your submission and contacted FBI FOIA Public Liaison regarding your request.

Due to discussions between OGIS and the FBI, the bureau reviewed its action on your initial request and determined that it misidentified the subject of the request as "Caporino, Gabe" and geared its search toward locating records relating to his 1974 disappearance. Upon further review, the FBI determined that you seek a copy of the FBI report that was generated as a result of your contact with SA Gagliano. The FBI will reopen your request and conduct a new search for the report you requested. You can expect to receive correspondence from the FBI concerning the outcome of its new search.

If the FBI's response to your request dissatisfies you, we strongly encourage you to file an appeal and you may contact OGIS for further assistance. For information on submitting a FOIA appeal, refer to DOJ's FOIA Reference Guide at https://www.justice.gov/oip/department-justice-freedom-information-act-reference-guide.

DOUGLAS CADDY
ATTORNEY-AT-LAW
7941 Katy Freeway
Suite 296
Houston, Texas 77024
713-867-3476
Email: douglascaddy@justice.com

February 9, 2018

Mr. David S. Ferriero
The Archivist of the United States
The National Archives and Records Administration
8601 Adelphi Road
College Park, MD 20740-6001

Re: Secret "Message to the American People" written by President Richard M. Nixon for posterity that he left hidden inside the White House

Dear Mr. Ferriero:

I am attorney admitted to the District of Columbia and Tcxas Bars and author of my forthcoming autobiography, "Being There: Eyewitness to History," that Trine Day Publishers will release on March 28, 2018. I am also co-author with Confidential Government Informant Robert Merritt of the book, "Watergate Exposed: How the President of the United States and the Watergate Burglars Were Set Up" that Trine Day published in 2011. A number of documents from the Watergate Special Prosecutor that the National Archives released to Mr. Merritt in 2010 are reproduced in our book, a copy of which is enclosed. Those documents are concerned with Mr. Merritt and with me as the original attorney for the Watergate seven burglars.

In my forthcoming autobiography I disclose new information revealed this year to me by Robert Merritt, information that he has been withholding for over four decades that deals with his role as the sole employee of the secret Huston Plan that was run out of President Nixon's White House. When White House Counsel John Dean was fired by President Nixon in April 1973 he took the only 31-page written copy of the Huston Plan with him and deposited it with Chief Judge John Sirica. This explosive document has been under court seal ever since, immune from being subpoenaed by any outside source.

In 1972 President Nixon summoned Mr. Merritt to three meetings that were held in a secure room far beneath the White House in the early morning hours after midnight. The first was held two days after J. Edgar Hoover died on May 2, 1972, the second about five days before the Watergate case broke with the arrests of five burglars on June 17, 1972, and the third in the second week of July 1972.

Page two of three pages

At the third and final meeting in July 1972 Mr. Merritt found the President distraught and near tears over an article on Watergate in the Washington Post that he said could destroy his presidency. Because of this unexpected turn of events he assigned Mr. Merritt to deliver clandestinely a three page letter handwritten by him and two tapes to Henry Kissinger at his home. The President described the letter, which he read aloud to Merritt, as the most important document he had ever written because its content dealt with the security of Planet Earth. In essence, Nixon talked about "life as we do not know it." The President said there was no one in the White House whom he could trust to deliver the letter to Mr. Kissinger, only Mr. Merritt.

President Nixon also disclosed to Mr. Merritt that he had written a "Message to the American People" that he had hidden at a location inside the White House for accidental discovery by someone in the future. He disclosed the location to Mr. Merritt with the stipulation that Mr. Merritt could reveal it at some future time if he deemed circumstances merited it.

Both Mr. Merritt and I know of its location. We believe the time has come for its disclosure and for it to be placed in the National Archives of the United States. To achieve this goal your cooperation and assistance are needed if in your judgment the existence of such a document is possible. There is no assurance that the document is still there. It may have been retrieved by President Nixon himself or discovered and not disclosed by some unknown person in the past.

We would like to request that you to arrange an unpublicized appointment with the White House in the near future at which time you or someone designated by you would meet with a small group of persons selected by Mr. Merritt and me when all of us would then proceed to the location of President Nixon's secret document. The only conditions that we impose if the document is discovered is that it immediately be read aloud to those present and that copies be made of it and distributed immediately to the public media and to those present after which the National Archives would take permanent possession of President Nixon's document.

To assist you in making a decision on our request for an appointment with the White House I encourage you to watch interviews of Mr. Merritt and me conducted by Daniel Liszt in a Dark Journalist video titled "Nixon's Secret Time Capsule" scheduled to be posted on YouTube on Thursday, February 15 of this month. Also Linda Mouton Howe will discuss this subject in her three hour segment scheduled for the radio show coasttocoastam on Thursday, Feb. 22.

Your attention to this public letter is appreciated.

Sincerely yours,

/S/

Douglas Caddy

Page three of three pages

Supplementary Information

Pulitzer Prize winning reporter Michael Powell authorized Attorney Douglas Caddy to use this character reference for Robert Merritt:

"I am a New York Times columnist and writer and I've worked on and off with Robert Merritt for many years. He can be excitable and passionate, but in my experience he is also remarkably level-headed and his work has benefited many federal and city investigations. He has worked everything from city investigations to the Watergate and the undermining of a president. He now appears to be the victim of a concerted attempt to undermine his credibility and it is taking a grievous and unfair toll on his health and safety."

Contact information:

Robert Merritt in the Bronx: ███████
Daniel Liszt in Boston: DJ@DarkJournalist.com and ███████
Linda Mouton Howe in Albuquerque: earthfiles@earthfiles.com
Trine Day Publisher Kris Millegan in Walterville, Oregon: 1-800-556-2012

Attorney Douglas Caddy in his autobiography, "Being There: Eyewitness to History," takes the reader through some of the greatest historical events of the past seventy years. In the 1950s while still in high school in New Orleans he worked with former FBI agent Gay Banister in combating organized crime in the Big Easy while Lee Harvey Oswald attended high school within walking distance. At Georgetown University in Washington, D.C. he formed the National Student Committee for the Loyalty Oath and Youth for Goldwater for Vice President. This led to the creation of Young Americans for Freedom in 1960 at William F. Buckley's family estate and marked the founding of the modern Conservative Movement. He worked in the New York City office of Governor Nelson Rockefeller for Lt.-Gov. Malcolm Wilson while attending New York University Law School. In the late 1960s General Foods Corporation sent him to the nation's capital to be its Washington Representative. Soon thereafter he met "retired" CIA agent E. Howard Hunt and became Hunt's personal attorney. In 1972 Hunt called him within hours after the arrests of the burglars at Watergate to retain him as the original attorney for the Watergate Seven. Hunt was also a major figure in the Kennedy assassination and confided in him why JFK was murdered. Koreagate followed Watergate and he was summoned by the House committee investigating that scandal that involved a large number of Congressmen. In the 1980s after he moved to Texas he represented notorious criminal Billie Sol Estes in Estes' attempt to get immunity to come clean about the murders and other crimes that he and his business partner, President Lyndon Johnson, had committed. His participation in more historical events continued right up to the publication of his autobiography and included submission to Special Counsel Robert Mueller of pertinent evidence of Russia's involvement in the 2016 presidential election.

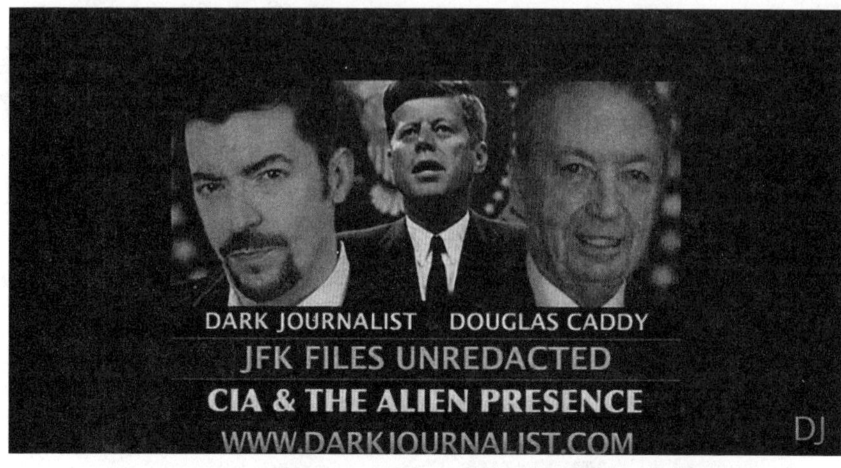

DARK JOURNALIST
DOUGLAS CADDY
JFK FILES UNREDACTED
CIA & THE ALIEN PRESENCE
WWW.DARKJOURNALIST.COM
DJ

The 4th Annual
JFK
The 4th Annual
JFK
Assassination

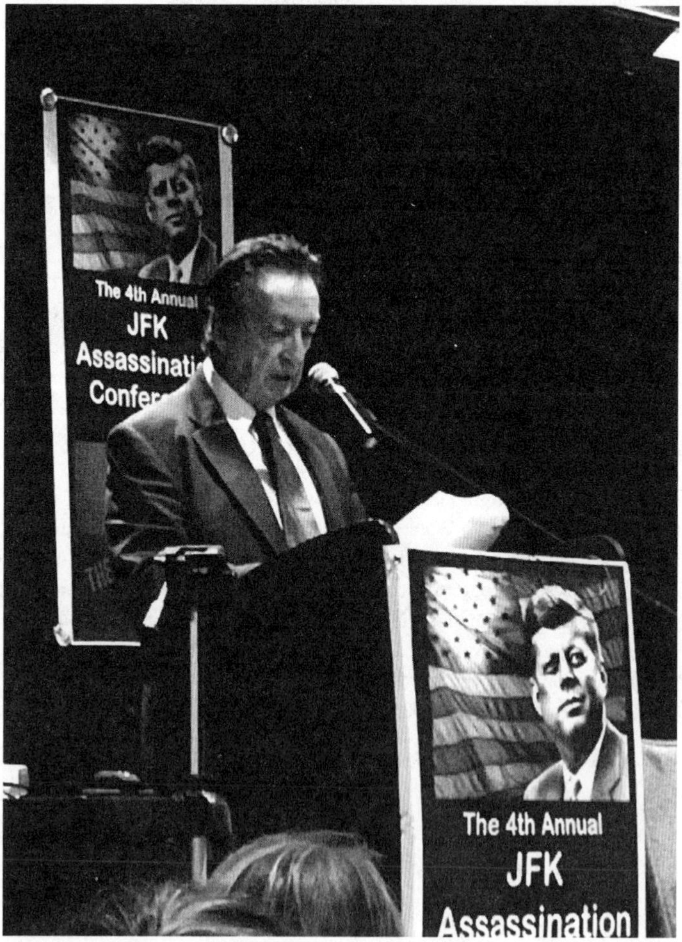

95th Congress }
2d Session }

COMMITTEE PRINT

ACTIVITIES OF "FRIENDLY" FOREIGN INTELLIGENCE SERVICES IN THE UNITED STATES: A CASE STUDY

REPORT

OF THE

SENATE SELECT COMMITTEE
ON INTELLIGENCE
UNITED STATES SENATE

JUNE 1978

Printed for the use of the Select Committee on Intelligence

U.S. GOVERNMENT PRINTING OFFICE
29-935 WASHINGTON : 1978

Man testifies that Moody asked him to hurt lawyer

9-18

By DIANNA HUNT
Houston Chronicle 9/18/87

Galveston insurance heir Shearn Moody Jr. tried to hire a former military explosives man to "cripple" a Houston attorney whose complaints led to an investigation of possible wrongdoing by Moody, the man testified Thursday.

David Hollaway of Houston said that when he rejected the idea, Moody suggested using a scope rifle to "take care of" the attorney, Douglas Caddy.

"Moody said, 'You could just cripple him,'" Hollaway told jurors in U.S. District Judge Ross Sterling's court.

"I told Moody it wouldn't take the FBI long to figure out who the culprits are. He (then) made some reference to perhaps using a scope rifle."

The conversation occurred in late 1985 in Moody's suite at the Hotel Washington in Washington, D.C., Hollaway said.

Caddy, who has since moved out of state, made initial complaints to the Moody Foundation that led to a widespread investigation.

Moody and two other men are on trial on charges they defrauded the foundation of nearly $1.5 million in grants.

Moody, ousted as a foundation trustee earlier this year, is accused of using the funds to finance his long-running bankruptcy case.

Hollaway's testimony is the first to link Moody directly with the alleged scheme, in which prosecutors say grants were funneled through phony foundations to Moody and others.

Hollaway said he first met Moody in the office of his former employer, William R. Pabst, a now-convicted con man who operated the now-defunct Centre for Independence of Judges and Lawyers in the United States Inc.

Hollaway said Moody complained about his problems over the bankruptcy of his Empire Life Insurance Co. — and that Pabst offered to help.

Pabst then began using non-profit foundations as fronts to obtain Moody

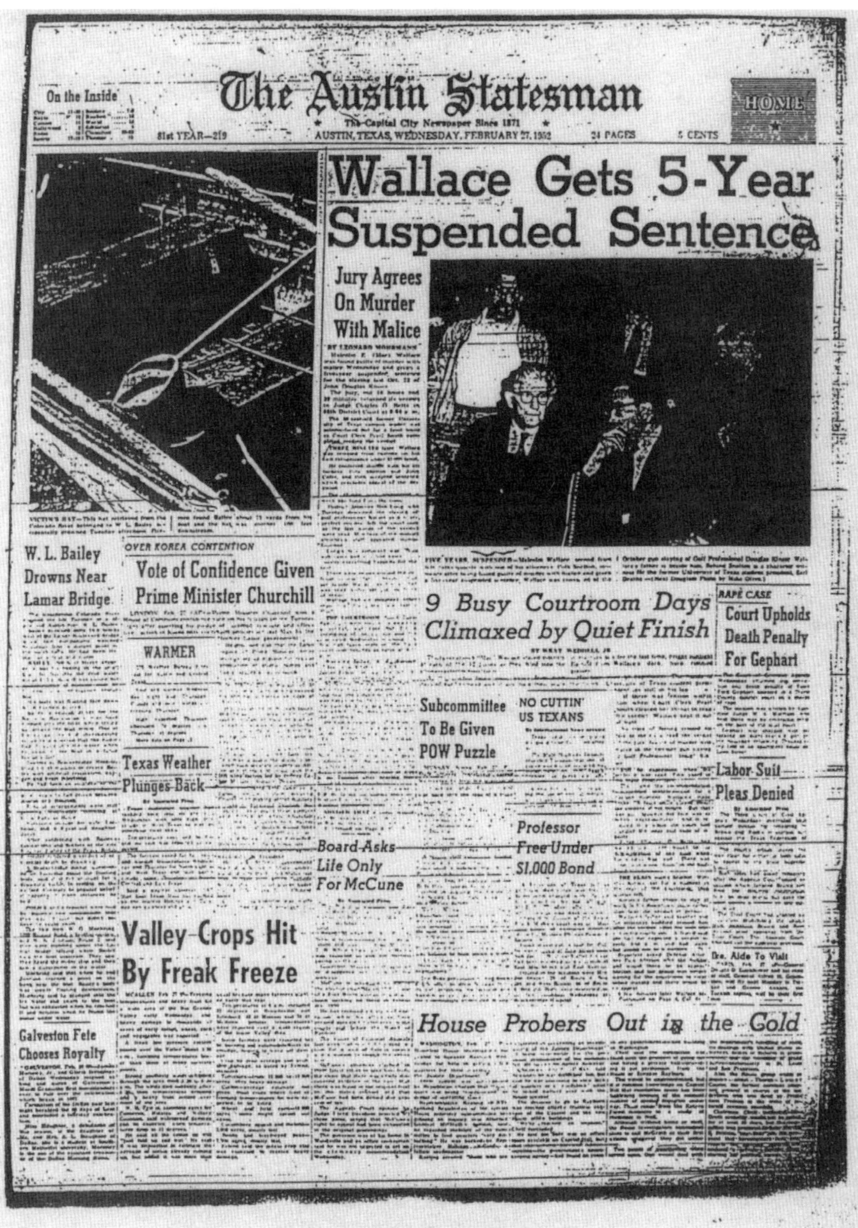

On the Inside

The Austin Statesman

★ The Capital City Newspaper Since 1871 ★

81st YEAR—219 AUSTIN, TEXAS, WEDNESDAY, FEBRUARY 27, 1952 24 PAGES 5 CENTS

HOME

Wallace Gets 5-Year Suspended Sentence

Jury Agrees On Murder With Malice

W. L. Bailey Drowns Near Lamar Bridge

OVER KOREA CONTENTION

Vote of Confidence Given Prime Minister Churchill

WARMER

9 Busy Courtroom Days Climaxed by Quiet Finish

RAPE CASE

Court Upholds Death Penalty For Gephart

Subcommittee To Be Given POW Puzzle

NO CUTTIN' US TEXANS

Texas Weather Plunges Back

Labor Suit Pleas Denied

Professor Free Under $1,000 Bond

Board Asks Life Only For McCune

Valley Crops Hit By Freak Freeze

House Probers Out in the Cold

Galveston Fete Chooses Royalty

The Austin American
February 27, 1952
Page 1 of 1 page

NOTE: This is the front page of *The Austin American* depicting the trial of Malcolm Everett Wallace, who shot and murdered John Dougla

331 x 22

STATE OF TEXAS 036-01-1 086-01 CERTIFICATE OF DEATH STATE FILE NO. 70698

1. PLACE OF DEATH a. COUNTY Gillespie
b. CITY OR TOWN Fredericksburg — c. LENGTH OF STAY 4 Yrs.
d. NAME OF HOSPITAL OR INSTITUTION 501 E. San Antono. St
e. IS PLACE OF DEATH INSIDE CITY LIMITS? YES ☑ NO ☐

2. USUAL RESIDENCE a. STATE Texas b. COUNTY Gillespie
c. CITY OR TOWN Fredericksburg
d. STREET ADDRESS 501 E. San Antonio St.
e. IS RESIDENCE INSIDE CITY LIMITS? YES ☑ NO ☐ f. IS RESIDENCE ON A FARM? YES ☐ NO ☑

3. NAME OF DECEASED (a) First Josefa (b) Middle Hermine (c) Last Moss
4. DATE OF DEATH December 25, 1961
5. SEX Female 6. COLOR OR RACE White 7. Married ☑ Never Married ☐ Widowed ☐ Divorced ☐
8. DATE OF BIRTH May 16, 1912 9. AGE 49
10a. USUAL OCCUPATION Housewife 10b. KIND OF BUSINESS OR INDUSTRY Home-making
11. BIRTHPLACE Texas 12. CITIZEN OF WHAT COUNTRY? U. S. A.
13. FATHER'S NAME Samuel Ealy Johnson 14. MOTHER'S MAIDEN NAME Rebekah Baines
15. WAS DECEASED EVER IN U.S. ARMED FORCES? No. — 16. SOCIAL SECURITY NO. — —
17. INFORMANT James D. Moss (Husband)

18. CAUSE OF DEATH PART I. DEATH WAS CAUSED BY: IMMEDIATE CAUSE (a) Cerebral Hemorrhage — Sudden
DUE TO (b)
DUE TO (c)
PART II. OTHER SIGNIFICANT CONDITIONS CONTRIBUTING TO DEATH BUT NOT RELATED TO THE TERMINAL DISEASE CONDITION GIVEN IN PART I(a)
19. WAS AUTOPSY PERFORMED? YES ☐ NO ☒
20a. ACCIDENT ☐ SUICIDE ☐ HOMICIDE ☐ 20b. DESCRIBE HOW INJURY OCCURRED.

TEXAS DEPARTMENT OF HEALTH REC'D. JAN 15 1962 BUREAU OF VITAL STATISTICS

21. I hereby certify that I attended the deceased from Nov. 1961 to December 1961 and last saw the deceased alive on December 11 1961. Death occurred at 3:15 a.m. on the date stated above, and to the best of my knowledge, from the causes stated.
22a. SIGNATURE [signature] M.D. 22b. ADDRESS Fredericksburg, Texas 22c. DATE SIGNED 12 26 61
23a. BURIAL, CREMATION, REMOVAL Burial 23b. DATE Dec. 26, 1961 23c. NAME OF CEMETERY OR CREMATORY Johnson Cemetery,
23d. LOCATION L.B. J. Ranch, Stonewall, Texas 24. FUNERAL DIRECTOR'S SIGNATURE J. H. Crofts — Crofts Funeral Home Johnson City, Texas
25a. REGISTRAR'S FILE NO. 118 25b. DATE REC'D BY LOCAL REGISTRAR Jan 13, 1962 25c. REGISTRAR'S SIGNATURE Felix Schinag, Co. Clerk

Death certificate of Josefa Johnson, LBJ's sister, who he allegedly murdered

The Dallas Morning News

Texas' Leading Newspaper — Dallas, Texas, Friday, March 23, 1984 — 25 Cents

Billie Sol links LBJ to murder

Sources also say grand jury told of plot

By David Hanners
Staff Writer of The News
©1984, The Dallas Morning News

FRANKLIN, Texas — Convicted swindler Billie Sol Estes told a grand jury that Lyndon B. Johnson was one of four men who planned the 1961 murder of an agriculture official, sources close to the grand jury said Thursday.

The sources said Estes testified that the group feared the official would link Estes' illegal activities to the vice president.

Estes, who testified with immunity from prosecution before the Robertson County Grand Jury Tuesday, told grand jurors that Johnson felt pressure to silence Henry Harvey Marshall of Bryan, a regional USDA official in charge of the federal cotton allotment program, sources said.

■ The Marshall case. 4A

Lady Bird Johnson, the president's widow, could not be reached for comment on Estes' testimony Thursday. "All we will say is that Mrs. Johnson does not answer scurrilous attacks and comments such as that," said Liz Carpenter, who served as Mrs. Johnson's press secretary when LBJ was president.

The sources, who asked to remain anonymous because grand jury testimony is secret under state law, said Estes testified that he had attended at least three meetings

Billie Sol Estes

Lyndon B. Johnson

Henry Marshall

Malcolm Wallace

with Johnson — two in Washington and one at the Driskill Hotel in Austin — during which they discussed the need to stop Marshall from disclosing Estes' fraudulent business dealings and his ties with Johnson.

Estes testified that he later balked at the idea of killing Marshall after Marshall had resisted attempts to have Marshall transferred from Bryan to USDA headquarters in Washington in order to silence him.

Sources said Estes' testimony implicated:

■ Johnson, who had just been elected vice-president. Estes and his family have repeatedly said that Estes was a political ally of LBJ, and that Estes made repeated campaign contributions to LBJ's campaigns. Johnson assumed the presidency on the death of John F. Kennedy, Nov. 22, 1963. He was elected in 1964 to a full term, but chose in 1968 not to seek re-election. He died at his ranch in Stonewall, Texas, on Jan. 22, 1973.

■ Clifton C. Carter, a close Johnson political aide and troubleshooter who later served as executive director and treasurer of the Democratic National Committee. Carter died of natural causes at Arlington (Va.) Hospital Sept. 2, 1971.

■ Malcolm Everette (Mac) Wallace, the president of the 1945 student body at the University of Texas at Austin and a onetime U.S. Agriculture Department economist. Wallace, who sources said Estes identified as Marshall's killer, previously had avoided a jail term on a 1952 murder conviction in Austin. Wallace died, sources

Please see BILLIE SOL on Page 4A.

AMENDMENT TO CERTIFICATE OF DEATH

TEXAS DEPARTMENT OF HEALTH — BUREAU OF VITAL STATISTICS

PART I. INFORMATION CONCERNING DECEASED AS SHOWN ON ORIGINAL DEATH CERTIFICATE.

NAME OF DECEASED	DATE OF DEATH
Henry Harvey Marshall	June 3, 1961
PLACE OF DEATH	**STATE FILE NO.**
Precinct 6, Robertson County, Texas	76879

PART II. ITEM(S) ON ORIGINAL DEATH CERTIFICATE TO BE CORRECTED.

ITEM OR ITEM NO.	ENTRY ON ORIGINAL CERTIFICATE	CORRECT INFORMATION
18	Wound by Gunshot Self inflicted	Wound by Gunshot
20a	Suicide	Homicide
20b	By Gunshot Wounds Self-inflicted	By Gunshot Wounds

PART III. ABSTRACT OF SUPPORTING DOCUMENTARY EVIDENCE

TYPE OF DOCUMENT	DATE OF ORIGINAL ENTRY	BY WHOM ISSUED AND SIGNED	DATE ISSUED
Certification of Judgement Cause #377991 261st Judicial District Court	9-26-1985	County Clerk Travis County, Texas	10-22-1985

PART IV. PERSON REQUESTING AMENDMENT.

NAME	ADDRESS	RELATIONSHIP TO DECEASED
Donald Marshall	Bryan, Texas	Son

PART V. CERTIFICATION BY STATE REGISTRAR.

I HEREBY CERTIFY THAT I HAVE EXAMINED THE DOCUMENTS LISTED ABOVE AND THAT THE ABSTRACT IS TRUE AND CORRECT.

DATE FILED October 22, 1985 STATE REGISTRAR M. Carroll

VS-173, REV. 1/60

Undated photograph of Malcolm "Mac" Wallace accompanied by law enforcement agents

THE TEXAS OBSERVER

A Journal of Free Voices *November 7, 1986* *One Dollar*

(12)

THE KILLING OF HENRY MARSHALL

In May of 1962, Marshall's body was exhumed for an autopsy.

Twenty five years ago a federal farm official was found dead on a remote corner of his central Texas ranch. It came out that he had been investigating the cotton operations of legendary swindler Billie Sol Estes. It came out that Estes had connections high up in the Kennedy-Johnson Administration. Much later, it came out that Estes had something to do with Henry Marshall's death. But a lot of things never did come out.

MINUTES OF THE COUNTY CRIMINAL COURT AT LAW NO. 14 OF HARRIS COUNTY, TEXAS

AT THE December TERM, A.D. 19 98

NO. 9744257

THE STATE OF TEXAS

VS. Michael Douglas Caddy Date of Judgment January 25, 19 99

Attorney for State : Asst. Dist. Atty. J. Jackson

Attorney for Defendant : G. Blass [ ] Appointed [X] Retained

Waiver of Attorney [ ] : The Defendant knowingly, intelligently and voluntarily waived the right to representation by counsel

Offense:

indecent exposure

RECORDER'S MEMORANDUM:
This instrument is of poor quality and not satisfactory for photographic recordation; and/or alterations were present at the time of filming.

V2621 P0682

Plea to Offense: NOT GUILTY

The Defendant having been charged in the above entitled and numbered cause for the misdemeanor offense shown above, and this cause being called for trial, the State appeared by her District Attorney as named above and the Defendant named above, appeared in person and either by Counsel as shown above or waived counsel as indicated above, and both parties announced ready for trial. The said Defendant was arraigned and in open court pleaded as indicated above to the charge contained in the information. Thereupon a Jury, composed of Sylvia Brady and five others was selected, impanelled, and sworn; and after having heard the information read, the Defendant's above indicated plea thereto, and the evidence submitted; and after having been charged by the Court as to their duty to determine the guilt or innocence of the Defendant; and after having heard the argument of counsel, they retired in charge of the proper officer, and on the 25 day of January, A.D., 19 99, returned into open court the following verdict, which was received by the Court and is here entered of record upon the minutes:

"We, the Jury, find the Defendant 'Not Guilty'.

/s/ Sylvia Brady
Foreperson"

It is therefore CONSIDERED, ORDERED, AND ADJUDGED by the Court that the Defendant is not guilty of the offense indicated above, a misdemeanor, as found by the jury, and that he be immediately discharged from further answering herein and go hence without day.

Signed and entered this the 25 day of January A.D. 19 99.

Judge, County Criminal Court at Law No. 14
of Harris County, Texas

ENTERED 23Jan99
VERIFIED

Plea Before the Jury-Finding of Not Guilty
CCCL-85 R07-30-93 -1-

Judgment of "Not Guilty" in my misdemeanor case on January 25, 1999, along with note signed by all the jurors on next page.

1/25/99

WE DO NOT BELIEVE RECKLESS INTENT WAS PROVEN DUE TO THE NATURE OF THE ESTABLISHMENT.

FILED
CHARLES BACARISSE
District Clerk
JAN 25 1999
Time: 8:08
Harris County, Texas
By ______ Deputy

Alicia K. Mcafee

Antonio Williams

Joey T. Lovett

Sylvia Brady
Foreperson

Photograph of Bob Woodward and Carl Bernstein taken in Houston in 2014 when the reporters spoke at the Brilliant Lecture Series; me feeding the ducks at Hermann Park in Houston in 2014

Index

E

F

G

H

Y

Dr. Mary's Monkey

How the Unsolved Murder of a Doctor, a Secret Laboratory in New Orleans and Cancer-Causing Monkey Viruses are Linked to Lee Harvey Oswald, the JFK Assassination and Emerging Global Epidemics

BY EDWARD T. HASLAM, FOREWORD BY JIM MARRS

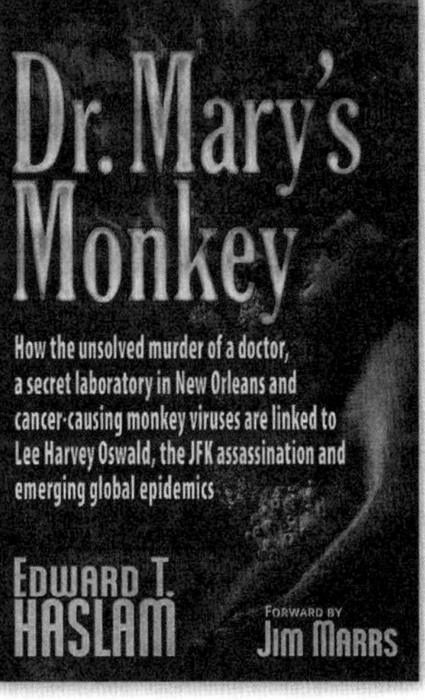

Evidence of top-secret medical experiments and cover-ups of clinical blunders
The 1964 murder of a nationally known cancer researcher sets the stage for this gripping exposé of medical professionals enmeshed in covert government operations over the course of three decades. Following a trail of police records, FBI files, cancer statistics, and medical journals, thisscontaminated polio vaccine, the genesis of the AIDS virus, and biological weapon research using infected monkeys.

Softcover: **$19.95** (ISBN: 9781634240307) • 432 pages • Size: 5 1/2 x 8 1/2
Hardcover: **$24.95** (ISBN: 9781937584597)

Me & Lee

How I Came to Know, Love and Lose Lee Harvey Oswald

BY JUDYTH VARY BAKER

FOREWORD BY EDWARD T. HASLAM

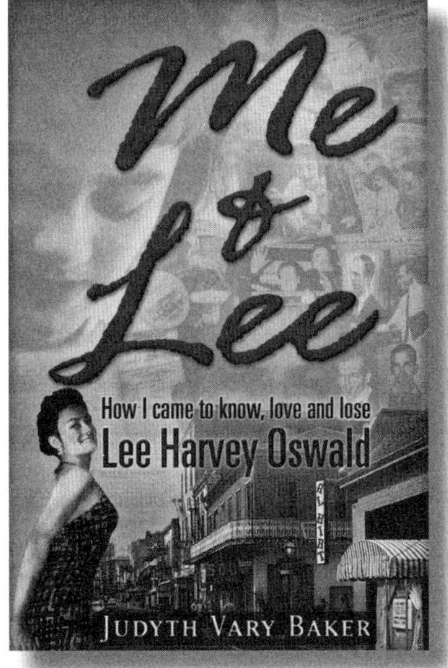

JUDYTH VARY WAS ONCE A PROMISING science student who dreamed of finding a cure for cancer; this exposé is her account of how she strayed from a path of mainstream scholarship at the University of Florida to a life of espionage in New Orleans with Lee Harvey Oswald. In her narrative she offers extensive documentation on how she came to be a cancer expert at such a young age, the personalities who urged her to relocate to New Orleans, and what lead to her involvement in the development of a biological weapon that Oswald was to smuggle into Cuba to eliminate Fidel Castro. Details on what she knew of Kennedy's impending assassination, her conversations with Oswald as late as two days before the killing, and her belief that Oswald was a deep-cover intelligence agent who was framed for an assassination he was actually trying to prevent, are also revealed.

JUDYTH VARY BAKER is a teacher, and artist. Edward T. Haslam is the author of *Dr. Mary's Monkey*.

Hardcover • $24.95 • Softrcover • $21.95 ISBN 9780979988677 / 978-1936296378 • 608 Pages

A Secret Order

Investigating the High Strangeness and Synchronicity in the JFK Assassination

by H. P. Albarelli, Jr.

Provocative new theories that uncover coincidences, connections, and unexplained details of the JFK assassination

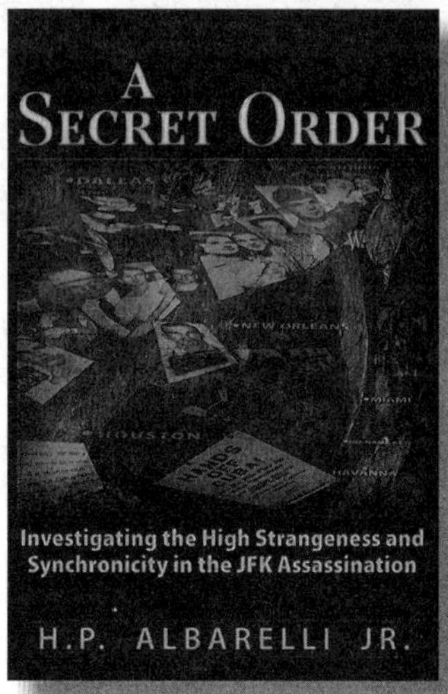

Reporting new and never-before-published information about the assassination of John F. Kennedy, this investigation dives straight into the deep end, and seeks to prove the CIA's involvement in one of the most controversial topics in American history. Featuring intelligence gathered from CIA agents who reported their involvement in the assassination, the case is broken wide open while covering unexplored ground. Gritty details about the assassination are interlaced throughout, while primary and secondary players to the murder are revealed in the in-depth analysis. Although a tremendous amount has been written in the nearly five decades since the assassination, there has never been, until now, a publication to explore the aspects of the case that seemed to defy explanation or logic.

H. P. Albarelli Jr. is an author and reporter whose previous works can be found in the Huffington Post, Pravda, and Counterpunch. His 10-year investigation into the death of biochemist Dr. Frank Olson was featured on A&E's Investigative Reports, and is the subject of his book, A Terrible Mistake. He lives in Indian Beach, Florida.

Softcover • **$24.95** • ISBN 9781936296552 • 469 Pages

Survivor's Guilt

The Secret Service and the Failure to Protect President Kennedy

by Vincent Michael Palamara

The actions and inactions of the Secret Service before, during, and after the Kennedy assassination

Painstakingly researched by an authority on the history of the Secret Service and based on primary, firsthand accounts from more than 80 former agents, White House aides, and family members, this is the definitive account of what went wrong with John F. Kennedy's security detail on the day he was assassinated.

The work provides a detailed look at how JFK could and should have been protected and debunks numerous fraudulent notions that persist about the day in question, including that JFK ordered agents off the rear of his limousine; demanded the removal of the bubble top that covered the vehicle; and was difficult to protect and somehow, directly or indirectly, made his own tragic death easier for an assassin or assassins. This book also thoroughly investigates the threats on the president's life before traveling to Texas; the presence of unauthorized Secret Service agents in Dealey Plaza, the site of the assassination; the failure of the Secret Service in monitoring and securing the surrounding buildings, overhangs, and rooftops; and the surprising conspiratorial beliefs of several former agents.

An important addition to the canon of works on JFK and his assassination, this study sheds light on the gross negligence and, in some cases, seeming culpability, of those sworn to protect the president.

Vincent Michael Palamara is an expert on the history of the Secret Service. He has appeared on the History Channel, C-SPAN, and numerous newspapers and journals, and his original research materials are stored in the National Archives. He lives in Pittsburgh, Pennsylvania.

Softcover • **$24.95** • ISBN 9781937584603 • 492 Pages

In the Eye of History

Disclosures in the JFK Assassination Medical Evidence

Second Edition

by William Matson Law

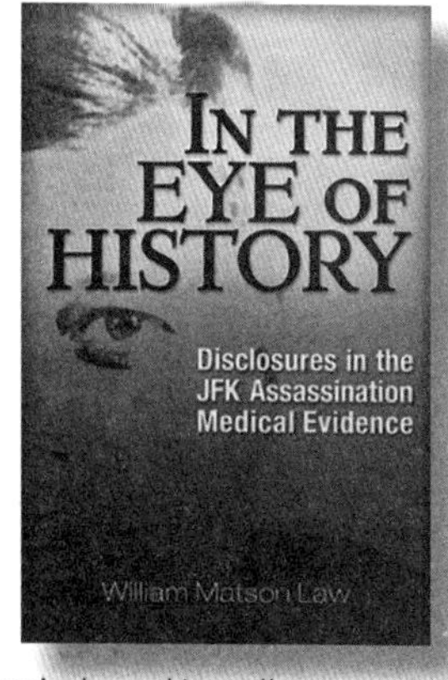

An oral history of the JFK autopsy

Anyone interested in the greatest mystery of the 20th century will benefit from the historic perspective of the attendees of President Kennedy's autopsy. For the first time in their own words these witnesses to history give firsthand accounts of what took place in the autopsy morgue at Bethesda, Maryland, on the night on November 22, 1963. Author William Matson Law set out on a personal quest to reach an understanding of the circumstances underpinning the assassination of John F. Kennedy. His investigation led him to the autopsy on the president's body at the National Naval Medical Center. In the Eye of History comprises conversations with eight individuals who agreed to talk: Dennis David, Paul O'Connor, James Jenkins, Jerrol Custer, Harold Rydberg, Saundra Spencer, and ex-FBI Special Agents James Sibert and Frances O'Neill. These eyewitnesses relate their stories comprehensively, and Law allows them to tell it as they remember it without attempting to fit any pro- or anticonspiracy agenda. The book also features a DVD featuring these firsthand interviews. Comes with DVD.

Softcover: **$29.95** (ISBN: 9781634240468) • 514 pages • Size: 6 x 9

JFK from Parkland to Bethesda

The Ultimate Kennedy Assassination Compendium

by Vincent Palamara

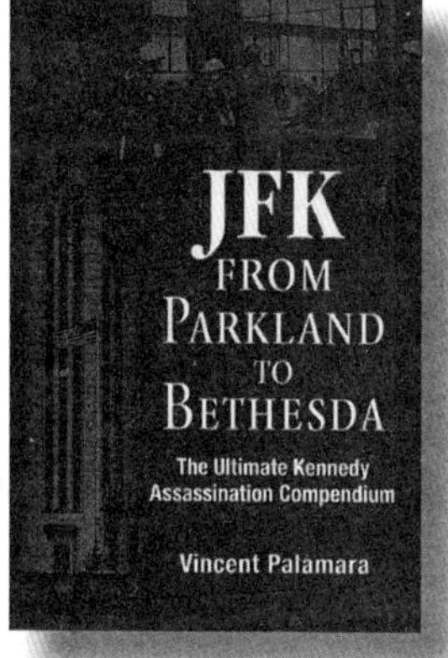

An all-in-one resource containing more than 15 years of research on the JFK assassination

A map through the jungle of statements, testimony, allegations, and theories relating to the assassination of John F. Kennedy, this compendium gives readers an all-in-one resource for facts from this intriguing slice of history. The book, which took more than 15 years to research and write, includes details on all of the most important aspects of the case, including old and new medical evidence from primary and secondary sources. JFK: From Parkland to Bethesda tackles the hard evidence of conspiracy and cover-up and presents a mass of sources and materials, making it an invaluable reference for anyone with interest in the President Kennedy and his assassination in 1963.

Softcover: **$19.95** (ISBN: 9781634240277) • 242 pages • Size: 6 x 9

The Polka Dot File on the Robert F. Kennedy Killing

Paris Peace Talks connection

by Fernando Faura

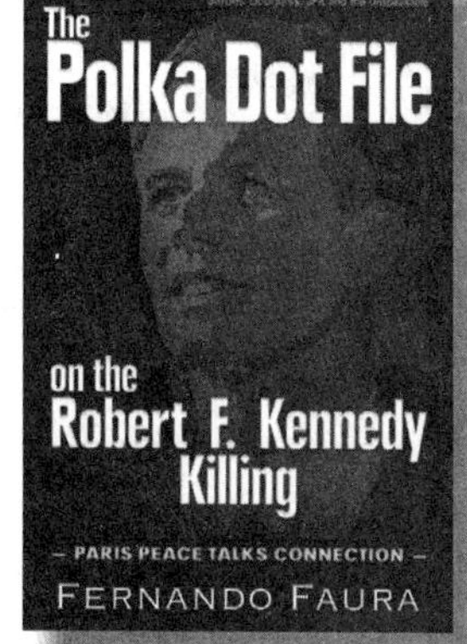

"The Polka Dot File is a gem in the field of RFK assassination research. Read it and learn."

—Jim Douglass, author, *JFK and the Unspeakable*

The Polka Dot File on the Robert F. Kennedy Killing describes the day-to-day chase for the mystery woman in the polka-dot dress. The book comments on but does not dwell on the police investigation, and reads like a detective thriller instead of an academic analysis of the investigation. It incorporates actual tapes made by an important witness, and introduces the testimony of witnesses not covered in other books and it is a new take on the assassination and the motives for it introduces a new theory for the reasons behind the assassination. Original and highly personal, it reaches a startling and different conclusion not exposed by other books.

Fernando Faura graduated cum laude with a degree in journalism from the California State University. In 1967 he joined *The Hollywood Citizens News.* Fernando has won awards from the Press Club, the National Newspaper Publishers Association, and was nominated for a Pulitzer Prize.

Softcover: **$24.95** (ISBN: 9781634240598) • 248 pages • Size: 6 x 9

From an Office Building with a High-Powered Rifle

A report to the public from an FBI agent involved in the official JFK assassination investigation

by Don Adams

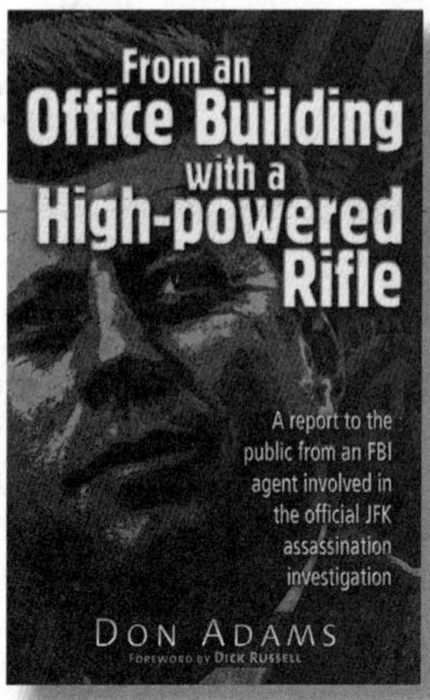

An insider's look at the mysteries behind the death of President Kennedy

The personal and professional story of a former FBI agent, this is the journey Don Adams has taken over the past 50 years that has connected him to the assassination of the 35th president of the United States. On November 13, 1963, Adams was given a priority assignment to investigate Joseph Milteer, a man who had made threats to assassinate the president. Two weeks later John F. Kennedy was dead, and Agent Adams was instructed to locate and question Milteer. Adams, however, was only allowed to ask the suspect five specific questions before being told to release him. He was puzzled by the bizarre orders but thought nothing more of it until years later when he read a report that stated that not only had Joseph Milteer made threats against the president, but also that he claimed Kennedy would be killed from an office building with a high-powered rifle. Since that time, Adams has compiled evidence and research from every avenue available to him, including his experiences in Georgia and Dallas FBI offices, to produce this compelling investigation that may just raise more questions than answers.

DON ADAMS is a former FBI agent who participated in the investigation of the assassination of John F. Kennedy. He is the author of numerous articles on the subject and is considered a respected authority on the topic. He lives in Akron, Ohio.

Softcover • **$24.95** • ISBN 9781936296866 • 236 Pages

Betrayal

A JFK Honor Guard Speaks

by Hugh Clark

with William Matson Law

The amazing story that William Law has documented with his historical interviews helps us to understanding our true history. This compelling information shreds the official narrative.In 2015, Law and fellow researcher Phil Singer got together the medical corpsman, who had been present at Bethesda Naval Hospital for President Kennedy's autopsy with some of the official honor guard, who had delivered the president's coffin. What happened next was extraordinary. The medical corpsmen told the honor guards that they had actually received the president's body almost a half-hour before the honor guard got there. The honor guard couldn't believe this. They had met the president's plane at Andrews, taken possession of his casket and shadowed it all the way to Bethesda. The two sides almost broke into fisticuffs, accusing the other of untruths. Once it was sifted out, and both sides came to the understanding that each was telling their own truths of their experience that fateful day, the feelings of betrayal experienced by the honor guards was deep and profound.

HUGH CLARK was a member of the honor guard that took President Kennedy's body to Arlington Cemetery for burial. He was an investigator for the United Nations. After Hugh left the service he became a New York City detective and held that position for 22 years.

WILLIAM MATSON LAW has been researching the Kennedy assassination for over 25 years. Results of that research have appeared in more than 30 books, including Douglas Horne's magnum opus Inside the Assassination Records Review Board. Law is the author of In the Eye of History and is working on a book about the murder of Robert F. Kennedy with the working title: Shadows and Light. He lives with his family in Central Oregon.

Softcover • **$19.95** • ISBN 9781634240932 • 144 Pages

Silent Coup

The Removal of a President

by Len Colodny & Robert Gettlin

25th Anniversay Edition – Includes Updates

Foreword by Roger Morris

This is the true story of betrayal at the nation's highest level. Unfolding with the suspenseful pace of a le Carre spy thriller, it reveals the personal motives and secret political goals that combined to cause the Watergate break-in and destroy Richard Nixon. Investigator Len Colodny and journalist Robert Gettlin relentlessly pursued the people who brought down the president. Their revelations shocked the world and forever changed our understanding of politics, of journalism, and of Washington behind closed doors. Dismantling decades of lies, *Silent Coup* tells the truth.

LEN COLODNY is a journalist. In 1992 he co-wrote with Robert Gettlin: *Silent Coup: The Removal Of Richard Nixon*. In the book the authors claim that John Dean ordered the Watergate break-in because he knew that a call-girl ring was operating out of the Democratic headquarters. The authors also argued that Alexander Haig was not Deep Throat but was a key source for Bob Woodward, who had briefed Haig at theWhite House in 1969 and 1970.

Softcover • **$24.95** • ISBN 9781634240536 • 520 Pages

Bond of Secrecy

My Life with CIA Spy and Watergate Conspirator E. Howard Hunt

by St. John Hunt

Foreword by Jesse Ventura

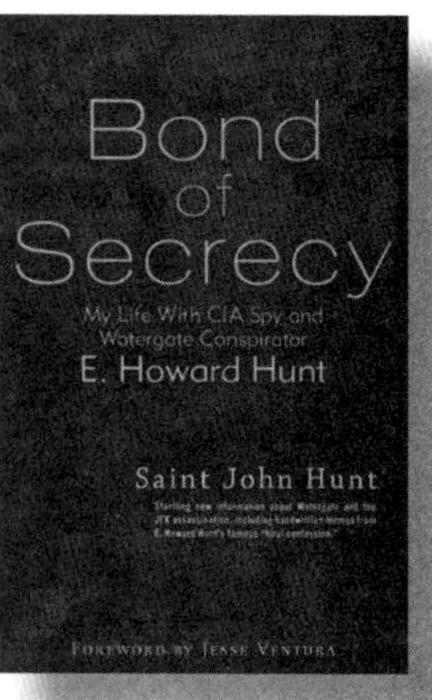

A father's last confession to his son about the CIA, Watergate, and the plot to assassinate President John F. Kennedy, this is the remarkable true story of St. John Hunt and his father E. Howard Hunt, the infamous Watergate burglar and CIA spymaster. In Howard Hunt's near-death confession to his son St. John, he revealed that key figures in the CIA were responsible for the plot to assassinate JFK in Dallas, and that Hunt himself was approached by the plotters, among whom included the CIA's David Atlee Phillips, Cord Meyer, Jr., and William Harvey, as well as future Watergate burglar Frank Sturgis. An incredible true story told from an inside, authoritative source, this is also a personal account of a uniquely dysfunctional American family caught up in two of the biggest political scandals of the 20th century.

Softcover • **$24.95** • ISBN 978-1936296835 • 192 Pages

Dorothy

The Murder of E. Howard Hunt's Wife – watergate's Darkest Secret

by St. John Hunt

Foreword by Roger Stone

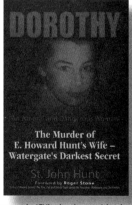

Dorothy Hunt, "An Amoral and Dangerous Woman" tells the life story of ex-CIA agent Dorothy Hunt, who married Watergate mastermind and confessed contributor to the assassination of JFK. The book chronicles her rise in the intelligence field after World War II, as well as her experiences in Shanghai, Calcutta, Mexico, and Washington, DC. It reveals her war with President Nixon and asserts that she was killed by the CIA in the crash of Flight 553. Written by the only person who was privy to the behind-the-scenes details of the Hunt family during Watergate, this book sheds light on a dark secret of the scandal.

Softcover • **$24.95** • ISBN 978-1634240376 • 192 Pages

Saint John Hunt is an author, a musician, and the son of the infamous and legendary CIA covert operative and author, E. Howard Hunt. Saint John spent more than ten years searching for the truth about his father's involvement in JFK's death, resulting in his first book Bond of Secrecy. In his second book, Dorothy, he explored his mother's life as a CIA spy and her war with Nixon, which resulted in her murder. He lives in south Florida.